Daw̄ David 27.8.83

Penguin Education

**Housing Policy**

D1335555

David Donnison and Clare Ungerson

# Housing Policy

 Penguin Books

Penguin Books Ltd, Harmondsworth, Middlesex, England
Penguin Books, 625 Madison Avenue, New York, New York 10022, U.S.A.
Penguin Books Australia Ltd, Ringwood, Victoria, Australia
Penguin Books Canada Ltd, 2801 John Street, Markham, Ontario, Canada L3R 1B4
Penguin Books (N.Z.) Ltd, 182–190 Wairau Road, Auckland 10, New Zealand

First published 1982

Made and printed in Great Britain by
Richard Clay (The Chaucer Press) Ltd,
Bungay, Suffolk
Set in Monophoto Times New Roman

# Contents

# Foreword

This book was at first intended to be a new edition of *The Government of Housing* which was written by David Donnison with the help of Clare Ungerson fifteen years ago. We should have foreseen that housing problems and policies have changed so much since then that we would have to write a new book. Parts of the original work remain in Chapters 3–6 and Chapter 9, but at least three quarters of this book are entirely new. Official statistics have improved enormously in recent years. Most of our figures are therefore derived not from our own research, as in the previous book, but from government and United Nations sources. However, we have gone much further in interpreting this evidence and drawing practical conclusions from it than we did before, and we have written more simply and clearly. *The Government of Housing* was intended mainly for specialists. *Housing Policy* is intended to help people who are only beginning to get to grips with this field – and to interest the specialists too.

Our work on this book, like its predecessor, was supported by the Joseph Rowntree Memorial Trust. We are enormously grateful for their generosity and patience. The University of Kent, the Centre for Environmental Studies and the Policy Studies Institute helped to administer the funds provided by the Trust; we thank them too.

We have consulted many people about various parts of the book – far more than we have space to acknowledge here. But we should particularly thank Professor Adam Andzrejewski, Derek Barton, Nick Beacock, Geoffrey Beltram, George Cunningham M P, Liam Gallacher, Professor Vic George, James Hannigan, Alan Holmans, Nora Hörcher, Dr Peter Levin, Professor Wanda Litterer-Marwege, Dr George Musil, Frederick Raes, Nick Raynsford, Stephen Ross M P, Hugh Rossi M P, Michael Tully, Elizabeth Vajdovich-Visy and Michael Whitbread. At the same time we absolve all of them from any responsibility for the use we have made of their help.

We were lucky to have the support of Irene Morrish, Sue Davies and Margery Russell, who did most of our typing and gave us a lot of practical help; Frances Hadden drew our map; we are very grateful to all of them.

# Part I
Problems and Policies

# 1
# Housing Problems and Policies

## Housing Problems

At first sight, housing problems seem obvious. Even in rich countries, most people have seen overcrowded, poorly equipped, decaying houses. The problems they present may be daunting in scale, but everyone knows what they are and everyone, it seems, should agree about solutions. Housing policy ought to be equally straightforward; much simpler than policies for education, health or the relief of poverty – fields in which the problems and their solutions are both harder to define.

But a second look shows that things are not so simple. House and home stand at the centre of people's lives, giving them a shelter for sleep and for half their waking activities, shielding them from the world yet admitting it in a controlled and selective fashion, and providing storage and a showcase for most of their possessions. Demands for housing are therefore complex and constantly changing as culture and living standards evolve and as families grow and disperse. They are also insatiable. Within the resources of current technology people's demands for spades, pens and motor cars can be – roughly speaking – satisfied. Not so with housing.

Other goods generally have a limited range of uses and meanings: a spade is a spade is a spade. But a house is not just a dwelling. It confers a bundle of rights and duties which may be distributed in various ways among various people – the occupier, the owner, tenants and sub-tenants, and the authorities responsible for taxation, town planning and public health. There is the right to occupy the house; rights to sell, let and sub-let it; rights to control the use which others make of it; rights to extend, demolish, rebuild and redecorate it; rights to benefit from tax concessions and subsidies; the right to hold an asset which generally retains its real value despite inflation; and the right to bequeath that asset to one's heirs. The duties attached to housing – duties to maintain it, and to pay various taxes on it, for example – can also take various forms and be distributed in various ways. Houses, moreover, are fixed to one place. With the house come the neighbours, the reputation of the neighbourhood, and the jobs, schools, doctors, shops and other opportunities within reach of that point on the map. A house which offers everything a man or woman could desire when considered as a building may be uninhabitable when considered as a location.

Finally, the home provides the setting within which men and women develop their own domestic economy and domestic roles. With bigger and better-equipped houses, this domestic economy has grown increasingly productive. Women, defined in industrial societies as 'housewives', have generally been responsible for most of that production. But men and children contribute to it too in changing ways, helping to produce domestic services, fresh fruit and vegetables, maintenance and repair work on the house, the motor car and other property of the household. What they can all do depends partly on the character of their housing.

Thus housing needs are neither simple nor self-evident. They are a collection of rights, opportunities, assets and attributes, about as complex, as liable to change and as difficult to define as needs for education, health and general prosperity.

Some simple definitions may help to find a way through this jungle. We have talked rather indiscriminately about demands, needs and problems. A 'demand' is something which people want. It becomes an 'effective' demand if they get it, whether through the market place or by administrative allocation. Otherwise it remains an unsatisfied or potential demand – perhaps a latent demand which people are as yet barely aware of. A 'need' is something which people believe they or others lack and ought to have. A 'problem' is a difficulty or dissatisfying circumstance which people want to see put right.

Effective demands can be defined and measured in fairly objective ways: that is to say, in terms which most people would agree about. Unsatisfied demands are harder to define and measure objectively. To assess their urgency or importance we must find ways of comparing such demands with unsatisfied demands for other things, and ranking the priority of one amongst the others. Needs and problems are still harder to define, and always subjective: that is to say, they are an interpretation of facts based partly on personal feeling and opinion – and no less important for that. (To call them 'economic' needs or problems means that a lot of the evidence about them can be expressed in terms of money or other exchangeable resources. They are no less subjective or questionable for that reason.) To assess the significance of needs and problems we must again consider priorities, comparing the prices we would pay to resolve them with those we would pay to resolve other needs and problems. Such 'prices' may be calculated in many different currencies – in money, time or political credit, for example.

## The Scope of Policy

Since housing problems are difficult to define and measure, the policies for tackling them may be equally difficult to plan and evaluate. Take the most obvious housing needs of a neighbourhood full of overcrowded, decaying slums: to demolish such houses and replace them with better, subsidized housing would in many places be considered the natural response of a humane government. But suppose that were impossible: the government may lack the powers, staff or funds for the job. Is there nothing else it can do? It could bring more work and better-paid jobs into the town. In this way it could equip people to earn more in the hope that they would then be able to spend more on housing. Town planning and transport policies might improve people's access to jobs. Better education and health may also increase earnings. Better pensions and family benefits, new tax policies and other redistributions of income may increase or redistribute expenditure on housing. Since poor people tend to spend proportionately more of their incomes on housing than rich people do, a transfer of income from rich to poor may increase total expenditure on housing. Landlords could be encouraged in various ways to improve their houses. People could be helped to buy and improve their own homes with subsidized savings, loans and repair work, and with free advice about all these things. Employers could be induced to contribute to the housing of their workers. Trade unions and voluntary associations might be induced to do likewise. Family planning services may help people to match the growth of their families more closely to the housing they can acquire to shelter their children. Almost every instrument of government could be – and somewhere has been – brought to bear on housing.

Thus housing 'policy' need not be confined to ministries and departments with a housing label on them. It may be as effectively – perhaps more effectively – pursued in other ways. Housing policy is any sustained course of action designed to affect housing conditions. It need not even be designed to improve these conditions: sometimes governments deliberately restrain investment in housing for the benefit of other sectors of the economy. The aims and instruments of housing policy will change as time goes by. Housing problems can be solved, and many have been. But the solution of one problem focuses attention on others. *The* housing

problem is never solved: it only changes. That may nevertheless constitute progress. Some problems are nicer to have than others. People may
protest more vociferously today about the lack of parking space than
their ancestors did about the lack of a water supply, but that does not
mean that these problems are equally urgent or severe.

Sometimes we shall talk about housing 'programmes' rather than
policies. By that we shall usually mean those parts of housing policy
which are carried out through ministries and departments of housing.
Some people use the term to refer to the nation's output of housing, or
to the steps taken by government to produce it. Sometimes, still more
narrowly, it refers only to the production of public housing.

The way in which housing policy evolves will become clearer if we look
back at a book we wrote fifteen years ago,[1] and note some of the new
problems to be explored in this book. When people say they have a housing
problem, what is that a problem about? If they have housing policies, what
are those policies about? How and why do the answers to those questions
change over time? These are the main themes of both books.


## Fifteen Years Ago

Starting from the simple observation that the population of a country
and the stock of houses they live in usually grow and change very slowly,
we explored fifteen years ago the ways in which housing and households
evolve – supply and demand each being shaped partly by the other.
Households form and re-form as people leave their parents' homes to
set up on their own, get married and start their own families. They
shrink again as a new generation moves out, and later as mortality takes
its toll of their parents. Meanwhile, people move from one country to
another and from place to place within their own country. In some
countries – usually those at an early stage of economic development –
these developments proceed quickly: people marry young, have large
families, and move in large numbers across frontiers or from the country
to the towns. Their governments have to cope with the rapidly growing
and changing demands of this turbulent demographic climate. In other
countries – usually those with mature urban industrial economies – the
demographic climate is much 'milder', housing conditions are better,
and governments have greater scope for improving things and a wider
range of policy options from which to choose.

Houses generally last longer than people, and much longer than the
households they shelter. They are like old clothes, handed down from

earlier generations and remodelled with varying success. Most of them are 'second-hand', previously occupied by someone else who had to move out before they became available to their present users. Thus households succeed each other as they move through the stock in a well-marked pattern of flows. During the 1960s new households in Britain usually started in privately rented housing – often in furnished rooms. They moved on either into council housing rented from the local authorities, or to buy homes of their own. Many moved within these sectors of the market. In privately rented housing they tended to move from furnished to unfurnished housing. In council and in owner-occupied housing they tended to move from smaller to larger houses, and sometimes back again to smaller houses in their old age. They also tended to move outwards from the inner to the outer parts of cities and the suburbs beyond.

Some of these patterns are changing: we shall show that, as privately rented housing dwindles, more people set up home for the first time in council or owner-occupied housing. As transport costs rise and as more women go to work, there are signs that more families are moving back from the suburbs to the inner city, or staying in more central neighbourhoods. But for most people these patterns remain unchanged: when they have children, most people value the space and privacy of the suburbs more highly and easy access to the city centre less highly than they did when the household was smaller and all its members had jobs or were students. Hence the outward flow of growing families towards cheaper, greener but less accessible neighbourhoods.

We must understand these flows, the demands they satisfy and the factors which determine who secures these opportunities and who is excluded from them, before we can talk sense about housing policies. The operations of government influence these processes in many ways, sometimes deliberately and sometimes accidentally. By encouraging or discouraging saving and by channelling savings towards various forms of investment, governments help to determine the flow of capital available for building, improving and maintaining houses. In Britain, as in many other countries, tax policies encourage investment in owner-occupation which is, in effect, heavily subsidized by tax reliefs on the mortgage interest payments of house buyers. Meanwhile they discourage investment in privately rented housing, from which the profits are taxed, while the depreciation of the landlord's capital is treated less favourably than depreciation of other forms of profit-making investment. The growth of higher education has created new demands from students, heavily concentrated in towns with polytechnics and universities – demands only partly met by the educational institutions involved. Social security policies put money in people's pockets which may help them to pay for housing: the big improvement in pensioners' incomes achieved in most industrial countries in recent years has enabled many old people to secure or retain better housing than their predecessors had. Changes in government expenditure and borrowing make an impact on the flow of funds to building societies and other institutions which lend to house buyers. Changes in the societies' interest rates exert their own influence on lending, and on the spending patterns of house buyers. Thus the operations of building societies have become an important political issue. Although governments in Britain and many other market economies have repeatedly tried to reduce their commitments in the housing field and draw housing programmes to a close, they have been compelled to recognize that many things which they do exert an influence on the housing market and the distribution of housing. They can within limits choose what kind of housing policy to adopt; but housing policies of *some* kind – explicit or implicit, deliberate or accidental – they must have.

In more rapidly developing countries, governments contending with turbulent growth in housing demands and desperate scarcities of resources often cannot do more than promote the rapid and regular development of land in their growing cities for house building, laying out a basic framework of streets, drains, water supply, electricity and other urban services, and imposing some minimum standards of building and helping people to help themselves. Later, with a more mature economy, a well-established building industry, a population growing and moving at a slower rate, more skilled workers and more experienced public services, the state generally adopts more active housing policies. Fifteen years ago we distinguished two roles assumed by governments in the more highly developed countries. We described one as a limited 'social' housing policy, confined to imposing some minimum standards on the operations of the market and meeting needs which the market cannot satisfy. The other we described as a more 'comprehensive' approach, leading governments to assume powers extending into every aspect of the production, distribution and management of the housing stock. We suggested that governments tend to move from the more limited to the more comprehensive role.

### Today's Debate

In this book we look again at this account of the matter. Although our main conclusions remain convincing, much of what we said must now be rephrased. Policies may be 'comprehensive' in the sense that many different programmes are closely coordinated to achieve particular ends. But unless the government gave housing priority over *every* other consideration – which is inconceivable – it could not keep up a complete and consistent coordination of every action which affects housing. What can be achieved is a more comprehensive approach to policy, calling for an alert and sophisticated understanding of the impact made on housing by every sector of the economy, and the avoidance of unnecessarily destructive conflicts between different programmes.

Policies may also be 'comprehensive' in the sense that they are designed to meet the needs of every citizen, and particularly the needs of those most likely to be neglected. Our original assessment bore the optimistic stamp of its era. In the 1960s the majority of people assumed that most of the world's economies would continue to grow, that the hardships of the poorest people could in time be eliminated without threatening the living standards of the mass of the population, that government and its public services would be the natural instruments for creating a society which would be both more equal and more prosperous, and, with the encouragement of sound research and regularly published government statistics, that a political consensus could be built to sustain programmes to attain better and more equal housing conditions. This was the liberal dream in many fields of government.

But storm warnings were already to be seen at that time. Unemployment in Britain doubled in 1966 (between completion and publication of our earlier book). With two brief intermissions it has gone on rising ever since. The economic crisis afflicting the advanced capitalist economies, and Britain in particular, is fundamental: depression and the rising price of oil have exacerbated it, but are not its main causes. As real living standards decline for several years at a time with no assurance that their upward trend will be resumed, the 'Butskellite' consensus sustaining policies which equalize opportunities and steadily extend the public sector of the economy has disintegrated. Minority parties have grown stronger, and at the time of writing we have a government with a mandate – largely secured from working-class votes – to cut down the scale of the public sector of the economy by reducing taxes, public expenditure and public officials. There is controversy about whether public services have exerted an equalizing influence on society, but everyone agrees that they are distributed more equally than wealth, wages, fringe benefits and other resources on which people rely for their living.[2] Thus the attack on public services is designed, as leading figures in the government have made clear, to create a less equal society.

Nevertheless, all over Europe, housing conditions measured in traditional ways (by counting rooms and persons per room, indoor toilets and other plumbing fixtures) have since the Second World War grown better and more equal. Thus the political battles which are fought over the growth and distribution of housing now centre increasingly on other things – particularly on questions of location, accessibility and the quality of neighbourhoods, and on questions of ownership and the financial status and benefits associated with housing, and the part it plays in the accumulation of wealth. The fundamental questions involved – questions of social justice – are the same as ever. But they must be argued in terms of new and more complex criteria. Useful though they still are, census figures of bathrooms, persons per room and the like are no longer sufficient. The whole discussion must be conducted in the more stringent political climate of a world in which people are less optimistic about growth, less friendly to government and the public services, and perhaps less generous towards the poor and the ill-housed than they used to be.

# 2
# Demands and Needs

## Introduction

In this chapter we look at demands and needs for housing. It is the
national scale we shall be concerned with. Had we been asking how
individuals and families fare, we would explore the workings of the
market place and the administrative procedures which distribute housing
amongst households. We have a good deal to say about those things in
later chapers, particularly Chapter 13 on housing tenure and finance.
Had we been asking about demands which operate at the scale of a
town or city, we would study the growth and decline of urban economies
and their changing structure. We have a good deal to say about those
things in Chapters 7 and 8, which put housing in an urban context and
compare different kinds of towns. But when the question is posed on a
national scale, the first questions to ask are demographic: about the
growth and migration of the population, and the changing proportions
of the population who form separate households.

Studies carried out by the United Nations show that the cost of building a house in Western European countries generally falls somewhere
between 3 and 4·5 times the average annual income of male workers.[1]
(Exceptions to this rule are found in the poorer countries where housing
is more expensive. But that is to be expected because the statistics from
these countries appear to compare the cost of good, urban housing with
average incomes derived partly from low-paid rural occupations.) More
important still, in particular countries the cost of a house expressed as a
multiple of the average annual wage tends to remain much the same
over long periods. A study made by the Building Research Station[2]
(now the Building Research Establishment) suggests that in Britain the
cost of building a new house has remained close to three times the
average annual earnings of male industrial workers for at least sixty
years, apart from brief intervals of higher costs after each World War
and during a bout of inflation which took place around 1973. Figures
for the USA covering the years from 1948 to 1960 showed a similar
pattern, although American earnings were much higher.

It is not surprising that the cost of a house tends roughly to keep pace with the growth of incomes. Because housing is so central a feature of living standards and personal expenditure, any major development in consumption patterns (the introduction of central heating, motor cars, frozen foods or television, for instance) makes some impact on the kind of houses which people want and the equipment they expect to find in those houses. As their incomes rise, they want more 'house' and are prepared to pay more for it. But a change in the numbers of people in the household-forming age groups, or changes in the proportions of people in various age groups who form separate households, will have a direct impact on the numbers and the types of houses demanded.

That is why we focus in this chapter mainly on demographic changes. What are the main changes now going on within European countries? What is happening to the flows of migration within and between these countries? What effects will these changes have on the demand for housing? And what general conclusions can we draw from this evidence about the capacity of governments to solve their countries' housing problems? These are the questions to be discussed here.

## Recent Demographic Changes in European Countries

A study[3] by the United Nations Economic Commission for Europe (ECE) of post-war European demographic trends stresses four major developments: **1.** the slow growth of Europe's population compared with that of the rest of the world; **2.** the ageing of Europe's populations and work forces; **3.** changes both in the age and in the duration of marriage; **4.** changes in the scale and direction of migrations. We will look at these in turn. These trends make it clear that the nations of Europe, once so different in demographic character, are converging towards similar patterns. They have all recently experienced a considerable fall in their birth rates, and final family sizes are becoming increasingly similar. Figures 3.2–3.5 on pages 46–7 illustrate these patterns. The age at which people in different countries marry is converging towards a similar average for the whole of Europe. And divorce – except in the Catholic south – is rising everywhere. There are fewer and fewer distinctions between north-western Europe on the one hand, and eastern Europe on the other. Only southern Europe remains distinct in some respects, particularly in the tendency of some of the Mediterranean countries to export migrant male workers to central and northern European countries. But more recently this flow of migrants, already declining, has been severely cut back by depression and rising unemployment in the receiving countries.[4]

We will look first at population growth. All European countries grew in population during the decade from 1960 to 1970. But most of them grew at a slower and slower rate; and the populations of some, such as West and East Germany, are now declining. Death rates have remained remarkably steady over most of Europe since the Second World War. There are now signs that they may be rising very slightly, particularly for males. The ECE's demographers believe that, with present scientific knowledge, there is probably a limit to the increase in longevity, and it may have already been reached in the richer European countries. Thus any future upturn in rates of natural increase would call for an upturn in birth rates. These declined almost everywhere between 1960 and 1970, with a few exceptions such as Romania, which in 1965 so tightened up its abortion laws that it produced a remarkable, but short-lived, increase. Since then, crude birth rates in some countries have risen slightly as the larger generations born just after the war have entered the child-bearing age groups. But age-specific fertility rates which discount the effect of a changing age-distribution are in most countries still moving downwards. Table 2.1 shows these trends. Unless governments take extreme steps, such as banning abortion or contraceptives, the decline of European birth rates is unlikely to be quickly reversed. Many European nations will in the 1980s have a very slow rate of natural increase. The growth of divorce, leading to second marriages producing new families, may halt the decline in some countries. But several – the United Kingdom, Switzerland, West Germany and Austria, for example – may experience a decline in total population. Only a sharp fall in the death rate, which seems most unlikely, can alter this forecast.

Therefore, for those planning to meet housing needs, the most urgent questions are no longer about the numbers of people to be sheltered but about how many of them will form separate households. Changes in demographic structure may produce growing numbers of households, even in falling populations. An increase in households may be brought about by a growth in numbers in the household-forming groups (married couples, for example) or by an increasing tendency to form separate households among people (such as the young and single) who previously lived in other people's homes. When trends in household formation are clear, the next questions to ask will be about the size and character of these households.

The dominant trend in Europe's demographic structure is the growth

**2.1** *Crude Rates of Birth, Death and Natural Increase*
(Per 1,000 population)

| Rates of | 1950–59 | | | 1970–78 | | |
|---|---|---|---|---|---|---|
| | Birth | Death | Natural increase | Birth | Death | Natural increase |
| Northern Europe [1] | 16·7 | 11·0 | 5·6 | 14·2 | 11·3 | 3·0 |
| Western Europe [2] | 17·6 | 11·2 | 6·3 | 13·1 | 11·0 | 2·1 |
| Eastern Europe [3] | 22·6 | 10·7 | 12·0 | 17·2 | 10·4 | 6·8 |
| Southern Europe [4] | 21·0 | 10·0 | 11·0 | 16·9 | 9·1 | 7·9 |
| Europe excluding USSR | 19·5 | 10·7 | 8·8 | 15·3 | 10·4 | 5·0 |
| USSR | 25·7 | 8·4 | 17·4 | 17·9 | 8·7 | 9·1 |

*Sources:* UN, *Demographic Yearbook. Special Issue: Historical Supplement, 1979.*

*Notes:*
1. Denmark, Finland, Ireland, Norway, Sweden, United Kingdom.
2. Austria, Belgium, France, West Germany, Luxemburg, Netherlands, Switzerland.
3. Bulgaria, Czechoslovakia, East Germany, Hungary, Poland, Romania.
4. Albania (1950–59 only), Greece, Italy, Malta, Portugal, Spain, Yugoslavia.

of the older age groups. Even in countries like the Netherlands, Spain, Portugal and the USSR (all of which have had high birth rates until recently and hence had high proportions of young people in the early 1970s), the proportions of people over 65 have increased considerably. The middle-aged groups have declined proportionately. It seems likely, therefore, that competition for housing, which used to be fiercest between young, newly married couples struggling to find their first homes, will in future arise increasingly between the smaller numbers of newly married couples and the growing cohorts of elderly people wishing to maintain their own homes. Who wins will depend on many factors, including the level of pensions, the spread of owner-occupation, the distribution of housing subsidies, the rules governing access to public housing, and the laws regarding rents and security of tenure. This competition between old and young is already building up in parts of western and northern Europe. It would be less severe if there were more small units of housing available at convenient rents and in convenient places for older people to move into as their households dwindle in size. The

problem, often presented as a financial one, has clearly foreseeable demographic causes.

The pensioners' growing numbers have given them increasing political
strength. All across Europe, from Ireland to the USSR, there have
been major increases in public commitments to present and future pensioners. Somehow, therefore, a labour force which will soon be recruiting
from age groups that will be declining in numbers will be expected to
provide larger pensions – along with housing, residential care and other
services – for growing numbers of retired people. The dependent proportion of the population will probably continue downwards for a while
because there will be fewer children at the other end of the age range.
But if gaps emerge in Europe's labour force in the 1980s, they are
unlikely to be filled, as they were in the 1950s and 1960s, by recruits
from the Mediterranean and north African countries, or from the West
Indies and other former colonial territories of once-imperial powers –
the 'guest workers' described in the 1960s as the 'stokers' of central
Europe's overheated economies. The growing demands for labour in
many of the countries which supplied these recruits, coupled with the
harsh experience of depression and unemployment in Britain and central
Europe, seem likely to deter the more affluent economies from ever
again recruiting foreign labour on such a scale. That means that gaps,
if they emerge, will have to be filled from elsewhere. Women are the
reserve army from which these additional workers are likely to come.
They have already made a major contribution. Between 1961 and 1975,
2·1 million more women had entered employment in Britain alone.[5]
The eastern countries have gone even further than the west in getting
women into industry. ('Socialism,' it has been said, 'is built on the
mother-in-law' – she minds the children while their mother goes out to
work.) The only other source to which Europe's hard-pressed work
forces may look for recruits is the elderly themselves. But that would
call for a reversal of current trends which have powerful political support. Increasingly early retirement is now being successfully pressed for
by trade unions representing workers in many depressed industries. In
the USA political pressure from the elderly – 'grey power' – is beginning
to reverse these trends. But there is no sign of that in Europe yet.

In 1980, with unemployment rising again all over western Europe,
speculation about labour shortages in the 1980s may seem unrealistic.
Although the ECE's demographers say that 'current fertility trends and
future work-force trends could make many of Europe's recent labour
shortages appear mild in comparison with the ones to come',[6] increases
in productivity, already within reach, may fill gaps in the labour force

without bringing the unemployed back to work.

The experience of each country is likely to vary. The mature capitalist economies are clearly going to pass through a difficult period of adjustment as scarcities of raw materials increase and manufacturing processes hitherto confined to the more advanced economies – the production of radios, cars and ships, for example – move into the Third World. Some of these mature economies may remain trapped in depression, unable to compete either with more sophisticated neighbouring countries or with the mass production of the Third World. In that case they will be unable to honour the commitments to better pensions and other benefits now being made to their ageing workers.

If the world economy recovers and general shortages of labour re-emerge in many places, we are likely to see varying mixtures of the following trends in European countries. There may be further growth in the numbers of married women in work, and that may lead to a further rise in the age at which people marry, and a further fall in the numbers of children they have. There may be a resumption of migration, in future drawing workers from Africa, Asia and other places farther away than the Mediterranean countries, where labour is likely to become increasingly scarce. Eventually, perhaps, retirement may be postponed in industries where the more severe scarcities of labour develop. Dramatic increases in productivity are likely to occur in some industries which will shed workers with obsolete skills who may find it difficult to get jobs elsewhere.

Whatever pattern emerges, it will have an important influence on demands for housing. If labour scarcities attract more women into work, the competition for housing between childless households in which everyone is earning and families with several children depending on one earner will become increasingly biased against the family – probably still further reducing birth rates as a result, unless governments give far more generous help to larger families (as they have done in France and Hungary). If large-scale migration between countries begins again, important decisions will have to be taken about the rights of migrant workers to bring their families with them, and about the opportunities they are to have, with or without families, for getting decent housing. The most constructive outcome – and one which would pose the least daunting problems for housing policy – will be achieved by those countries in which productivity increases rapidly, unemployed workers are promptly retrained and redeployed, family benefits are sufficiently generous to enable those who choose to have children to compete on equal terms for space with the childless, and pensioners are enabled to go on working for as long as they wish.

If people can afford to buy their own homes, that helps to minimize their housing costs later in life. For many people house purchase is growing easier. Already the most common type of household in many parts of Europe, other than the south, contains two adults of working age and no dependent children or elderly parents. In Great Britain, by 1971, 27 per cent of households were of this kind.[7] If more and more women complete their families before the age of 30, this type of household will become more common throughout Europe. Most of these are middle-aged couples. Affluent middle age is, on this scale, a new phenomenon. When Booth and Rowntree made their first studies at the end of the nineteenth century, most women were on the brink of old age by the time their last children were off their hands. But now, with no dependants to care for, both partners will often be free to earn and to spend their earnings largely on themselves for as long as twenty years. Table 2.2 illustrates the trend. In nine different countries, for women

**2.2** *Average Numbers of Births Expected, and Numbers Achieved during First Six Years of Marriage*

(Averages per woman and percentages)

|  | Cohorts married | | | |
|  | Before 1951 | 1951–5 | 1956–60 | 1961–5 |
| --- | --- | --- | --- | --- |
| *Northern Europe* | | | | |
| England and Wales: | | | | |
| Nos. expected | 2·6 | 2·4 | 2·2 | 1·8 |
| Nos. achieved as % of those expected | 48 | 52 | 65 | 82 |
| Denmark: | | | | |
| Nos. expected | 2·7 | 2·6 | 2·7 | 2·5 |
| Nos. achieved as % of those expected | 48 | 52 | 54 | 59 |
| Finland: | | | | |
| Nos. expected | 4·0 | 3·1 | 2·8 | 2·3 |
| Nos. achieved as % of those expected | 39 | 53 | 57 | 65 |
| *Western Europe* | | | | |
| Belgium: | | | | |
| Nos. expected | 2·7 | 2·4 | 2·3 | 2·2 |
| Nos. achieved as % of those expected | 52 | 61 | 67 | 73 |
| France: | | | | |
| Nos. expected | 2·9 | 2·9 | 2·6 | 2·6 |
| Nos. achieved as % of those expected | 52 | 53 | 61 | 64 |

**2.2**—*Continued*

| | Before 1951 | Cohorts married 1951–5 | 1956–60 | 1961–5 |
|---|---|---|---|---|
| *Eastern Europe* | | | | |
| Czechoslovakia: | | | | |
| Nos. expected | 2·8 | 2·4 | 2·5 | 2·3 |
| Nos. achieved as % of those expected | 55 | 63 | 61 | 63 |
| Hungary: | | | | |
| Nos. expected | 2·5 | 2·2 | 2·1 | 1·9 |
| Nos. achieved as % of those expected | 58 | 57 | 57 | 63 |
| Poland: | | | | |
| Nos. expected | 3·2 | 2·9 | 2·6 | 2·4 |
| Nos. achieved as % of those expected | | 66 | 69 | 66 |
| *Southern Europe* | | | | |
| Yugoslavia: | | | | |
| Nos. expected | 3·4 | 3·1 | 2·7 | 2·5 |
| Nos. achieved as % of those expected | | 52 | 56 | 59 |

*Source:* United Nations Population Studies, *Fertility and Family Planning in Europe around 1970: A Comparative Study of 12 National Surveys.* Reproduced in *Economic Survey of Europe in 1974*, p. 105.

married in four successive periods, it shows the numbers of children born during the first six years of marriage as a percentage of the total number they expected to bear. The results were strikingly uniform. In all countries the expected size of family was falling, and mothers were in nearly every country getting closer to completing their expected families within six years. The decline in final family size and the earlier completion of child rearing will make a major contribution to the independence, affluence and housing conditions of retired people. Household earnings per person rise during the early years of a household's life, then dip during the period of family-building as children are born and wives often cease work, rise to a high plateau during middle age, and finally decline steeply in old age. The plateau is growing longer.

But young children do not cost as much to maintain as adults. How severely a household's income appears to fluctuate over its life span in relation to its needs depends largely on the weight given to the needs of children, and on whether any account is taken of the additional services a non-earning housewife contributes to the family. G. C. Fiegehen and his colleagues have traced a poverty cycle which fluctuates in much the same way as the one traced by Peter Townsend.[8] They show income per 'equivalent couple' in relation to supplementary benefit scales for households with heads of different ages. At each age they show the incomes of those at the fifth, tenth, fiftieth and ninetieth percentiles from the bottom (i.e., those poorer than all but 5 per cent, 10 per cent, etc. of households with heads of the same age). The resulting curves, traced in Figure 2.3, show that rich and poor alike experience a rather similar life cycle of alternating poverty and affluence. At all social levels the youngest and oldest households are poorest, and middle-aged households with heads aged between about 50 and 55 are richest.

**2.3** *Percentiles of Equivalent Household Income by Age of Head of Household, 1971*

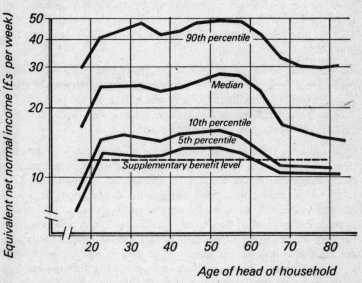

*Source:* G. C. Fiegehen, P. S. Lansley and A. D. Smith, *Poverty and Progress in Britain 1953–73*, Cambridge University Press, 1977, p. 55.

*Notes:*

1. Left-hand point on each curve based on 23 households with heads aged under 20, and subject to large sampling error.

2. Net normal income shown on a logarithmic scale.

## Marriage Patterns

We turn next to changes in patterns of marriage. Several important developments have taken place during the past ten years. The age of marriage in different countries is converging. In some parts of eastern Europe, where marriages have for at least a century taken place very early, the age of marriage has risen very slightly. In western European countries, where marriage has traditionally taken place later, marriage age has dropped – quite dramatically in some countries such as Holland and Austria. In parts of northern Europe, however, a different phenomenon is emerging: the age of marriage, particularly in Denmark and Sweden, is rising significantly. Somewhat similar trends are beginning to appear in France and in England and Wales. Meanwhile marriage rates as a whole have been declining, particularly in Sweden, and there has been a sharp increase in divorce rates everywhere except in Catholic southern Europe and Romania. As the ECE demographers point out:

> The facts no longer rule out the possibility that major questions of change may be at stake, possibly involving the survival of the traditional family unit, and in any case having central policy and behavioural implications for fertility, the role of women, labour force and housing, among other factors.[9]

It is difficult to foresee the implications of these trends for housing policy. Postponement of marriage in countries where people used to marry earlier may reduce demands for housing. But if couples then have their children more quickly, that may improve their capacity to pay for housing by reducing the period during which they have to live on one income. The meaning of these trends is not at all clear. A rising marriage age may only reflect a postponement of formal commitments until children are expected. If so, men and women may be forming households as early as ever – or earlier – and seeking housing through building societies, housing authorities and other institutions which may regard them as 'unstable' and their claims as 'illegitimate', following the conventions of earlier times. These conventions generally give way eventually to new patterns. In Britain the barriers which used to keep unmarried mothers out of municipal housing have been greatly reduced. So have those which made it difficult for unmarried couples and couples of the same sex to borrow money from building societies on their joint incomes. 'We will lend to two of anybody,' said the head of one of Britain's biggest building societies at a recent conference.[10] But more generous lending to 'two of anybody' may bode ill for single-person households and households with only one earner.

The implications for housing policy of the increase in divorce rates and, in some countries, a genuine drop in marriage rates are clearer. The numbers of people seeking to set up home on their own are likely to increase. Moreover, divorced and separated households will want larger, better houses than young single people will: they may have children, new partners, and furniture accumulated during previous years. Growing numbers of independent, unattached or semi-attached people are a new phenomenon. Their housing needs may not differ greatly from those of the married couples of the previous generation. But between them they will want more separate units, and more flexible allocation procedures capable of responding to more varied and rapidly changing needs. In countries where vast numbers of publicly owned houses, designed almost entirely for conventional families, have been built since the war, these new social patterns are already creating serious strains. Divorced people may be compelled to remarry as soon as possible in order to get housed, or to stay with their divorced spouses until another divorcee with access to housing appears on the scene to rescue one or other of them. This is not an uncommon situation in eastern Europe. In 1977 Hungary and East Germany had, along with Denmark and England and Wales, the highest divorce rates in Europe.

## Fertility

Trends in fertility follow partly from these trends in marriage. Completed family size seems to be declining towards a norm of two children throughout Europe, and more than three quarters of all births now occur when mothers are under the age of 30. As the ECE demographers point out, this early fertility, achieved with the help of simpler, safer and cheaper contraception, is particularly sensitive to economic, social and political conditions. Childbirth can be easily postponed in times of inflation or general uncertainty. This means, for example, that when house prices increase rapidly, as they did in Britain during the early 1970s, couples can postpone having children – although in that case other factors may also have been at work.

As the two-child family becomes the European norm, this may affect the ways in which the housing market works. Larger families with more than two children will find that potential demand for larger dwellings grows less severe. But the pattern of taxes, social benefits and prices has in many countries – and notably in Britain – grown less favourable to families with children. Thus, as small families become the rule, larger families may find it harder to gain a hearing in the market place and in the political arena. Only if government intervenes to help them with more generous child benefits, housing subsidies and other forms of family support can their demands become effective and their living standards keep pace with those of the rest of the population.

Figure 2.4 compares for countries in the EEC the value of child benefits for families of different sizes, expressing these benefits as a proportion of the average wage. It shows that Great Britain does reasonably well for the smaller family because, unlike some countries, it pays fairly generous benefits for the first child. It is for families of three or more children that this country falls behind her neighbours.

Particularly, perhaps, in Protestant countries, many have regarded the larger family as a parasite on the ordinary taxpayer. That is a shortsighted as well as an inhumane view. The social costs of overcrowded, unhealthy, poorly educated childhood are ultimately paid by the whole society. Moreover, the social benefits which the electorate is prepared to provide for average families and the childless when they are out of work depend in practice on the living standards attained by low-paid workers with several children when they are in work. These standards come to be regarded as the 'ceiling' to the whole structure of benefits which society is prepared to pay to people who are not able to earn their own living. Smaller families then have to survive on still lower benefits. The incomes of low-paid workers with several children – the 'working poor' – are thus the fulcrum on which everyone else's social benefits and living standards have to be levered forward. Poverty in larger working families holds down the living standards of all who are hard pressed.

## International Migration

Turning finally to questions of migration, we look first at international movements. After the Second World War, mass emigration from Europe on the scale experienced in the late nineteenth and early twentieth centuries came to an end. There was a net emigration of more than 3 million people from Europe to other continents between 1950 and 1970, but more than three quarters of that took place during the 1950s. This change arose partly from restrictions imposed by the receiving countries,

**2.4** *Child Benefits as a Percentage of Average Earnings*

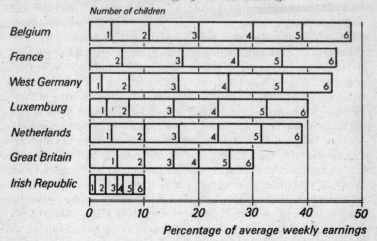

Number of children

Percentage of average weekly earnings

*Source:* Supplementary Benefits Commission, *Annual Report, 1979*, HMSO, Cmnd 8033, 1980, p. 82.

**Benefits**

1. All data on rates for July 1979 based on latest available information.

2. Sterling equivalents are for 9 July 1979.

3. In Belgium additional allowances of up to £3.03 are payable for each child aged 6 or over, according to age.

4. In France additional family allowances of up to £3.62 are payable for each child other than the first if there are children aged 10 or over, according to age. A separate benefit, family supplement, may also be paid for families with three or more children or for those with a child under 3 (even if it is the only child).

5. In Luxemburg additional allowances of up to £1.50 are payable for each child aged 6 or over.

6. In the Netherlands double the allowance can be paid for a child who is a student, apprentice or disabled person and who is substantially maintained by its parents. If born after 1 January 1979, the first child in the family qualifies for only half the normal rate until its third year.

7. In the United Kingdom an additional allowance of £2.00 is payable for the first child of a lone parent.

**Earnings**

8. Sterling equivalents are for 9 July 1979.

9. Earnings are based on the average gross hourly earnings in April 1979 of male manual workers in all industries except electricity, gas, steam and water (except for Ireland, see below).

10. In all cases weekly earnings have been derived by multiplying hourly rates by 40.

11. For Ireland figures relate to adult (21+) male workers (including non-manual) in manufacturing industry only.

and partly from Europe's economic recovery. Europeans need no longer look to New Worlds across the oceans for better opportunities: they can find them closer to home.

These opportunities have been found mainly in France and West Germany, although most of the countries of north-western Europe have recruited their share of immigrants. Between 1951 and 1970, West Germany and France accounted for 8 million out of a net immigration balance of 9·2 million for the whole of western Europe – many of West Germany's recruits coming initially from East Germany. In these two countries immigration accounted for 40 per cent of population growth between 1950 and 1970. The migrants came mainly from the Mediterranean countries: Italy, Greece, Turkey, Yugoslavia, the Iberian peninsula and north Africa. Then, as first the Italian and Spanish economies 'took off', followed by others, migrants from these more prosperous countries found better opportunities within their own borders – moving from southern to northern Italy, for example. The highly industrialized but demographically sluggish economies further north had to look to Turkey, north Africa and further afield for workers.

Since 1970, immigration has in West Germany been the only factor which has turned a natural decrease into a slow rate of growth. The country with the largest proportion of foreigners in its labour force is Switzerland. There, in 1970, 22 per cent of the economically active were 'aliens'.[11] The United Kingdom's immigrants have come from different sources – mainly Ireland and the New Commonwealth – and they have been offset in most years since the war by an even larger outflow of emigrants. Holland has also recruited people from her ex-colonies, particularly in recent years from the new republic of Surinam. Most of these movements have been prompted by economic motives. Large numbers of men aged between 20 and 44 came from countries where unemployment was widespread and birth rates were – and still often are – high. They came to work in countries where greater prosperity, declining birth rates, longer education, and earlier retirement combined to produce labour shortages, increasing the dependent and reducing the working proportions of their populations.

Three characteristics followed from the economic motivation of these migrations. First, the flow was perceived by the importing countries and often by the migrants themselves as a temporary one. The newcomers came strictly as workers, and in most of the receiving countries severe restrictions were imposed on residence and citizenship rights, and the rights of entry of dependants. Many of the immigrants intended to go home again once they had earned and saved enough to do so. Secondly, these short-term perceptions meant that the flow was particularly sensitive to economic upturns and downturns. Thirdly, the migrants had distinctive demographic characteristics, generally being male and considerably younger than the indigenous population. Increasingly too, they have been non-Europeans.

The effects of these migrations on the housing market, particularly in the receiving countries, can be striking. Some countries – Switzerland and West Germany are the most important examples – insist that employers provide at least initial housing for migrant workers. Often this housing has been of poor quality, never intended for families.[12] While the numbers of immigrants may remain fairly stable for long periods, their composition has changed rapidly. In 1973 in Switzerland, for example, 78 per cent of foreign workers had lived in the country for less than five years. Such countries need a substantial pool of housing which is available at short notice for a mobile population. Turnover costs, such as those experienced by owner-occupiers when they buy and sell houses, need to be very low. Most of this housing has therefore been rented. The spread of owner-occupation, which has been encouraged all over Europe by inflation and tax advantages, has therefore excluded short-term migrants from much of the housing stock. Subsidized rented housing, provided by public authorities, accountable to local electorates, has also tended to exclude them. On the continent immigrants generally found shelter in privately rented dwellings or, where they were not available, in second-class publicly financed dwellings. In countries such as West Germany, where privately rented housing remains fairly plentiful, their situation has generally not been too bad. But in Britain the influx of migrants during the 1950s and 1960s created more serious problems because many of the immigrants came to stay, and privately rented housing was declining fast. Here the solution of owner-occupation, sometimes financed by local authority loans, was more often adopted. Because British immigrants differed from those going to continental countries in more frequently seeking to settle, their demographic structure was correspondingly different: they included women as well as men, children of all ages, and old people too.

In all these countries, the housing stresses of overcrowded migrants, often living in rather decrepit property, gave rise to tensions amongst the immigrants themselves, and encouraged popular notions linking colour with overcrowding and squalor. Such notions lead to racial discrimination, and the concentration of immigrants into 'ghetto' neighbourhoods.

International migration may pose problems for the exporting countries too. Difficulties arise when large numbers of single men leave home, and other troubles may follow when they return. In Portugal between 1960 and 1970, for example, more than the entire natural increase was wiped out by emigration: well over a million people left this small country. The remaining families must have had an extremely difficult time, because less than a quarter of Portuguese women are in paid work. Many must have depended on remittances sent home to them, or on the generosity of their relatives. When the men return home, either as a result of economic recession elsewhere in Europe, or (as in Portugal) when an army is brought home from overseas, the effect on marriage rates, birth rates, housing demands and prices can be dramatic.[13]

Since the economic recession of the mid 1970s, these patterns have changed. The flow of migrants into European countries virtually ceased in 1973. Some of the workers already in northern and western Europe returned home, as they had done in previous recessions. But many stayed. That was because a great deal had been done to integrate immigrants into the societies where they had settled. Sweden gave immigrants the vote, and West Germany offered them unlimited residence rights after they had lived for eight years in the country. Governments became more willing to accept or even encourage the entry of dependants, while severely restricting the entry of new workers. Thus the demographic profile of the aliens became more like that of their hosts. If severe labour shortages reappear in the 1980s, whole families rather than workers alone may be accepted as migrants. But, as neighbouring economies prosper, the migrants are likely in future to come from further afield. So long as they are not excluded by racial discrimination, these families may make their way into the dominant social structure and find their feet, as families, in local housing markets. Their need for small dwellings or other special provisions may decrease because their households and housing requirements are more like those of the rest of the community.

## Internal Migration

As far as internal migration is concerned, the ECE demographers have pointed to its 'remarkable diversity'.[14] On the whole, three features have stood out. Firstly, urban growth has virtually ceased in northern and western Europe, where about three quarters of the population now live in areas defined as 'urban'. Generally it has been the suburbs and middle-sized towns which have grown most rapidly. Secondly, in the less developed parts of eastern Europe, such as Bulgaria and Romania, and in most countries of southern Europe, such as Spain and Greece, migration from rural areas to the big cities is still flowing strongly. Thirdly, some countries have experienced major inter-regional movements, usually allied to the pattern of employment opportunities – from the *Mezzogiorno* in southern Italy to the industrial north, for example, and from Clydeside to more prosperous parts of Britain. Most important for housing is the general conclusion that 'Europe as a whole . . . is rapidly approaching a stage of almost total urbanization, if not in residential patterns as such, then at least in socio-economic functional terms.'[15] Most Europeans have a fundamentally urban life style, but many of them can sustain that without actually living in a town. We discuss in Chapter 7 some of the patterns of urban settlement which result.

Some countries try by administrative regulation to restrict urbanization. They may then find that they have growing numbers of workers who commute to the towns each day from the countryside. That is very common in eastern Europe. In Hungary, Poland and Czechoslovakia, for example, such commuting has been encouraged by residential licensing systems. In western market economies the long-distance commuters are usually the richer people who can afford higher transport costs than most, and who often start work later in the morning. But in eastern Europe workers with high status in their enterprises are more likely to get the scarce supply of housing built in the cities. It is those with lower status and pay who are then compelled to commute long distances, catching buses early in the morning from distant villages. The results have been described by east European scholars as 'underurbanization' following from a policy of rapid industrialization. Perhaps because they have difficulty in translating popular pressure into public policy, the governments of these countries perceive housing as unproductive and therefore give it low priority for investment.

If younger workers move in large numbers to the cities, they may leave behind them an impoverished, elderly and declining population in remote communities which lack housing of the small size and good quality that old people need. The fate of such communities depends heavily on their political power and the generosity of the cities. In Norway, where many younger townspeople still have relatives in distant rural communities and the wartime sufferings of these communities are still vividly remembered, the response has been generous – in housing as in other matters.

In eastern and western Europe alike, a new pattern is emerging in some of these declining areas. They are being transformed by the more affluent city dwellers who use them as leisure areas. Rural slums have been taken over by weekenders, holiday-makers and the more affluent pensioners. The housing stock is improved, house prices soar, and some services, such as the shops, garages and telephones, are improved. But public transport often remains poor, since the weekenders generally have private cars, and education and health services may remain unchanged, since most of the newcomers are not permanent residents. Those of the original residents who can participate in the transition to a more affluent urban life style will prosper. They sell the weekenders petrol and groceries, rebuild and maintain their houses, work in the expanding hotels and so on. But older and more isolated people, who find that difficult, may gain little or nothing from the change. As the price of housing and much else rises, their opportunities may be increasingly restricted. There has been much more concern about the process of 'gentrification', which occurs when middle-class people move into inner-city neighbourhoods long occupied by the working class, but less concern about similar – and possibly more destructive – developments in the countryside.

## In Conclusion

Changes in demographic structure remain embedded in the population for the lifetimes of the people concerned, and through their children may imprint further effects on the next generation. This meant in the past that, barring disasters like wars and famines, fairly accurate predictions of the numbers and sizes of future households could be made. It is twenty years or more before the newborn show up in figures for new households.

In Europe, the numbers of households newly formed because of a first marriage will decline for many years to come as a result of the fall in birth rates. That decline is partly offset by the growing numbers of divorces and remarriages. There will be more old people in the housing market – particularly very old people, many of whom will be frail and in need of constant care as well as shelter. If Europe's ageing and currently underemployed work forces eventually need an injection of new recruits from elsewhere, a new generation of immigrant workers may more often bring their families with them. That much is clear.

But forecasting is growing harder. When the main factors shaping demands for housing were births and marriages, and nearly everyone got – and stayed – married, the forecasters had ample warning of changes in demand. Now that migration, divorce, new styles of human relationships which fall short of marriage, and more effective means of birth control have all come to play larger parts in shaping demands for housing, prediction grows more difficult. Demographic changes which affect demands will in future give less warning and will be harder to foresee.

Housing demands and needs still reflect the phase of social development attained by the country concerned. Countries depending largely on the simpler forms of agriculture and primary production usually have a poor and rapidly growing population; the revenues of government are correspondingly low, trained administrators are scarce and the techniques of administration unsophisticated. There is little that government can do to improve housing conditions quickly. Its resources may be better deployed in educating people for the work that must be done to increase productivity, in providing them with the capital equipment they need to prepare the groundwork of roads, drainage, water supplies, town plans and the supporting administrative structure which will be required to sustain the growth of cities, and in giving people scope to develop productive enterprises of various kinds. The fate of future generations will be determined for years to come by the standards of building, planning and urban equipment achieved at this stage.

Governments may feel compelled to give first priority to industrial investment, defence, health and education, but they can impose minimum standards of town planning without much cost to the community, and can direct building resources to the most rapidly growing centres and to the most urgent needs within these centres. They must frequently make unpopular decisions, choosing, for example, between a restricted, high-quality building programme – often popular with the rising urban middle class – and a numerically larger housing programme built at lower standards with local materials. The acquisition of land in advance of development and the imposition of wise controls on its use, though never popular with landowners, will pay handsome dividends for future generations. In major cities throughout Europe, the point at which effective controls over building and layout were first imposed is still clearly visible to anyone walking outwards from the town centre. During this stage of rapid growth, ten years' delay in taking control may condemn thousands to live in slums from which their successors are still struggling to escape sixty years later.

Most European countries have moved beyond this stage. At the next stage of development, many countries have a less mobile and more slowly growing population, and they become richer. This is the point at which fundamental changes occur in the conditions under which housing policies are made. The policy-makers have hitherto been responding with scanty resources to major increases in population, major flows of migration and major changes in industrial structure – factors they can do little to control. Henceforth the needs generated by these forces, considerable though they may be, no longer exceed the capacity of a properly organized building industry. Improvements in the quality of housing and greater opportunities for the establishment of separate households in unshared housing then play an increasingly important part amongst the requirements to be met. These are factors over which the policy-maker can exercise considerable control. Meanwhile, the resources which can be devoted to housing by government and private households alike grow larger. The payments which people make for housing and the revenues of government generally take a larger proportion of the growing national income. But the wages they earn in industrial economies are not adjusted to the needs of households at different phases of their families' development. When they have young children to feed and clothe, their housing needs are most urgent but they have least money available to spend on housing. Hence the nation's capacity to raise housing standards will depend on the government's capacity to subsidize housing for families or to redistribute income in ways which make subsidies less necessary.

The next phase of development, into which the wealthiest countries of eastern and western Europe are now moving, cannot be so clearly foreseen, but some of its characteristics are already apparent. The drive to establish more, and smaller, separate households has reached no ceiling. But the rise in headship rates – the proportions of people who are heads of households – is concentrated increasingly among the single, the young and the old, since nearly everyone else by now has a home of some kind. Growing demands for second homes must be met in ways which do not injure the communities amongst whom the weekenders and holiday-makers come to stay. Greater attention must be given to the needs of groups hitherto neglected – large families, the physically and mentally handicapped, students and foreign immigrants, for example. Resorts at spas and beside lakes or the sea attract tourists and growing numbers of retired people to what amounts to a new form of urban settlement with its own problems. These problems include sharp seasonal fluctuations in income and the demand for housing, the presence of many home owners with low incomes who are reluctant or unable to pay for better services, and a growing population of elderly frail people who need adaptations to their homes and good social and medical services to enable them to retain as much independence as possible.

Meanwhile, with the spread of the electric railway, followed by the motor car, people and their jobs move out of the biggest cities into the surrounding suburbs and middle-sized towns, leaving impoverished 'inner' cities behind them. Severe stresses may result as people redistribute themselves into increasingly polarized districts, each of which houses distinctive social classes, age groups, and household types. The attempt to bring about in the inner city a wholesale replacement of the first generation of urban housing provokes further losses of people and industry, and a decline in skills and taxable capacity, which may impoverish these neighbourhoods still more. The rebuilding, once it is completed, may bring people back to the centre. Rising fuel prices which increase the cost of commuting also hasten that removal. The least attractive peripheral neighbourhoods, often built originally by public housing authorities for people rehoused from downtown slums, may then become the most deprived urban areas.

The housing problem at this stage disintegrates into many different problems. These are not simply a matter of bricks and mortar. They arise from social changes which polarize or impoverish particular neighbourhoods, and from the difficulties of rebuilding cities and villages without destroying communities, their services, and the whole economy on which they depend.

In the next phase of development, the pressures compelling governments to assume responsibility for the solution of housing problems are unlikely to diminish. But these problems will not in future be solvable by housing production alone. They will call for a more complex and sophisticated response, involving many departments of government. Similar developments can be seen in other branches of the public services – in the health services, for example. That helps to explain the paradox that government's 'interventions' in the economy tend to increase, both absolutely and as a proportion of the national product, as wealth increases and as needs become, in a world context, less urgent. More recently, depression has provoked a new attempt by governments in some of the richer countries to extricate themselves from these responsibilities and reduce the whole scale of their commitments. Past experience suggests that they are unlikely to succeed for long.

These generalizations should not be taken to mean that governments are compelled by irresistible impersonal forces to embark on steadily more comprehensive attempts to improve housing standards. The decision to assume or decline responsibility, to develop or preserve existing structures and methods, has to be made by each government, again and again, through the usual processes of controversy, experiment and improvisation. Policy making is a learning process. We turn to these processes in Chapter 4. But first we must consider the supply of housing.

# 3
# The Supply of Housing

## Introduction

Having considered demands for housing, we must turn to the supply. Although many of the most urgent housing needs of the more highly developed European economies now have little to do with the physical character of the housing stock, it is with this that our discussion begins. Since the stock grows so slowly, the scope for solving housing problems depends for many years ahead on the houses already in being. What shapes this supply and determines its capacity to meet the demands made on it? These are the questions discussed in this chapter.

In the countries of Europe for which published data are available, the numbers of houses grew in the mid 1970s by an average of just under 2 per cent each year. In some parts of Europe, particularly in the east and in the increasingly affluent countries of southern Europe, the rates of growth were often a little higher – up to 2·7 per cent in Spain, for example. But the pace is generally slow. In the United Kingdom it has been even slower in recent years: between 1965 and 1968 the annual growth in the stock was about 1·7 per cent, but since 1969 it has dropped to little more than 1' per cent and is now well below that. In time the stock is increased and renewed, but how far housing conditions are improved depends on the rate at which needs are growing.

The international comparisons presented here may be read as 'league tables' of housing progress, but that is not their purpose. Each country's policies reflect its own needs, resources and aspirations. The main purpose of this chapter is to show how a country's housing situation evolves, to identify strengths and weaknesses in this situation which are typical of particular phases of economic and social development, and to explore the opportunities available during each phase for improving housing conditions.

A country's housing standards can be clarified by asking four questions about them. 1. How many separate dwellings are there in relation to the population to be housed? (This is an attempt to assess the opportunities potentially available to people for setting up separate households and finding a home to live in – an approximate measure of the family's independence and privacy.) **2.** How large are these dwellings? (An attempt to assess the opportunities for personal independence and privacy which these houses afford to the individual.) **3.** How much living space do people have in practice? (An attempt to measure the living space people actually secure from the distribution of houses amongst households.) **4.** How good is this housing? (An attempt to assess the quality of housing and the convenience and comfort it provides.) These questions will be considered in turn. They are not the only questions which might be asked. They do not tell us, for example, what these houses cost, or whether they stand in the right places, or what the quality of the surrounding environment is.

## The Quantity of Houses

At a conference called in 1966 by the United Nations Economic Commission for Europe,[1] the definition of 'dwelling' was more or less settled for the whole of Europe. Since then, 'households' have almost always been conceptually distinct from 'dwellings' or 'housing units'. 'Dwellings' are structurally separate units built for people to live in, with an entrance opening on to the street or a space within the building to which the public has access. There are, however, a few European countries which continue to publish data that do not conform to the general guidelines of the ECE. These are noted in Table 3.1 and some of the following tables.

Table 3.1 shows populations, changes in population, and the ratio of dwellings to people for European countries between 1960 and 1978.

**3.1** *Population, Population Growth and Quantity of Dwellings, 1960–78*

| | Population (millions) | | Average annual rate of change per 1,000 | Number of dwellings per 1,000 inhabitants | | Percentage change |
| --- | --- | --- | --- | --- | --- | --- |
| | 1960 | 1975 | 1960–75 | 1960 | 1978 | 1960–78 |
| United Kingdom | 52·7 | 55·8 | 0·9 | 315 | 378[1] | +20 |
| Austria | 7·1 | 7·5 | 1·3 | 304 | 399 | +31 |
| Belgium | 9·2 | 9·8 | 2·3 | 328 | 410[2] | +25 |
| Bulgaria | 7·6 | 8·8 | 4·6 | 228 | 300[2] | +32 |
| Czechoslovakia | 13·7 | 15·1 | 6·9 | 278 | 337[1] | +21 |

| | Population (millions) | | Average annual rate of change per 1,000 | Number of dwellings per 1,000 inhabitants | | Percentage change |
|---|---|---|---|---|---|---|
| | 1960 | 1975 | 1960–75 | 1960 | 1978 | 1960–78 |
| Denmark | 4·6 | 5·1 | 4·2 | 323 | 406[1] | +26 |
| East Germany[5] | 17·1 | 16·8 | −2·2 | 321 | 395[2] | +23 |
| Finland | 4·4 | 4·8 | 3·8 | 272 | 344[7] | +26 |
| France | 46·5 | 53·3 | 6·0 | 313 | 399[7] | +27 |
| Greece[6] | 8·4 | 9·3[2] | 7·8[3] | 229[4] | * | * |
| Hungary | 10·0 | 10·7 | 4·2 | 272 | 352 | +29 |
| Ireland | 2·8 | 3·2[2] | 11·7[3] | 240 | 266[1] | +11 |
| Italy | 50·6 | 56·7 | 6·9 | 257 | 321[2] | +25 |
| Netherlands | 11·5 | 13·9 | 8·5 | 244 | 334[1] | +37 |
| Norway | 3·6 | 4·1 | 5·7 | 299 | * | * |
| Poland | 29·8 | 35·0 | 9·2 | 236 | 275[1] | +17 |
| Portugal | 8·8 | 9·8 | 10·1 | 267 | * | * |
| Spain | 30·6 | 37·1 | 11·8 | 240 | 345[2] | +44 |
| Sweden | 7·5 | 8·3 | 3·7 | 344 | 431[7] | +25 |
| Switzerland | 5·4 | 6·3 | 3·0 | 291 | 414 | +42 |
| USSR | 214·4 | 261·3 | 9·2 | 244 | * | * |
| West Germany | 54·0 | 61·3 | 1·2 | 288 | 403[1] | +40 |
| Yugoslavia | 18·6 | 21·9 | 9·2 | 220 | 272[2] | +24 |

*Source:* UN, *Annual Bulletins of Housing and Building Statistics for Europe.*

*Notes:*
1. Estimated.
2. Figure for 1977
3. 1970–77.
4. Authorized dwellings only.
5. All data refer to dwellings in residential buildings only.
6. All data refer to dwellings authorized, not built.
7. Figure for 1975.
* No figures available.

The dwelling stock does not include rustic (semi-permanent) and improvised housing units (e.g., huts, cabins, shanties), mobile housing units (e.g., trailers, caravans, tents, wagons, boats) and housing units not intended for human habitation but in use for the purpose (e.g., stables, barns, mills, garages, warehouses).

Except where otherwise indicated, a dwelling is a room or suite of rooms and its accessories in a permanent building or structurally separated part thereof which by the way it has been built, rebuilt, converted, etc. is intended for private habitation. It should have a separate access to a street (direct or via a garden or grounds) or to a common space within the building (staircase, passage, gallery, etc.).

Population has generally grown most slowly in northern and western Europe. But advances in the ratio of dwellings to people have not necessarily been greatest in these countries. Some – notably the UK – have made less progress than more recently industrialized nations such as Spain and Bulgaria, which have had higher rates of demographic growth and have also built a lot of new houses. The east European countries began the 1960s with a relatively small stock of housing in relation to their needs, but they have now gone ahead so fast that in terms of dwellings per thousand population they are beginning to catch up with the more sluggish of the 'older' industrialized nations of Europe.

A simple comparison between the numbers of people and the numbers of dwellings takes no account of differences in need, of which those arising from differences in the demographic structure of the population are among the most important. A country with many widows and old people, for example, will need more and smaller houses than a country with a lot of children because the old form smaller and more numerous households than the young. There are differences in the age distributions of European countries, owing to long-term divergences in the pace and pattern of their demographic growth and the devastating effects of war on the death rates and (particularly) the birth rates of the generations affected. However, as Figures 3.2–3.5 illustrate, these demographic differences are becoming less pronounced. Differences in living standards are also narrowing, as we shall show. If peace and reasonable prosperity continue, European demographic profiles are likely to converge.

We have picked four countries to illustrate the trends already noted in the previous chapter. Poland's massive post-war birth rates have fallen to much lower levels, and the generations now growing fastest in numbers are the middle-aged and the 15–30-year-olds. Her population looks less like a pyramid as it moves towards the 'beehive' shape typical of north-western European countries such as the UK. Other countries of eastern Europe show similar trends. West Germany's war-ravaged age groups are growing older and have been succeeded by generations of more uniform size. France and East Germany, with similar wartime experience, show rather similar patterns. Greece, like other Mediterranean countries, is also moving towards a beehive-shaped distribution, with more old people and fewer children.

Henceforth, the housing opportunities of particular generations will depend less on their position in Europe's varied demographic structures, and more on other factors such as the supply of housing available, the financial status of the particular groups concerned and the general distribution of incomes.

**The Size of Houses**

As Valerie Karn pointed out, 'the UN statistics on room numbers in dwellings have such copious footnotes that one begins to devise riddles based on them'.[2] The notes to Table 3.6 show some of the difficulties; in fact, most countries stick to their idiosyncrasies over the years, so comparisons over time for each country are somewhat safer than comparisons between countries. In almost every country for which data are available, the average size of dwellings has increased. The sharper differences between countries were reduced over the decade 1960–70. Thus, while Swiss houses are still among the largest, they are no longer so far ahead of the rest in numbers of rooms as they used to be. In most countries the average dwelling has between 3 and 4 rooms. The countries of eastern Europe still have the smallest dwellings, but they are slowly catching up with the west. Similarly, the densities of occupation measured in persons per room have declined, particularly in the most crowded countries. But the average densities in eastern Europe are still generally over one person per room – about twice the figure for the United Kingdom.

Occupancy rates and the average sizes of houses measured in numbers of rooms are slowly converging all over Europe. Yet major differences persist. Traditions of building vary from country to country. The Norwegians have always lived mainly in houses, while their neighbours, the Swedes, with similar climate and living standards, have relied far more on flats. The countries of eastern Europe have long had a policy of mass-producing small flats. In 1978, for example, the average number of rooms per dwelling completed was 4·9 in West Germany and 2·8 in East Germany. The countries of eastern Europe are now building more houses, but the low space standards of previous building will impose higher occupancy rates on them for many years to come. These lower standards arise from a deliberate policy of getting as many dwellings as possible from restricted resources. The British have achieved their more spacious standards partly by economizing on the insulation, equipment and 'finish' of their houses, and partly by devoting fewer resources to industrial investment.

Just as important as the size of houses is their distribution. Do they stand where people want to live? Do the market and administrative systems of allocation ensure that households of different sizes get houses to suit their needs? The richer countries have generally succeeded in

## Population by Age and Sex Groups, 1977

### 3.2 United Kingdom

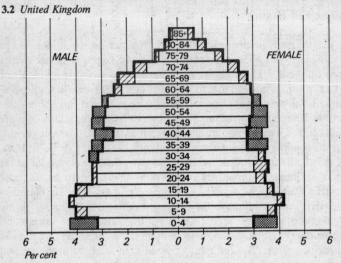

*Source:* Eurostat, *Demographic Statistics, 1977*, Statistical Office of the European Communities, 1978; and UN, *Demographic Yearbook, 1962*.

### 3.3 West Germany

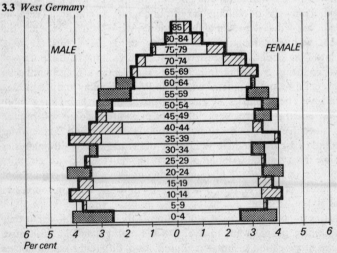

*Source:* Eurostat, *Demographic Statistics, 1977*, Statistical Office of the European Communities, 1978; and UN, *Demographic Yearbook, 1963*.

**3.4** *Poland*

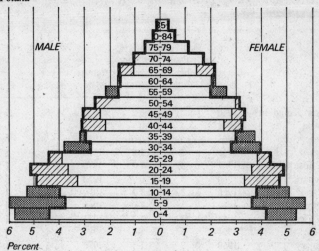

*Note:* Data for age bands of 70+ not comparable for 1961.

**3.5** *Greece*

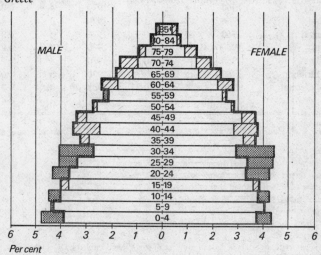

*Source:* UN, *Demographic Yearbook, 1963* and *1977*.

**Key**

1977 population over 1961 population.
1961 population over 1977 population.

**3.6** *Occupied Dwellings by Size and Density of Occupation around 1960 and 1970*

| | Census date | Average rooms per dwelling | Average persons per room | Census date | Average rooms per dwelling | Average persons per room |
|---|---|---|---|---|---|---|
| United Kingdom[1] | 1960 | 5 | 0·7 | 1970 | 5 | 0·6 |
| Austria | 1961 | 4 | 0·9 | 1971 | 4 | 0·8 |
| Belgium | 1961 | 5 | 0·6 | 1970 | 5 | 0·6 |
| Bulgaria[2] | 1965 | 3 | 1·3 | 1975 | 4 | 1·0 |
| Czechoslovakia | 1961 | 3 | 1·3 | 1970 | 3 | 1·1 |
| Denmark[3] | 1960 | 3 | 0·9 | 1970 | 4 | 0·8 |
| Finland[4] | 1960 | 3 | 1·3 | 1970 | 3 | 1·0 |
| France | 1962 | 3[5] | 1·0[6] | 1968 | 3 | 0·9 |
| East Germany[3] | 1961 | 3 | 1·2 | 1971 | 3 | 1·1[7] |
| Greece[4] | 1961 | 3[7] | 1·5 | 1971 | 4[3] | 0·9[1] |
| Hungary | 1960 | 2 | 1·5 | 1970 | 3 | 1·3 |
| Ireland | 1961 | 4 | 0·9 | 1971 | 5 | 0·9[8] |
| Italy | 1961 | 3 | 1·2 | 1971 | 4 | 1·0 |
| Netherlands | 1960 | 5[4] | 0·8 | 1971 | 5 | 0·7 |
| Norway[2] | 1960 | 4 | 0·8 | 1970 | 4 | 0·7 |
| Poland | 1960 | 3 | 1·7 | 1970 | 3 | 1·4 |
| Portugal | 1960 | 4 | 0·9 | 1970 | 4 | 0·8 |
| Spain | 1960 | 4 | 0·9[4] | 1970 | 4 | 0·8[4] |
| Sweden[4] | 1960 | – | 0·8 | 1970 | 4[9] | 0·7 |
| Switzerland | 1960 | 5 | 0·7 | 1970 | 5 | 0·6 |
| West Germany | 1960 | 4 | 0·9[4] | 1968 | 4 | 0·7 |
| Yugoslavia | 1961 | 3 | 1·6 | 1971 | 3 | 1·4 |

*Source:* U N, *Statistical Survey of the Housing Situation in the ECE Countries around 1970.*

*Notes:*
1. Data refer to households in conventional dwellings.
2. Data refer to all occupied living quarters rather than dwellings.
3. Kitchens are not counted as rooms.
4. Data from U N, *Statistical Yearbooks.*
5. Principal residences only.
6. Kitchens count as rooms only if 12m² or more.
7. Estimated.
8. A set of living quarters is defined in terms of the space occupied by a household.
9. Number of rooms includes rooms used only for professional or business purposes.

reducing serious overcrowding to very low levels. Table 3.7 compares six of these countries, all of which had low occupancy rates around 1960. All are countries in northern and western Europe which industrialized relatively early. They have, for at least half a century, been amongst the richest nations of the world, and they have more dwellings per 1,000 inhabitants than most countries. But the sizes of their dwellings are quite dissimilar: for example, only a quarter of Sweden's had five or more rooms, compared to two thirds of those in the Netherlands and three quarters of those in England and Wales.

The histories of these countries differ too. Some were devastated during the war; others escaped destruction in neutrality. Their demographic patterns are different, and so are their traditions of government. The Swiss, for example, with a federal constitution and a very small public sector of the housing market, were unwilling at this time to recognize that government had any permanent commitment to provide housing; West Germany had no publicly owned civilian housing at all.

**3.7** *Distribution of Dwelling Stock in Countries with Similar and Dissimilar Stocks and Occupancy Rates*

| Per cent of dwellings with: | Rooms | | | Persons per room | | | |
|---|---|---|---|---|---|---|---|
| | 1–2 | 3–4 | 5+ | Less than 1·5 | 1·5 or more | 2·0 or more | 3·0 or more |
| England and Wales (1966) | 1 | 24 | 75 | 98 | 2 | 1 | * |
| Belgium (1961) | 10 | 38 | 52 | 96 | 4 | 1 | * |
| West Germany (1960) | 10 | 61 | 29 | 92 | 9 | 3 | * |
| Netherlands (1956) | 5 | 28 | 66 | 90 | 10 | 4 | 1 |
| Sweden (1965) | 22 | 54 | 24 | 93 | 7 | 3 | * |
| Switzerland (1960) | 7 | 45 | 49 | 97 | 4 | 1 | * |
| Greece (1961) | 53 | 39 | 9 | 49 | 51 | 38 | 16 |
| Yugoslavia (1961) | 47 | 45 | 9 | 45 | 55 | 37 | 15 |
| Poland (1960) | 58 | 38 | 4 | 40 | 60 | 43 | 17 |

*Source:* UN, *Statistical Yearbooks*, 1969 and 1971.

*Notes:*
The census years in the table are the latest dates at which comparable data are available in this form.

* Less than 0·5 per cent.

The Swedes, on the other hand, had pursued an ambitious public housing programme under social-democratic governments for a generation. Yet, despite these differences, all six countries succeeded in reducing severe overcrowding to similarly low levels. Sweden and West Germany both had relatively few large houses, yet they had managed to achieve occupancy rates about as low as the others. Political systems and ideologies play only a small part in shaping housing standards and the distributions of housing space.

The same conclusions can be drawn for poorer countries. Table 3.7 also compares Greece, Yugoslavia and Poland. Despite their different political régimes, all have very similar housing stocks and occupancy rates. They share other fundamental characteristics: rapid rates of economic growth, similar living standards and demographic structure. These comparisons suggest that the quantitative supply of houses and the standards of space and privacy these houses provide depend mainly on the stage of demographic and economic development attained. The political and the economic market places are each capable of communicating housing demands reasonably effectively to the suppliers.

That is what we would expect. Housing is not just another durable consumer good. It is the setting for most of the household's activity and consumption, it stores most of their possessions, and it is related – both as cause and as effect – to every aspect of their life style and living standards. It cannot be understood or planned for in isolation from the rest of the economy. Housing evolves in step with the general development of the whole society.

## The Quality of Housing

Assessments of the quality of housing may distinguish the tolerable from the bad or the good from the tolerable. Table 3.8 deals with the lower of these levels, showing the percentages of dwellings which are supplied with water and electricity and have a flush lavatory. In the 1970s nearly all European houses had electricity, but many lacked the other things. Electricity can be quickly provided as the table makes clear. Rapid progress in electrification was made in Bulgaria, Greece, Poland, Portugal and Yugoslavia. Starting from low levels in 1960, all but Portugal had by 1970 caught up with the standards attained in the rest of Europe. Poland made particularly dramatic progress, raising the percentage of houses with electricity from 14 to 96 per cent.

**3.8** *Equipment within Dwellings around 1960 and 1970*

| Per cent of dwellings with: | Census dates | Piped water Around 1960 | Piped water Around 1970 | Flush WC Around 1960 | Flush WC Around 1970 | Electricity Around 1960 | Electricity Around 1970 |
|---|---|---|---|---|---|---|---|
| United Kingdom | '61, '71 | 98 | — | 87[1] | 85 | — | — |
| Austria | '61, '71 | 64 | 84 | — | 70 | 98 | — |
| Belgium | '61, '70 | 77 | 90 | 48 | 53 | 100 | 100 |
| Bulgaria | '65, '75 | 28 | 66 | 12 | 28 | 64 | 95 |
| Czechoslovakia | '61, '70 | 49 | 75 | 28 | 49 | 97 | 100 |
| Denmark | '60, '70 | 93 | 99 | 74 | 90 | 99 | — |
| East Germany | '61, '71 | 66 | 82 | — | 41 | — | 100 |
| Finland[3] | '60, '70 | 47 | 72 | 35 | 61 | 89 | 96 |
| France | '62, '68 | 78 | 91 | 37 | 52 | 98 | 99 |
| Greece[3] | '61, '71 | 29 | 65 | 15 | 45 | 53 | 88 |
| Hungary | '60, '70 | 23 | 36 | 16 | 27 | 81 | 92 |
| Ireland | '61, '71 | 51 | 73 | — | 62 | 83 | 95 |
| Italy | '61, '71 | 62 | 86 | — | — | 96 | 99 |
| Netherlands | '56, '71 | 90 | 97[2] | — | 81 | 98 | — |
| Norway | '60, '70 | 93 | 98 | 40 | 69 | — | — |
| Poland | '60, '70 | 30 | 47 | 19 | 33 | 14 | 96 |
| Portugal | '60, '70 | 29 | 48 | — | 34 | 41 | 64 |
| Spain | '60, '70 | 45 | 71 | — | 71 | 89 | — |
| Sweden[3] | '60, '75 | 90 | 98 | 76 | 95 | — | — |
| Switzerland | '60, '70 | 96 | — | — | 93 | — | — |
| West Germany | '60, '72 | 85 | 99 | 75 | 94 | 99 | 100 |
| Yugoslavia | '61, '71 | — | 34 | — | 26 | 56 | 88 |

*Source:* Data on electricity from UN, *Statistical Yearbooks.* Remainder from UN, *Statistical Survey of the Housing Situation in the ECE Countries around 1970*.

*Notes:*
1. 1961. All flush toilets, inside or outside the dwelling.
2. Piped water inside dwelling or outside within 100m.
3. Data from UN *Statistical Yearbooks*.

The great majority of European dwellings have an internal supply of piped water. But outside north-western Europe many people still have to rely on wells, street pumps, or taps in yards or on landings. It is only in the United Kingdom, Scandinavia, West Germany and the Netherlands that almost every home has piped water. In affluent countries such as Belgium and Austria, between 10 and 15 per cent of dwellings had no internal piped water around 1970. In eastern Europe standards were lower – particularly in Bulgaria, Hungary, Poland and Yugoslavia, all of which have large rural populations.

Europe has even further to go in providing water-borne sanitation. Although piped water inside the dwelling is a prerequisite for flush lavatories, one is not necessarily provided with the other. In France, where nearly all houses had piped water by 1970, little more than half had flush lavatories, although by 1975 nearly three quarters had attained this standard. Many other European countries fare worse than the French in this respect. But rapid progress can be made within a decade: Finland, Greece and Poland all achieved that during the 1960s, and many countries must have gone much further since then. (Since progress can be so rapid, comparisons should not be made between countries without carefully checking the dates concerned.)

These figures distinguish roughly between bad and tolerable housing. To distinguish between the tolerable and the good a more sophisticated assessment is needed. It would deal with such things as the design and 'finish' of buildings, insulation for sound and temperature, heating systems, waste-disposal services, built-in storage and other equipment, and – outside the dwelling itself – the provision of gardens, lifts, garages, laundries, nurseries, play space and other services. If statistics about such things were available, they would show that new building in the United Kingdom generally falls below that of Scandinavia, Switzerland, West Germany and parts of eastern Europe in some of these respects – particularly in the scale and efficiency of heating systems and insulation, and the provision of nurseries and built-in storage. However, the introduction of mandatory Parker Morris standards for local authority housing in the United Kingdom in 1967 brought central heating to most new council houses – too often at excessive cost to the users. The private sector has also made rapid progress in providing central heating for new houses. Nevertheless, housing over much of western Europe is more comfortably equipped. These are not mere frills. If most of the rooms in the United Kingdom are too expensive to heat to a tolerable temperature for several months of the year, and if many children have nowhere to play outside their homes, then this country may have less *usable* living space than other countries which have smaller houses or fewer rooms per head.

In one extremely important respect, however, British house design is coming to be regarded as among the best in Europe. Despite the recent furore about high-rise building, it is clear from Figures 3.9–3.12 that the United Kingdom's proportion of new housing built in the form of one- and two-dwelling units – usually with a private garden – has been amongst the highest in Europe. Norway has always been high in this league, and other countries such as West Germany, Denmark and Sweden are now catching up. Nowhere has the general revulsion against high-rise building in western Europe been sharper than in Sweden. Here, the voluntary housing societies which build a large share of the country's housing were so alarmed at the numbers of flats in tall blocks standing empty (27,000 dwellings built since 1967 were empty in 1974) that they drastically changed their policies: between 1971 and 1978 the proportion of new dwellings built in the form of one or two units rose from just over 30 per cent to over 70 per cent. Whether these policies will reduce the growing numbers of empty new dwellings now to be found in Denmark, Sweden and (to a lesser extent) West Germany, remains to be seen. Other factors, to be discussed in Chapter 15, also lie at the root of this problem. The east Europeans show no sign of changing their policies about the design of housing. Although most of them have large rural populations, the construction industries in many of these countries lack the tradition of good, solid rural building found in countries like Germany, Norway and Britain. Thus they have adopted large-scale industrial building techniques which have proved comparatively cheaper and quicker than their traditional methods for building small houses. Eastern Europeans will therefore continue for a long time to live in smaller dwellings built in larger, taller blocks than their western neighbours. Figure 6.2 on page 99 shows some typical examples of the flats now being built in these countries.

Government policies about the design of housing are shaped by assumptions originating many years ago. Some of these assumptions remain sound while others have grown obsolete. Since the First World War the British local housing authorities have generally sought to provide for the working class a cheaper version of the houses being built for those who could afford to buy a house of their own. Since the Second World War, under alternating governments of the left, backing public enterprise, and the right, backing private enterprise, competition between the public and private sectors has sharpened, and public housing has often been built to slightly higher standards than private housing. In England and Wales this tradition generally led to the building of small houses with gardens, for that was what was wanted by the home buyer whose preferences set a national standard. In Scotland, where many of the well-to-do had long chosen to live in flats, a different tradition developed.

Giving the public tenant what the private buyer chooses for himself has a lot to be said for it. But less appropriate policies have been fostered

## Percentage of Houses Built in Units of One or Two, 1965–78

**3.9** Northern Europe

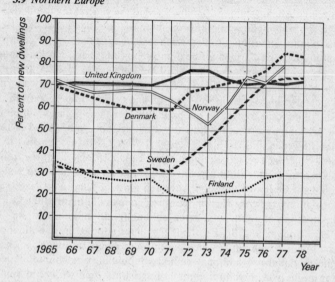

**3.10** Western Europe

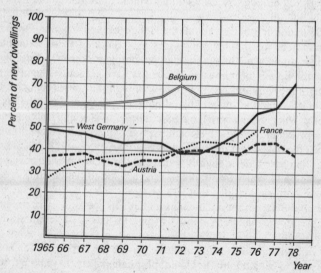

**3.11** *Eastern Europe*

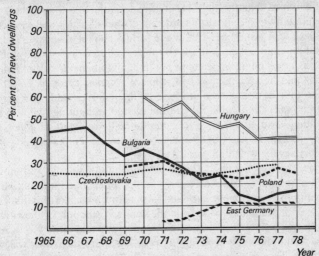

*Note:* No earlier figures available for Hungary, Poland or East Germany.

**3.12** *Southern Europe*

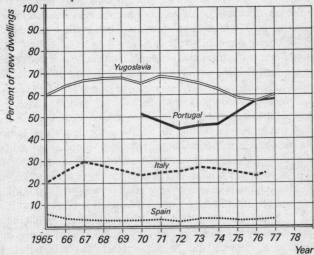

*Note:* No earlier figures available for Portugal.

*Source:* UN Economic Commission for Europe, *Annual Bulletins of Housing and Building Statistics for Europe.*

by economists, planners and senior officials throughout Europe who have assumed that the only productive activities are those which are recognized by governments, recorded in official statistics, and subject to tax and social insurance. This is the formal market economy. The informal economy or 'black market', which is outside this officially recognized economy but in which money or its equivalent nevertheless changes hands, tends to be neglected by designers, planners and policy-makers, and so they have not been sensitive to the demands and satisfactions which it generates, particularly in the context of housing policy. Similarly, they have tended to ignore the domestic economy in which the family, its friends, relatives and neighbours produce and exchange goods and services for which no price is charged.

These three economies – formal, informal and domestic – cannot in practice be distinguished as clearly as this brief description suggests. Activities constantly move back and forth between them. Much domestic laundry, for example, moved from the domestic economy of the kitchen sink to the formal economy of the launderette and is now returning again to the domestic economy as people acquire their own washing machines. The three economies are closely related to each other. The movement of millions of 'housewives' into paid jobs in the formal economy which has occurred in recent years has been made possible partly by the services of cleaners, baby-sitters, child-minders and others whose work – often paid, but more rarely insured and taxed – may figure in any of the three economies.

It is said that rising taxes and insurance contributions levied on earnings in the formal economy, coupled with the decline of this economy from which growing numbers of unemployed people are being excluded, have led to massive enlargement of the informal economy. Even in the centrally planned east European countries, where unemployment is not generally recognized as existing at all, there are flourishing informal economies. But it is difficult to gain reliable evidence about activities which, by definition, cannot be systematically recorded in any way. And it would be wrong to assume that it is the unemployed who are most active in the informal economy: those most successful in the legitimate market place are often better equipped to succeed in black markets too.

What is much clearer is that since the industrial revolution the domestic economy has grown enormously in scale. In the middle of the nineteenth century, when the British were arguing about their first housing and public health legislation, very little happened in people's homes. Working hours were cruelly long, education was brief and retirement virtually unheard of. For most people the home provided no more than the minimum shelter for sleeping, eating, and the production and rearing of children. But today the home may have a well-equipped kitchen, a garage or workshop, a garden and potting shed, a television set, music centre, playroom, and much else besides. In more and more homes central heating has made all the rooms comfortably usable throughout the year. Well under half the population is working. Far more are at school, rearing children or retired. Even the workers usually spend longer each week at home than at their place of work. For many people the activities which go on at home are more attractive, creative and productive than anything they do at work. But there are no official statistics of the domestic economy. Thus these activities, along with the people who perform them, tend to be neglected when governments make plans. When a redundant steelworker is compelled to retire early, the labour thereby lost to the formal economy is not offset against the extra care he may give to his family, his garden, his car or his house. If his wife 'goes to work', the extra labour she contributes to the formal economy is recorded in official statistics, but no account is taken of the loss of her services in the domestic economy. At home she is, officially speaking, unproductive. So are her children and their retired grandparents.

The misleading and damaging effects of these biases are now being recognized.[3] That recognition has implications for fiscal, social security, educational and many other policies; but some of the most important arise in the field of housing. The activities of children play a large part in the domestic economy. A study made for UNESCO[4] shows how children in different countries gain stimulation and self-confidence, or are deprived of both, as a result of the quality of the urban environment in which they grow up. Research monitoring the development of some 15,000 British children born in 1958[5] shows that even when the effects on children of every other discernible factor are discounted, the degree of crowding in their homes exerts an important influence on their attainment in school: children from crowded homes are handicapped. Other studies suggest that people's mental health and happiness depend to a considerable extent on the character of their housing. Neglect of the domestic economy and the informal economy has led planners, architects and the makers of housing policy under widely differing régimes to undervalue space – indoors and outdoors – and the scope which people can be given to extend and adapt their homes and gardens.[6] They have instead been too ready to build flats without gardens or even balconies, too reluctant to give tenants a stake in their homes or any scope for changing them, and too prone to admire the inflexible, unresponsive bureaucracies which too many housing authorities have made of themselves. The determination of the present British government to compel these authorities to make their housing available to the tenants at almost any price may prove to be a clumsy attack on complex problems. But it is not surprising that these authorities now have powerful enemies with a good deal of electoral support.

It is difficult to compare the scope which different kinds of housing offer for the domestic economy. Table 3.13 provides figures for electricity consumption and for some of the more readily comparable household equipment in eight countries of western Europe. It shows that in the early 1970s about half the dwellings in Belgium and Ireland

**3.13** *Electricity Consumption and Household Equipment around 1975*

| | Bath-room | Central heating | Freezer | Dish-washer | Phones | TVs | Household electricity consumption |
|---|---|---|---|---|---|---|---|
| | (Per cent of dwellings[1]) | | (Per cent of households[2]) | | (Per 1,000 inhabitants[3]) | | (kWh per person) |
| United Kingdom | 87[4] | — | 20 | 3 | 39 | 32 | 1,536 |
| Belgium | 55[5] | 37[5] | 28 | 7 | 31 | 29 | 978 |
| Denmark | 71[6] | 84[6] | 39 | 12 | 53 | 35 | 1,356 |
| France | 70[2] | 53[2] | 15 | 8 | — | 28 | 893 |
| West Germany | 82[7] | 45[7] | 40 | 10 | 37 | 31 | 1,224 |
| Ireland | 56[4] | — | 12 | 4 | 15 | 17 | 859 |
| Italy | 65[4] | 28[4] | — | 15 | 27 | 23 | 564 |
| Netherlands | 81[4] | 29[4] | 29 | 7 | — | 28 | 993 |

*Source:* Statistical Office of the European Communities, *Regional Statistics: Population, Employment, Living Standards*, 1978; and Central Statistical Office, *Social Trends, 7*, 1976.

*Notes:*
1. Dwellings include second residences and vacant dwellings, irrespective of whether the latter are part of residential or non-residential buildings.
2. 1975.
3. 1977.
4. 1971.
5. 1976.
6. 1970.
7. 1972.

had bathrooms, compared with about three quarters of the dwellings in most of the other countries listed. Electricity consumption varied widely, being highest in Denmark and the United Kingdom, where there were also most television sets. (The British fell further behind on freezers and dishwashers.)

The recent upsurge in ownership of cars and domestic equipment has important implications for housing. It means that many people need room somewhere in or around their homes for these large possessions. Thus a new source of housing obsolescence has appeared, for those households which do not have the space to accommodate cars, freezers, dishwashers or washing machines will eventually perceive themselves as deprived – and not without reason. There are already signs that, as more women take paid work and more houses have central heating and refrigerators, *unfrozen* food is becoming an expensive luxury. The spread of washing machines means that people have to travel further to find a launderette – preferably by car. Housing which prevents people from sharing in this way of life will become the slums of to-morrow.


## Conclusion

Thanks largely to studies made by the United Nations, most of these comparisons are already familiar to those who know where to find them. But the origins and evolution of the housing situations they portray are less clear. A country's housing conditions are both a cause and an effect of its current standard of living. But they are the outcome of a much longer history.

The quantity of houses in comparison with the numbers to be housed – and hence the opportunities potentially available to people for setting up home on their own – depends mainly on the comparative rates at which the population and the housing stock have grown over the past fifty years or so. In most of the poorer and less industrialized countries of Europe, populations have grown fairly rapidly; investment has been restricted, and concentrated until recently on the expansion of 'productive' resources rather than on the improvement of urban housing; and there has been no widespread easing of rural shortages through de-population of the countryside. Starting from low standards, the rate of building in these countries for a long while did not greatly outpace the growth in their needs. Meanwhile, in countries with higher living standards, a long industrial history and slow rates of population increase, the stock of dwellings is correspondingly more plentiful and progress has been easier. During the last twenty years a number of countries in southern and eastern Europe have moved from the former to the latter category. That is why basic standards of housing are now beginning to converge.

The living space available to people depends on the size and structure as well as the numbers of houses. In most European countries, rural housing tends to be slightly larger than urban housing, though less well equipped. In the country land is cheaper, but electricity, main drainage and water supplies are more expensive. The largest houses, however, are not found in the least urbanized countries, such as Greece and Yugoslavia; in those countries the average size of the whole stock tends to be smallest. It would be nearer the truth to say that the largest houses are found in countries in which wealth (in England and Switzerland, for example), large families (in Ireland and the Netherlands, for example) and other features of the cultural pattern established an early tradition of spacious building, which was carried over into the towns and adapted to urban life – usually in the form of houses rather than flats. Norwegians, for example, have until recently built larger houses than the wealthier Swedes, who have smaller families and in the past seemed to prefer living in flats. The space standards actually achieved and the extent of overcrowding depend on the location of houses, their distribution amongst households and many other factors. But the numbers overcrowded depend largely on the general wealth of the country and the stage of economic development it has reached.

The quality and equipment of the housing stock follow a somewhat different pattern, reflecting different aspects of a country's history. They naturally depend on the living standards the economy permits and the aspirations it encourages. Industrial revolutions creating the major industrial centres, followed by transport revolutions creating the suburbs surrounding these centres, produced the great housing inheritance of the wealthier countries. But the quality of this inheritance depends largely on the date at which these social changes took place, the living standards considered acceptable at that time, and the willingness of governments to enforce these standards. Thus the quality of housing tends to be best in countries where industrial revolutions created or expanded the cities at a point when wealth permitted, and government imposed, the most rigorous standards for new building. Long-industrialized and wealthy countries, like Belgium and France, therefore have housing of poorer quality than the Scandinavian countries where cities have been created more recently, or West Germany, where wartime devastation was followed by the most extensive rebuilding programme in Europe.

These observations may be summarized by saying that the *quantity* of housing depends mainly on the relationship between the rates at which housing and population have grown in the past fifty years. It therefore tends to be most plentiful in countries which are economically and demographically 'mature'. The *quality* of housing depends mainly on the age of the housing stock, and therefore tends to be best in countries which have built and replaced most housing since the point in their history at which adequate water, main drainage, gas and electricity services became available, and modern building standards were effectively enforced.

# 4
# First Interventions
# in the Housing Market

## The Role of Government

We have outlined in previous chapters some of the main social trends which shape Europe's changing demands for housing and the supply available to meet these demands. We can now turn to the response made by governments. Their policies change from year to year and a description of them would soon be out of date. We offer instead an outline of the roles which governments assume in this field. That may help readers to appreciate some of the strengths and weaknesses of their own government's approach.

Housing policies evolve over the years, bearing traces of the political history and administrative culture of the country concerned. That process may be illustrated by British patterns which most of our countrymen would probably regard as part of the natural order of things.

The life styles and living standards of the different regions of the British Isles are, by European standards, remarkably uniform – and growing more so.[1] In normal times the British expect to be able to borrow 80 or 90 per cent of the price of a new house at an interest rate of about 10–12 per cent and to repay this over twenty-five years, provided their income and age clearly demonstrate that they will be capable of honouring their obligations. Every part of the country has its elected local authority with similar powers for the provision of housing, depending in similar ways on subsidies from the central government; and, despite an infinite local variety in minor matters, the Department of the Environment and other central departments treat them all as having equal responsibilities for meeting housing needs. Housing for rent is still regarded as the natural instrument for sheltering people who cannot afford to meet their own needs unaided. The uses to which land can be put are now controlled by the state, but the land itself is normally owned privately. The state buys land from time to time, but its operations, though conducted through special procedures for purchase, valuation and appeal, are not regarded as being in principle very different from those of any other body that buys and sells in the market. Taxation is now used as an instrument for regulating the general development of the economy, but its principal function is still assumed to be the raising of revenue to pay for public services. Although grossly over-simplified, this glimpse of our world is a reasonably accurate summary of British assumptions, and these assumptions exercise a profound influence on our rulers, whether in Whitehall or town hall. Yet in countries not far away, this picture would seem incomprehensibly exotic.

Even in Norway and Italy, where living standards do not diverge greatly from our own, there are major economic, cultural, climatic and linguistic differences between regions. (North Italians are accustomed to say that 'Africa begins in Sicily' – if not closer.) Such differences, coupled with a sparsely scattered population – Oslo is as far from the North Cape as London is from Belgrade – make it impossible to establish a uniform system of independent local authorities or to treat each authority on the same footing. Altogether different institutions have therefore been created to build and manage housing. In many countries it is only the rich who can borrow money in the open market, and it is normal to raise two or three separate loans from different sources to buy a house. (The French have a saying: 'On ne prête qu'aux riches.') The money may then be repaid over ten years, forty years or sixty years.

As far as public housing is concerned, Britain seems to have a system unlike any other in the western world. Only in this country do public authorities acquire the land, build the dwellings, receive the subsidies, allocate the completed accommodation and collect the rents. No other market economy has so much publicly owned housing. No other country anywhere has demolished and rebuilt so much slum housing. In this country, voluntary bodies, which play so large a part elsewhere, soon abandoned the attempt to build working-class housing on a massive scale. Henceforth, they and the Labour movement relied increasingly on local government to provide for those who could not secure loans from the growing array of building societies. But in France, Austria, Germany, Scandinavia and the Netherlands, industrial, political and religious movements developed various patterns of voluntary and cooperative association which were later adopted by governments as their principal instruments for the provision of housing – just as our own friendly societies were called upon to administer national health insurance between 1911 and 1948. In some countries, repeated changes of régime have taught people that services which are to survive must not be too closely identified with government. People who originate from an independent, yeoman farming tradition do not necessarily assume that weekly tenancies provide the natural system of housing rights and tenures. They may devise other patterns which combine features of owner-occupation and tenancy. In Sweden and Norway – and, much earlier, in Germany too – it was more readily assumed that municipal governments had a duty to acquire land in advance of development in order to shape, rather than merely regulate, the growth of cities. Where much of the land was literally created by government, as in the Netherlands, it was natural for the state to adopt rather different attitudes to its ownership and use.

Government's first interventions in the housing field are not necessarily prompted by the need to protect public health and provide homes for heroes. The story may have begun with, or been carried forward by, attempts to bring about agricultural reforms and assist poverty-stricken regions (as in Italy and Ireland), to combat depression and mop up unemployment in the building trades (as in Sweden), to rebuild a war-shattered economy and erect a defence against Communism (as in West Germany), to increase the quantity of housing in times of scarcity without much regard for those in greatest need (as in France), or to attract key workers to growing industries (as in several east European countries). Several such potentially conflicting motives are usually to be found embedded somewhere in a housing policy.

The role of civil servants and of government itself varies from country to country. Where British administrators generally speak with the tact and reticence that befit secretaries of the minister, their French counterparts have the authority and directness of spokesmen of the Republic – slightly misleading though both guises may be. Where foreign visitors pursuing research in a British provincial town may be received by councillors and chief officers in the town hall, they would in France be received by the prefect and his staff in the local offices of the central government. Tracing the sinews of power to their source, they will eventually come to the politicians, but their route will lead in some countries through the Ministry of Finance, in others through the Central Planning Commission – with detours on the way which may pass through the Church, the trade unions or the banks. The officials they meet may be aware of the world beyond their departments and national frontiers, quoting the findings of research in several disciplines and three languages, or they may be able to tell them only about their own department's work – the next budget or the next election forming the outermost horizons of thought. When officials talk about 'housing needs', they may be referring to the requirements of a whole nation over the next decade, or to the current waiting-lists for public housing. When they talk of short-term programmes and the immediate future, they may be referring to the next five years or the next five months.

It is obvious that each country is different, and to multiply illustrations of this platitude is of little value unless it demonstrates the impact such differences make upon policy. The British experience may help to show how that comes about. This country's policies have long relied heavily on two great engines of housing finance. The building societies harvest repayments from their borrowers and deposits from millions of small savers. They then lend this money to house buyers, who are supported by tax reliefs and the conviction that inflation will steadily reduce the burden of their debts. The local housing authorities, subsidized by the Exchequer and the ratepayers and (thanks to inflation again) deriving constantly rising rents from their tenants, have also invested a steady flow of funds in houses. Both engines have until recently been used mainly to build for young families. Later it was natural that the work of clearing the slums and rehousing those who lived in them should be taken on by local councils, whose origins lie in the nineteenth-century sanitary and poor law authorities, and whose presiding ministry has descended in direct line through the Ministry of Health from the Poor Law Board. The dominant influence and the best-trained staff in this service were not housing managers but sanitary inspectors – as they were called until recently – concerned for more than a century with the prevention of overcrowding, the closure of unfit houses, and the removal of nuisances. This system tends to harden the social distinctions of a class-ridden society, by perpetuating them in bricks and mortar and street plans. Tenanted council estates are clearly distinguished from the speculative builders' owner-occupied suburbs, despite the basic uniformity of the houses in each, while the private landlord dies out, unable to contend with their subsidized competition. Our housing system – including the terms on which money can be borrowed – makes it increasingly difficult for people as they approach middle age to cross these boundaries and move from one kind of housing to the other. Meanwhile the housing debate between the political parties has been orchestrated to dramatize the competition between private enterprise (owner-occupation) and public enterprise (council housing).

Countries which have had a greater variety of institutions – cooperatives, housing associations, banks and so on – building houses with the aid of more varied forms of subsidy have generally been more successful in avoiding the social and spatial polarization of people, and the oversimplification of political issues which have afflicted Britain. But their builders and designers may have been less successful in housing those in greatest need and in replacing property which is unfit for human habitation. The voluntary organizations which built so much of the housing in these countries were accountable not to the whole electorate, but to cooperatives, trade unions, church groups and other bodies which generally represented the middle strata of society, not the working class or the poorest people.

The British tax system exercises a growing influence over the types and numbers of houses built and their distribution amongst households, as rising incomes and the spread of owner-occupation give greater play to the effect of various forms of tax relief. Taxation plays an important part in the housing systems of many other countries, but in some its influence has been more deliberately planned; it need not be just an accidental outcome of a revenue-raising process – as it was in Britain until quite recently. Elsewhere in western Europe, the private landlord has generally been regulated and subsidized; restrictions on his rents have been repeatedly modified and relaxed, and have been concentrated most heavily upon selected areas of shortage. In this way landlords have been employed, unwillingly maybe, as instruments of housing policy, and in return they have sometimes been more willing to retain a foothold in the housing market. In Britain landlords have been treated sometimes as parasites to be ruthlessly suppressed, and sometimes as paragons of free enterprise to be unleashed in haphazard and unselective fashion. Not surprisingly, they have extricated themselves from the market whenever they got the chance to escape with profit.

Policies do not follow from administrative structure and tradition in some inevitable, mechanistic way. But structure and tradition, by determining the means for getting things done and the people who must be convinced in the process, help to determine the way in which a problem is perceived and approached. In practice the aims of the people involved are likely to conflict. A policy of housing those in most urgent need may conflict with a policy of replacing the worst houses, and both will conflict with a policy of stimulating demand through subsidies directed to those who are most likely to be persuaded by such help to build or buy homes for themselves: different people will benefit from the pursuit of each of these objectives. An attempt to keep pace with the housing needs of expanding industrial centres will conflict with an attempt to revive poverty-stricken areas. A policy designed to improve productivity in the building industry will not be best suited for eliminating unemployment in the building trades. A policy designed to eliminate rent controls and create a 'free market' in housing may conflict with the need to avoid inflation of living costs and wages. A policy intended to put a stop to exploitative rents may also put a stop to maintenance and repairs. Every country's housing policies contain the seeds of several such conflicts, for housing is so central a feature of the economy and the way of life it supports that many of the competing aspirations at work in society gain a hearing in branches of government operating in this field. We should neither deplore these contradictions nor complacently tolerate them. For it is these contradictions which allow the more effective policy-makers, be they politicians or administrators, to seize opportunities for pursuing new objectives and modifying administrative structure and tradition. History exerts an influence on housing policies which is always important, but never all-important.

In this chapter and the next we shall briefly outline three roles, or patterns of responsibility, to be seen amongst the governments of the market economies of Europe, contrasting the distinctive features of each. Simplifying the constantly changing complexities of real life, this picture may be a bit of a caricature – but at least, we hope, a revealing one.

## First Objectives and Second Thoughts

Examples of the first pattern of housing responsibilities to be outlined are to be seen amongst the countries of southern Europe, stretching from Turkey to Portugal. These countries have recently passed through – some are still going through – the enormous social, economic and political changes which occurred in the other market economies of Europe many years ago. Spain, Portugal, Greece and Turkey have all experienced revolutions or *coups d'état* within the past few years. All of them were growing very fast economically until the recession which began in 1973. Along with the United Kingdom, all suffer from higher rates of inflation than occur elsewhere in western Europe. Some – notably Greece – have recently experienced a sharp fall in demographic growth. But everywhere people are flooding into the towns from the country and adopting urban life styles. Unemployment is relatively high in all these countries, but it has been masked by seasonal employment, military conscription, and particularly by emigration. The recent recession has reduced emigration, and this has made unemployment worse at home. That has been coupled with severe balance-of-payments problems, previously eased by the remittances of expatriates working abroad. Many of those who would previously have left their villages for a city elsewhere in Europe, now migrate to their own country's cities instead. Thus, although economic and demographic growth are slowing down in most of the Mediterranean countries, rapid changes are still taking place in their cities. Table 4.1 shows that the countries of southern Europe have a more rapidly growing proportion of their people living in towns than any other region of Europe. Warm climates and plentiful building skills and materials make housing problems easier to tackle (every Greek and Turk, it seems, knows how to build a house), but these problems are now particularly acute.

Although governments in all these countries have tried to restrict the movement of jobs and people to the towns, that has proved very difficult. It is easier to control the centrally planned countries of eastern Europe, where government has greater powers. In east and west alike, governments of the rapidly growing but poorer economies are committed to industrial growth. Because they tend to undervalue service industries, small-scale enterprise and the activities of the informal and domestic economies, they give low priority to housing. Even where capital is available for construction, most of it goes into factories, transport and

**4.1** *Changes in Urban and Rural Populations, by Regions, around 1950, 1960, 1970 and 1975*
(Percentages)

| | Year (approx.)[1] | Annual rate of change since preceding census | | Index of population change (1950 = 100·0) | | | Urban population as percentage of total population |
|---|---|---|---|---|---|---|---|
| | | Urban[2] | Rural | Total | Urban[2] | Rural | |
| Eastern | 1950(C) | — | — | 100·0 | 100·0 | 100·0 | 43·2 |
| Europe[3] | 1960(C) | 2·1 | −0·2 | 108·8 | 123·2 | 97·9 | 48·8 |
| | 1970(C) | 1·5 | −0·3 | 115·8 | 143·5 | 94·7 | 53·5 |
| | 1975(E)[4] | 1·8 | −0·8 | 121·1 | 158·8 | 92·4 | 56·6 |
| Northern | 1950(C) | — | — | 100·0 | 100·0 | 100·0 | 67·9 |
| Europe[5] | 1960(C) | 0·9 | −0·2 | 105·3 | 109·0 | 97·6 | 70·2 |
| | 1970(C) | 1·1 | −0·8 | 111·4 | 121·5 | 89·9 | 74·1 |
| | 1975(E)[4] | 0·7 | −0·5 | 114·1 | 126·0 | 88·7 | 75·1 |
| Western | 1950(C) | — | — | 100·0 | 100·0 | 100·0 | 62·8 |
| Europe[6] | 1960(C) | 2·2 | −1·0 | 111·0 | 123·3 | 90·2 | 69·8 |
| | 1970(C) | 1·5 | −1·0 | 119·8 | 142·9 | 80·9 | 74·9 |
| | 1975(E)[4] | 1·2 | −1·4 | 124·3 | 152·7 | 76·4 | 77·1 |

| | Year (approx.)[1] | Annual rate of change since preceding census | | Index of population change (1950 = 100·0) | | | Urban population as percentage of total population |
|---|---|---|---|---|---|---|---|
| | | Urban[2] | Rural | Total | Urban[2] | Rural | |
| Southern | 1950(C) | — | — | 100·0 | 100·0 | 100·0 | 35·5 |
| Europe[7] | 1960(C) | 2·3 | −0·2 | 107·8 | 125·1 | 98·2 | 41·2 |
| | 1970(C) | 2·5 | −0·7 | 116·1 | 160·7 | 91·7 | 49·1 |
| | 1975(E)[4, 8] | 1·7 | −0·7 | 121·8 | 203·6 | 76·9 | 59·2 |
| Europe | 1950(C) | — | — | 100·0 | 100·0 | 100·0 | 51·7 |
| excluding | 1960(C) | 1·9 | −0·4 | 108·6 | 120·2 | 96·1 | 57·3 |
| USSR | 1970(C) | 1·6 | −0·7 | 116·3 | 141·2 | 89·7 | 62·8 |
| | 1975(E)[4] | 1·4 | −0·8 | 121·0 | 157·1 | 82·4 | 67·1 |
| USSR | 1950(E) | — | — | 100·0 | 100·0 | 100·0 | 38·9 |
| | 1960(E) | 4·1 | −0·1 | 118·9 | 149·6 | 99·4 | 48·9 |
| | 1970(E) | 2·7 | −0·3 | 135·4 | 196·0 | 96·9 | 56·3 |
| | 1975(E)[4] | 2·3 | −0·9 | 142·9 | 222·3 | 92·3 | 60·5 |

*Source:* UN, *Economic Survey of Europe in 1977, Part II*, op. cit., p. 179.

*Notes:*

1. (C) = censuses around stated year; (E) = estimates for stated year.
2. As a general rule, national definitions of 'urban' have been accepted.
3. Bulgaria, Czechoslovakia, East Germany, Hungary, Poland, Romania.
4. Based on information for 1973–4.
5. Denmark, Finland, Ireland, Norway, Sweden, United Kingdom.
6. Austria, Belgium, France, West Germany, Netherlands, Switzerland.
7. Greece, Italy, Portugal, Spain, Yugoslavia.
8. In addition to the countries included under footnote 7, in 1975 Albania and several smaller countries were also included.

other investments, rather than housing. It is unusual in market economies of this kind to find large-scale state intervention in the housing market. The great majority of houses are privately owned – often owner-occupied, both in rural areas, where a peasant economy has usually existed for many centuries, and also in the towns, where recent migrants often own their own homes. Such migrants may squat on land illegally and build their own shacks on it, or they may buy their way into more substantial apartments, often built by illegal developers who may themselves be ex-squatters.

The pace of social and economic change in these countries is so rapid and their administrative and technical resources so limited that governments have great difficulties in getting to grips with housing problems.

But as they become more like the rest of Europe, their housing problems and policies grow more like those of the countries to the north and west. Turkey and Greece provide contrasting examples of these changes.

Turkey is still very poor, with an income of $1000 per head in 1976, and her population is growing at a phenomenal rate – from 29 million in 1962 to 43 million in 1977.[2] The rate at which her urban population is growing is unprecedented in Europe, although fairly commonplace in the Far East and Latin America: Istanbul's population grows by 9 per cent a year. Unemployment is difficult to estimate because so many Turks work in very small-scale enterprises, but the fact that such a large number of Turks have left the country (the 1977 National Plan estimated there were 1·1 million Turkish workers living abroad in that year) shows that many of them believe job opportunities are better elsewhere. When they return home, these workers usually bring money for housing and consumer goods, and – wherever they originated – they usually settle in the two major cities of Istanbul and Ankara. Thus emigration delays the growth of Turkish cities but does not prevent it.

Turkey's housing problems are unlike those to be seen elsewhere in Europe, although most European countries have at some time had similar experience. In one sense, the Turks do not have a housing problem: they are extraordinarily adept at building for themselves and their administrative system has accommodated every kind of building, whether or not it is strictly lawful. Most migrants to the city put up *gecekondu* (literally 'built overnight'). These are squatters' shacks on illegally occupied land, for which a capital sum is paid to a local *gecekondu* 'boss'. Once settled into these shacks, they set about improving them, inside and out, cultivating subsistence crops and working hard at street-dealing to buy the 'luxuries' which become 'necessities' once they have attained an urban life style. The municipal authorities may grant squatters a legal right to their land, especially around election time. Later they will provide communal taps, electricity and even a few local buses. A local philanthropist – often an ex-squatter who has become wealthy through sales of land and apartment blocks, legal and illegal – may endow a local school or mosque. This is how 55 per cent of Istanbul's population live at the moment. Their housing standards vary greatly, depending on how long they have lived in the city, the amount of capital with which they arrived, and the support they have been able to gain from kin already in the town. Some of this housing is dreadful by western European standards, lacking running water, drains and heating. Large families often live in single rooms adorned by one beautiful Anatolian carpet (soon to be discarded for imported nylon) and a washing machine which formed part of the wife's trousseau but for which there is no water supply. But the rapid growth of the city means that land, whether sold legally or not, may rise enormously in value, providing large capital windfalls for the more fortunate squatters. They may sell their illegally acquired land to property developers for a capital sum and the ownership of one or two flats in the apartment block to be built on the site. These blocks, containing large flats with splendid internal fittings, sit cheek by jowl with shacks roofed with corrugated iron. At first the apartments probably lack drains, running water, electricity and paved roads. But once the municipality has caught up with this free enterprise main services are installed, and such housing can provide desirable homes for the new urban middle-class. Housing themselves in this way, the Turks acquire personal wealth and pursue a strange route to 'social mix'.

Over 90 per cent of new Turkish dwellings are built privately, many in this 'illegal' way. But the government is beginning to intervene in the housing market. The chief thing it does is to lend money at very low rates of interest to housing cooperatives, mainly through national banks and the Social Security Fund. Although these cooperatives are supposed to be for workers, most have an entirely middle-class membership. Many are run by property developers whose main operations are illegal. There is no sign that the central government intends to abandon this regressive policy, but local municipalities are beginning to recognize that they should also do something for the poorest migrants. Thus Istanbul has recently developed two areas on a 'sites and services' model, providing basic services before the land is squatted, and building simple dwelling shells for which people pay a very low rent. These sites are proving very popular, and they may eventually become a more common feature of Turkish housing policy.

Greece's economy has developed further than Turkey's, but her housing problems are similar. Income per head is still very low, but roughly double Turkey's. The response of the government provides an interesting contrast. Greece was until recently a predominantly agricultural country, but the 1971 census showed that the proportion of economically active people working in agriculture had fallen to less than half. In value produced, trade, transport and services are now the most important sector of the economy, with manufacturing a fairly close second. With this transformation has come rapid growth of cities, particularly around Salonika and Athens. The latter now houses over half of Greece's urban population. Although these cities have been growing more slowly than Turkey's, they have generated similar housing problems. Meanwhile, the total population of Greece grows slowly – between 1963 and 1973 at an annual average of 0·6 per cent, which was slower than France, Germany and Scandinavia at that time, and considerably slower than Spain. Many Greeks leave their country permanently: between 1955 and 1970 over 1 million left in this way, and many others emigrated temporarily. Greece's housing situation is correspondingly less critical than Turkey's: household densities and sizes even in the most densely settled areas have fallen a great deal in recent years. But Greece, more often than Turkey, has been shaken by earthquakes, leaving thousands homeless in their wake, and this has led the Ministry of Social Services to set up emergency housing services run by the central government to deal with the problem. These have been provided in conjunction with housing services for refugees. Turkey has no arrangements of this kind.

In Greece, as in Turkey, squatting has been the normal way for newcomers to gain a foothold in the city. Their settlements have provided rich pickings for illegal property developers who have often persuaded local politicians to 'legalize' these areas later. No reliable count has been made of these illegal settlements, but it is estimated that between 1945 and 1966 380,000 people were illegally housed in Athens alone. Although this housing may be little better than a shanty town to start with, the residents constantly develop and improve it, and in time they create what can be a very attractive environment. The government's attitude towards such settlements is ambivalent but, in contrast to Turkey, where it is impossible to find a housing expert prepared to defend such a 'policy', the Greeks take a more positive view. In a recent report to the UN on 'Housing Tomorrow', a group of Greek housing experts working in government wrote as follows:

> The state appears to tolerate or even encourage unauthorized building. How else can one explain the fact that, contrary to official prohibition, unauthorized building has been continuously taking place from 1945 to the present? And, moreover, that in Athens alone the population that has moved into such areas in this period – mostly of provincial origin – amounts to about 45 per cent of the total population growth of the basin? Or that the unauthorized houses built have probably reached a figure of 150,000? . . . The state may present itself as a 'scarecrow' chasing illegal squatters away, but this only happens in order to keep up appearances and avoid the implication that it is itself encouraging illegal building. In essence, this constitutes a support of the latter, because in fact it does the state a service. And this is for the following reason.

Through unauthorized building, the state solves the problem of popular housing, almost without any initial cost to the state budget. It certainly solves it in an unorthodox way; while no public investment is required in the short term, in the long term heavy expenditures will be necessary for the development of illegal settlements, their servicing with urban infrastructure and, generally, the establishment of a human environment in public spaces.

The report goes on to discuss the costs and benefits of illegal housing, illustrating the social and architectural benefits of such settlements, likening them to rural villages with a strong sense of community and pleasing design. It concludes:

If organized house building in Greece today adopts the sterile model of large housing complexes, a model which European countries are now beginning to reject after 40 years of application, then there will come a day when we shall grow nostalgic for the dynamism and freshness of unauthorized settlements. The classes of people who manage to house themselves in the urban fringes outside official, planned areas, with economic sacrifice and legal dangers and despite the burden of various private exploiters and the negative attitude of the authorities, these classes prove the existence of a dynamism and creativity which today take the road of illegal building.

The Greek government is more tolerant of squatter settlements than the Turks are: there is less breast-beating about it, more pragmatic acceptance. Recent housing policies build on the individualism which such housing displays. Previous legislation, introduced in 1959, provided for the demolition of illegal slums and their replacement by small apartments to be built on small estates by the Ministry of Public Works. Similar estates were also built by the Ministry of Social Services for refugees and by the Organization for Workers' Housing for low-income workers. All this housing was free to the occupiers, funded by taxation raised particularly from employers. Not surprisingly, perhaps, it tended to stigmatize the people who lived in it, its quality was poor, it cramped the individualism of the occupiers, and was not popular. In 1972, the building of mass-produced state dwellings was abandoned and replaced by loans to individual households. Subsequent economic crises have held back the development of this policy, but it remains the intention of the government to concentrate on helping people find their own housing solutions. This policy seems better suited than Turkey's government-backed cooperatives to the industrious individualism which is characteristic of the people in both countries. It is also less likely to be abused by speculators, for whom the cooperatives have proved to be a very profitable form of investment.

As these Mediterranean countries grow richer and their administrative and professional services develop, housing policy is accepted as an essential part of industrial and urban planning. Spain is developing a more comprehensive housing policy of this kind. A Ministry of Housing was established in 1957, combining many functions previously exercised by different agencies, and a long-term projection of housing needs and the resources required to meet them was drawn up for the period 1961–76. The annual output of dwellings rose from 4 or 5 per 1,000 population in 1961–2 to 9 or 10 per 1,000 in 1971–5,[3] and there has been a steady growth in the proportion of the capital required for this programme which has come from private sources. Government funds have been increasingly used to ensure continuity of demand by reducing fluctuations in output, and to provide help for households in greater need of it. Building has been concentrated in the major industrial centres where population is now growing very fast, and it is intended that a start should soon be made on the major programme of replacement which will be required and on the provision of housing for the elderly, whose expectation of life is rising rapidly. These developments were made possible by the pace of economic growth and by the rising trend of saving and investment achieved in Spain during recent years, and carried forward by general political pressures for an improvement in living standards. The relaxation of central controls which followed Franco's death makes it harder to discern current trends. But the government's housing responsibilities appear to be taking an increasingly comprehensive form which can no longer be classed among the first group discussed here, since they are assuming patterns more like those to be described in the next chapter.

## Social Housing Policies

The next countries to be considered have a longer industrial history. This, in conjunction with other characteristics, goes far to explain the different pattern of housing responsibilities assumed by their governments. Switzerland and the United Kingdom, though dissimilar in many respects, followed 'residual' or 'social' housing policies for many years, although the UK is now in a more confused intermediate state. Further away, the USA, Canada and Australia have similar features.[4] Other countries in northern Europe – Norway and Sweden, for example –

once had the same sort of system, and Ireland and Belgium still exhibit some of the same characteristics. These countries are not classed together because their governments intervene in the housing market on a similar scale. The extent of government intervention amongst these countries varies widely, ranging from the UK, where high proportions of the housing stock belong to government, to Switzerland and North America, where the public sector is much smaller. The total number of dwellings produced annually also varies widely: until recently Switzerland built far more than the UK in relation to her population, but each of these countries is now producing much fewer houses when compared with the more rapidly developing economies of Europe.

Despite these differences, however, the character and intentions of housing policies in this group of countries have many similarities. The government's principal role is to come to the aid of selected groups in the population and help those who cannot secure housing for themselves in the 'open market'. Its operations are designed to meet particular needs and solve particular problems; and, whether they consist of building, lending, subsidy, rent controls or other measures, these operations are regarded as exceptional 'interventions' – often temporary interventions – within an otherwise 'normal' system. Thus government is not assumed to be responsible for the housing conditions of the whole population, except in the negative sense of enforcing certain minimum standards for the protection of public health, and it is not expected to prepare and implement a long-term national housing programme. It has a residual role. There is no national target figure for the building of new homes, no systematic attempt to relate public to private investment in housing, and little research into the interdependencies between different sectors of the housing market. In short, government does not have a perspective in which *all* consumers of housing and *all* sources of housing appear together. Instead, there is much discussion of the needs of special groups, such as the residents of inner-city areas, lone parents, migrant workers and others who are distinguished by the difficulties they have in the labour market and hence in the 'normal' housing market.

For a period during the mid 1960s, the United Kingdom adopted more comprehensive policies. But under the pressure from recession and balance-of-payments crises, through a period of minority government followed by a Conservative government intent on reducing the whole scale of the public sector of the economy, the UK has resumed a pattern of policies which gives government a more limited 'social' role.

Countries adopting this pattern have a number of common features. For various reasons their shortage of houses has not been as severe as that which has afflicted most of Europe. The population to be housed in Ireland fell for more than a century until the 1960s, and the United Kingdom's rates of population growth and internal migration are well below the averages for western Europe. Their major centres of population were established long ago, at a time when the state was not expected to build houses. They have a well-developed system of local government with a strong poor law and public health tradition, making it natural for the state to employ local authorities as the principal instrument of its housing policies, and for their efforts to be concentrated mainly upon problems of squalor and overcrowding. To these characteristics the Swiss add a distrust of government itself, which springs from a long republican tradition and an administrative system which is more completely decentralized than that of any other industrial country: the cantons – often minute in size – still constitute the principal unit for citizenship and administration.

The restricted and specialized role of governments in these countries has been made possible by well-organized and long-established private capital markets which enable the credit-worthy to borrow money for the building and purchase of houses. London, Brussels and Zurich are three of the world's principal financial centres, and the scope for lending and borrowing they provide has major implications for housing, as for other forms of capital investment: Switzerland's system has for many years been extraordinarily generous, offering at low interest rates loans which in effect need never be repaid. In Britain, too, the existence of a long-established nationwide system for lending money through building societies and insurance companies at what amount to negative real interest rates (because inflation generally proceeds faster) has permitted government to restrict its contribution in a way that would have been intolerable in countries with more severe housing shortages, greater scarcities of capital, greater regional disparities in living standards, or greater wartime devastation. Another factor enabling British governments to restrict their housing responsibilities has been the low cost of building in relation to the average wage: the domestic building industry works in a highly competitive way to produce buildings of modest standards at modest prices. In addition, a number of these countries have tax systems which enable borrowers to deduct interest payments on housing loans from their taxable incomes. This practice constitutes a major subsidy to investment in housing, but the influence it exerts on the housing market has not until recently been seen as an instrument of policy to be used for deliberate social purposes. It has been simply an accidental outcome of tax-gathering procedures.

The countries we have described as pursuing 'social' housing policies differ in all sorts of ways. In Switzerland the role of government is severely limited, being based on short-term legislation, typically authorizing no more than a four-year programme, with the intention – so far unrealized – that these powers be eventually terminated altogether. But in the United Kingdom the government financed the bulk of the house-building programme for several years after the war, and in 1949 it removed the restrictive phrases about 'housing for the working classes' which had hitherto confined the powers conferred by Housing Acts. Later, in the 1960s, a massive programme of grant-aided improvement and the development of publicly funded housing associations extended the role of the state well beyond its traditional function of helping those unable to fend for themselves in the market. But these attempts to take on a more comprehensive role were repeatedly abandoned, by Conservative and Labour governments alike.

Yet, despite their diversity, the essentially residual roles assumed by the state in these countries can be distinguished from the more ambitious patterns found in the countries to be considered in the next chapter.

# 5
# Towards a Comprehensive Commitment

## More Comprehensive Policies

Most of the countries with long industrial histories and high living standards have followed 'social' housing policies at some stage of their development. But since the Second World War several of them have extended their commitments to a point at which they can no longer be regarded as residual 'interventions' within an otherwise 'normal' market; governments now shape and control this market to such an extent that their housing responsibilities have assumed a national or 'comprehensive' form.

All these countries have attained high levels of industrial and urban development. But, although it is easier for the governments of rich countries to secure the resources for a big housing programme, that alone does not explain the form their housing policies take. All have highly developed welfare systems which give their governments major responsibilities for medical care, education, social insurance, town planning and employment services. Such services cannot be taken far without it becoming obvious that housing plays an important part in their work. Housing standards may have a bigger influence on health than medicine; educational attainment depends partly on the pupils' home environment; opportunities for work and the scope for regenerating backward regional economies depend partly on the location and mobility of labour, and hence again upon housing. Governments in such countries are therefore less likely to regard housing as 'unproductive', and more likely to recognize that it makes a fundamental contribution to economic development. They also have, at central and local levels, a large, well-trained and reliable body of administrative and technical staff who are capable not only of operating a powerful and sophisticated bureaucracy, but also of forging strong links with other groups in society – cooperatives, trade unions, the building industry, the money-lenders or whoever they may be – which have an interest in sustaining a major housing programme.

It is for these reasons that a 'comprehensive' housing policy may appear to be the ultimate stage which sufficiently advanced economies attain. But that conclusion would ignore advanced economies, such as the United States, which have retained 'social' housing policies. To take the discussion further we must explain what we are talking about. It is a tendency, rather than a complete and consistent pattern. Comprehensive policies show the following characteristics to a more pronounced degree than the policies to be seen elsewhere:

**1.** Estimates and projections of housing requirements are prepared for the whole country and revised from time to time, contrasting the implications of different assumptions, and showing the programmes envisaged for the next five or ten years: thus the needs to be met are defined and discussed in a comprehensive fashion.

**2.** The government may itself commission a large or small proportion of the houses in the programme, or it may (as in West Germany) build no houses at all. But it draws up a long-term programme, which includes all forms of house building, and its own contribution is regarded as an integral part of that total. Policy will be revised and modified from time to time, often at fairly short notice, but builders, lenders, town planners and the public at large have confidence that building will continue in a reasonably predictable fashion. Thus the housing programme is comprehensively defined and, despite variations, underwritten by government. The government's own contribution to this programme is not regarded as a 'marginal' intervention designed only to meet residual needs which cannot be met by other investors.

**3.** By whatever means seem appropriate – and we shall see that many are available – government secures control of a sufficient volume of savings to ensure that money is available to sustain the level of building it requires.

**4.** Government does not merely predict but actively controls the total output of housing – often with great precision – and it relates this programme to other sectors of the economy. Therefore it is responsible both for expanding and for restricting output when either appears to be called for, and for ensuring that appropriate numbers of households will buy or rent the houses built. It may not always succeed in doing that, but if it fails it bears a heavy responsibility for the resulting mismatch between demand and supply.

**5.** The government has means for relating the output and geographical distribution of new houses to the general development of the whole economy and of particular industries and regions within it. This is a peculiarly difficult task which cannot be performed with precision in a changing society – even in centrally planned economies where government owns all the principal means of production – but systematic and increasingly effective attempts are made to forecast the growth and distribution of employment, population and households, and to show the relationships between these trends and the demands for housing and transport, and the pattern of land uses.

6. In times of general scarcity – now receding – the government, besides controlling new building, also has some control over the distribution of existing housing, particularly in the areas of greatest shortage, and takes responsibility for getting obsolete housing and its surrounding environment improved. These powers are usually exercised through municipal authorities. Thus housing policy deals with the use and condition of the whole stock of housing, not only with the distribution of new houses. To be effective such policies may call for fairly extensive regulation of rents in areas of shortage, and for new forms of subsidy to help the poorer people who often live in the housing which needs to be improved.

7. The government finds it has to assume a large measure of control over the standards, types and sizes of the new houses built, in order to ensure that the existing stock is increased in ways which match the needs to be met, and that its resources are used in an economical fashion to produce a sufficient quantity of houses which can be let or sold at prices which the people who are to go into them can afford.

8. The development of the building industry which has to fulfil these programmes cannot be left to chance without jeopardizing the rest of the system, and the government therefore assumes increasing responsibility for improving the technology, organization and general efficiency of the industry through research, education, practical demonstrations, development projects and other means.

9. These responsibilities cannot be fulfilled unless government knows a lot about the general development of the economy, makes fairly long-term forecasts of future needs and resources, and is briefed by officials familiar with current research in a variety of technical and social fields. Thus government conducts, promotes and uses research on a considerable scale.

Governments of the countries mentioned vary in the extent to which they abide by these requirements, and none completely fulfils all the conditions listed. Moreover, the list does not exhaust the characteristics of a genuinely 'comprehensive' housing system: little has been said, for example, about the links which have to be created between housing and the planning of urban development, transport and the location of jobs, and social and commercial services. (This omission reflects a weakness in the policies of many of these countries.) But the validity of the criteria in this list does not depend simply on the observed performance of governments. The rest of the list could be more or less predicted from the first two responsibilities which appear on it. Any government which is sufficiently committed to meeting housing needs in a comprehensive and ambitious fashion must in time be led, as a matter of logical necessity, to assume most of the remaining commitments. Governments which pursue these aims far enough find they are applying, in the sphere of housing, a new conception of the state. They are no longer regulating, supplementing, or restraining the operations of an independent market. They have assumed responsibility for shaping the kind of world their people are to live in, and hence for mobilizing the resources and creating the conditions required for that purpose. Distinctions between the 'public' and 'private' sectors of housing, which are central to the thinking of those accustomed to a 'social' pattern of housing policies, lose most of their significance. Private enterprise usually has as large and secure a part to play as ever – often a larger one – and its spokesmen do not for long oppose trends which help them to keep their capital productively employed within the context of a plan determined by government.

Opponents of this development will justifiably point out that our list of the components which together constitute a comprehensive policy explains how government intervention in one part of the economy leads to interventions everywhere else. Reactionaries in Britain – or, as they now often call themselves, 'liberals' – would on principle oppose all interventions and reject the competence of government to formulate any vision of the future. Conservatives in other European countries have generally been more sophisticated. The French, for example, have been ruled by conservative régimes with scant interruption since the Second World War, but their governments have never doubted the need for a large public sector and a comprehensively planned housing programme.

## How These Policies Developed

The main levers which governments have used to create a more comprehensive pattern of policies have been financial rather than administrative. The French and German governments used subsidies, taxes and loans to regulate new building and control the use of the existing housing stock. Instead of the complex criteria of housing 'need' used for the allocation of subsidized housing in Britain (an administrative system), the French and the Germans relied more heavily on broad criteria of income, using readily understood maxima and minima for different types of accommodation. The development of a comprehensive housing programme calls for control over a continuing flow of small savings and other payments, and the capacity to direct these funds into investment in housing. That control may be exercised in a variety of ways, and it is not necessary for the funds to pass through the hands of public authorities. In each country savings are garnered from several different sources; there is no single device or institution which provides all that is required. Although the people currently being rehoused pay quite heavily for the privilege, it is not principally from their savings that the capital resources for the programme are derived; nor does the scale of the housing programme depend directly on the income expectations of individual households. It depends on the growth and resources of the whole economy and on government decisions about the allocation of those resources.

The capital controlled by government is invested by different means in different types of housing and is not concentrated upon one sector of the programme. By offering money on different terms to a wide selection of investors – owner-occupiers, municipal housing authorities, private landlords, housing associations and cooperatives, for example – and by direct control of bank lending and the final, comparatively small, 'top loans' which actually determine whether particular building schemes proceed, governments can spread their influence through every sector of the market. Thus they can secure extensive and sensitive control of the programme, and provide a greater variety of housing for a wider variety of households, although the capital they invest may be no greater than the contribution made by British public authorities to the financing of council houses.

The Swedish system illustrates this pattern particularly well. There has never been an extensive private capital market in Sweden, and the costs of building are high, owing to the excellent quality of Swedish housing and the rigours of the climate and the terrain. Government has therefore provided three types of loan for house builders: first loans, at a rate of interest slightly below the market level, calling for no repayment until other loans have been repaid; and second and third loans, at similar privileged rates of interest, repaid over thirty to forty years. All three types of loan are available to all the principal types of investor, but their size varies: municipal authorities borrow 100 per cent of the capital cost of their building; non-profit-making cooperatives borrow slightly less; and owner-occupiers and private landlords successively less still. The distribution of these credits among the different investors and the different geographical regions of the country is planned with care in the light of up-to-date reports on building capacity furnished by local Labour Market Boards. The short-term credits covering the remaining margins of capital cost are provided by the banks, which work in close collaboration with government. The cost and quality of housing financed in this way are subject, respectively, to upper and lower limits. Since the war, more than 90 per cent of Sweden's large housing programme has depended on government lending and controls of this kind.

If this account suggests that the transition to comprehensive housing policies came about smoothly and deliberately, it would be misleading. All the countries which moved in this direction were jolted by a crisis of some kind which occurred at a time when the political climate permitted bold interventions by government. In Sweden this sense of crisis appears to have been provoked by the collapse of the building industry during the early years of the Second World War. In France the shock of defeat was followed after the war by a determination to shake off the years of stagnation and to fashion a more dynamic society. This development wrought changes which eventually had an effect on housing as on other sectors of the economy. Similar developments appear to have been provoked in the Netherlands by wartime devastation, a rapid growth in population and the loss of empire; in Norway by wartime devastation – particularly of the northern territories – and the rapid post-war growth of population and cities, coupled with the paucity of this small nation's capital resources; and in West Germany by the obliteration of most of her principal cities, the collapse of the currency, the threat of Communism and the flood of refugees from the east.

The development of more comprehensive housing responsibilities sprang at first from urgent needs, the capacity to meet these needs – given time – and the determination to do so. Then the housing market in turn began to generate its own 'crises'. Shortages of building materials often presented the first problem to be surmounted. Sites had then to be acquired and equipped with the services needed for housing. Then labour became increasingly scarce. As building costs rose in response to these shortages, the size and standards of housing had to be reappraised – and were frequently reduced to secure more houses from the resources available. The order and the severity of these bottlenecks varied from one country to another, but each government had to contend with successive crises on most of these fronts – crises which followed from their success in solving earlier problems on the road towards a solution of their country's housing problems. Thus policies designed at first to cope with massive losses from the housing stock or huge shifts and changes in population evolved to cope with the problems which arose from a large-scale housing drive.

Countries which have adopted 'comprehensive' policies are not compelled to maintain them. But powerful forces help to ensure that they do. Their governments do not usually mount large state housing programmes. They maintain a complex and essentially financial relationship with private and voluntary housing institutions, which have an interest in maintaining close collaboration with their paymaster. The main issues to be resolved are often settled without much public debate by officials and well-informed professionals working in the field. Most of the countries concerned – France, West Germany, the Netherlands, Sweden, Norway and Denmark – elect their parliaments by proportional representation, which often produces multi-party coalition governments. Lacking clearly defined political ideologies, these governments have been inclined to regard housing as a 'technical' matter to be left to the experts.

We do not conclude that one of the three patterns of housing policy which we have described is necessarily the best. International comparisons provide an education in the scope and limits, the strengths and weaknesses, of the various roles which government may adopt, not a 'best buy' formula for Housing Ministers. Dutch reliance on building by housing associations is to be expected of a nation which has achieved peaceful mutual toleration between its deeply entrenched religious denominations by ensuring that adherents of each have their own trade unions, their own radio and television stations, and – naturally – their own publicly funded housing associations. The West Germans' determination to enlarge owner-occupation, and to avoid building publicly owned housing at all costs, came equally naturally to people who were constantly trying to create defences against the Communist menace to the east, just as their innovative ways of encouraging saving and deploying loans were derived from long experience of inflation and currency reforms. Their desperate need for rebuilding after the war meant that every source of investment was regarded as legitimate.

Likewise, it was probably inevitable that Britain's two-party system would make housing a major political issue to be presented to the public as a contest between the party of free enterprise and the party of public enterprise. As the parties succeeded each other in power, this formula has probably produced more dramatic oscillations in policy than any other country has experienced. Decisions about complex issues of housing finance, rent levels and so on, which have in other countries been taken privately by expert professionals and administrators following consistent policies over long periods, have in Britain been taken – and constantly reversed – in heated political debates. This pattern has strengths as well as weaknesses. The poorest and worst-housed people have generally been rehoused, whereas the less accountable housing agencies of other countries have often neglected those in greatest need. Britain has carried through the biggest slum-clearance programme in the world, followed by the biggest subsidized home-improvement programme; and although 'hard-to-let' blocks of flats are now beginning to appear in many of Britain's biggest cities, that problem is nothing like so daunting as it is in several other European countries – for reasons we discuss below.

## New Problems, New Policies

New problems now confront the market economies of northern and western Europe. Their responses may prove to be a turning-point in the housing policies of the more affluent countries. The main developments now under way can be summarized under four related headings.

The quantitative problems – the sheer scarcities which dominated the policy-makers' concerns for a generation – have largely disappeared. That emerged dramatically in the early 1970s with the appearance of empty new housing in Sweden, Switzerland, the Netherlands, Denmark and West Germany – all of them for years at the top of Europe's production league tables, building ten or more dwellings per thousand population, as Figures 5.1 and 5.2 show. In 1973 and 1974, West Germany had about 300,000 new houses which no one was prepared to buy. Building was hurriedly cut back – too hurriedly in some places. These surpluses arose partly from the inflation of prices, the misjudgement of the types of housing in demand, and other factors we shall discuss. But, whatever their causes, they made it clear that Europe's main housing problem would henceforth centre on questions of quality rather than quantity and of distribution rather than production.

Growing attention is now being given to the replacement and improvement of obsolete housing. Table 5.4, listing proportions of older housing in many European countries, shows that this problem is most heavily concentrated in the older, industrial countries of the east and west – those with the longest-established cities and the more slowly growing populations. Successful policies for dealing with these problems will call for new resources and skills. High amongst these will be the

Dwellings Completed per 1,000 Inhabitants, 1970–79

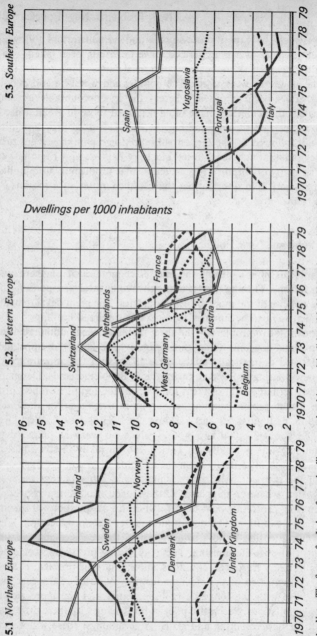

5.1 Northern Europe    5.2 Western Europe    5.3 Southern Europe

Dwellings per 1,000 inhabitants

1. *Note:* The figures for Italy refer to dwellings completed in municipalities with 20,000 and more inhabitants.

*Source:* UN Economic Commission for Europe, *Annual Bulletin of Housing and Building Statistics for Europe*, United Nations, Vols. XVIII, XX and XXII, 1974, 1976 and 1978.

**5.4** *Housing Built between the Wars and before the First World War, Europe 1968–71*

| Percentage of housing stock built: | before 1919 | 1919–46 |
| --- | --- | --- |
| United Kingdom | 36 | 23 |
| East Germany | 57 | 23 |
| France | 51 | 20 |
| Ireland | 45 | 20 |
| Austria | 42 | 14 |
| Hungary | 36 | 27 |
| Belgium | 33 | 27 |
| Czechoslovakia | 33 | 28 |
| West Germany | 32 | 17 |
| Italy | 31 | 14 |
| Poland | 30 | 27 |
| Sweden | 20 | 32 |
| Yugoslavia | 18 | 21 |
| Finland | 12 | 22 |
| Bulgaria | 8 | 22 |

*Source:* UN Economic Commission for Europe, *Major Trends in Housing Policy in ECE Countries*, 1980.

capacity to revive the economies as well as rebuild the housing of decaying neighbourhoods. Housing which is poorly maintained and poorly equipped is generally occupied by poor people. Those of them who are capable of working need, first and foremost, opportunities for earning more money: with larger incomes they can often improve their own houses, but with no increase in their incomes they will perforce allow housing somewhere to decay unless they are continuously subsidized to prevent that. Too often, slum-clearance and urban-renewal programmes have simply shifted around the map the unresolved problems of poverty which gave rise to the poor housing conditions which the programmes were intended to eliminate. Worse still, these programmes may break up and disperse communities which gave poor people some support in coping with a hard life. Worldwide recession is now making these problems more urgent, but harder to resolve.

All across western Europe, growing attempts are being made to reduce subsidies which give indiscriminate support to whole categories of housing and to replace them with more selective help for the people in greatest need – a switch to subsidies designed to manipulate distribution rather than to promote production. These developments produce new problems – a poverty trap for low-wage earners, who find that means-tested rent allowances coupled with progressive income tax and insurance contributions may together make it impossible for them to attain higher living standards, no matter how hard they try. We discuss the British version of these difficulties and some potential solutions in Part II of this book. Meanwhile, grants for the rehabilitation of older housing – now widely preferred to wholesale demolition and rebuilding – tend to flow in the opposite directions, being taken up not by the poor and the elderly, who are most likely to live in such houses, but by younger, richer and more mobile people, who have greater opportunities and incentives to raise the capital contributions usually required of those who seek improvement grants.

The second, and closely related, group of problems gaining increasing attention in these countries arises from the transformation of the ownership of housing. In virtually all the market economies of Europe, owner-occupied housing and housing rented from non-profit public agencies – each heavily subsidized in different ways – have been growing, while housing let by private landlords has, not surprisingly, been declining. During the 1960s, only Switzerland showed a reduction in the proportion of its stock which was owner-occupied.[1] Table 5.5 shows that at least half the houses are owner-occupied in nearly half the market economies for which we have figures – and this proportion is growing. Well over half the British now live in owner-occupied homes. The highest figures, however, are not found in the most affluent economies: Ireland comes top of this league, followed by Spain and Finland.

Most of these countries permit house buyers to deduct mortgage interest from their incomes for tax purposes. Some of them tax the imputed rent of owner-occupied houses, regarding the services these homes provide as being a source of income equivalent to the interest which the owner would have earned had he invested his capital in some other way. But the net effect of these fiscal operations now amounts in most of the market economies to a larger subsidy to owner-occupiers than the total distributed through subsidies to individual householders and in interest subsidies on government loans for housing.[2] This trend will not easily be reversed: as the numbers of home owners increase, so does their political power, and it would be a brave politician who proposed any major assault upon their tax privileges. The more modest aims of realistic policy-makers are therefore likely to be to monitor and publish the extent of the revenue lost in this way, to restrict the number and value of the loans on which tax relief may be claimed, and to confer similar

**5.5** *Tenure of Housing in the Market Economies, 1970*
    (Percentages)

|  | Owner-occupied | Let | Other |
|---|---|---|---|
| United Kingdom | 49 | 51 | — |
| Ireland | 71 | 27 | 2 |
| Spain | 64 | 28 | 9 |
| Finland | 60 | 39 | — |
| Belgium | 55 | 42 | 3 |
| Norway | 53 | 42 | 5 |
| Italy | 51 | 44 | 5 |
| Denmark | 49 | 47 | 5 |
| France | 45 | 43 | 12 |
| Austria | 41 | 47 | 12 |
| West Germany | 36 | 64 | — |
| Netherlands | 35 | 65 | — |
| Sweden | 35 | 52 | 13 |
| Switzerland | 28 | 69 | 3 |

*Source:* UN Economic Commission for Europe, *A Statistical Survey of the Housing Situation in the ECE Countries around 1970*, pp. 80–90 and 270–71.

benefits on house buyers too poor to pay tax. The United Kingdom has made some progress in all these directions.

As larger numbers of people have bought their own homes, the house builders have had to reach further down-market to households with lower and lower incomes. Extensions of the period for repaying loans and new subsidies of various kinds have helped them to achieve that. But if houses are to be built to a standard that will still be acceptable towards the end of their life – sixty years or more hence – promoting the further expansion of owner-occupation becomes an increasingly expensive and difficult task. In response to this dilemma, governments in many parts of Europe have been inventing new forms of tenure which fall somewhere between renting and owner-occupation: co-ownership schemes, condominiums, renting with an option to purchase, equity sharing – all are designed to give people tax reliefs, a stake in the equity of their house and other advantages of owner-occupation, but with lower monthly payments and greater protection than the ordinary house buyer has.

The third group of problems now attracting growing attention in the market economies arises from inflation. Although inflation was endemic, it was usually fairly gentle until the oil price increases in 1973. Since then it has become so rapid that borrowers, lenders and governments have had to give it a central place in their calculations. Several major problems follow. One is the constant tendency of new housing built at rising prices with money borrowed at rising rates of interest to be far more expensive than older housing of equal quality. That tendency grows worse still when coupled with rent controls, for they generally bite hardest on old housing and on housing which has been occupied by the same tenants for many years. Many countries have been seeking ways of rationalizing subsidies, loan charges and rent controls so that rents reflect more accurately the value of the accommodation offered. The task has been easier in the United Kingdom, thanks to the capacity of this country's large housing authorities to pool and rationalize rents and subsidies on property built over many years, than it has been in countries relying on a large number of small, independent housing associations and cooperatives.

Similar problems arise for house buyers on modest incomes, and those who build for them. New houses have to be sold at inflated prices to people borrowing from lenders who must add whatever real return they hope for to the 10 or 20 per cent decline in the real value of their savings which they have learnt to expect each year. Many potential buyers are priced right out of the market. Yet even Europe's increasingly high interest rates have in most years failed to compensate lenders for the effects of inflation. Thus those buyers who can surmount the hurdle of their initial payments generally do very well later, as their incomes overtake the repayments due on their loans. Faced with this dilemma, people are now seeking ways of reducing the early payments made by borrowers and of increasing the payments due later when their incomes have risen. Many lenders would be content with a very modest rate of interest if only they could be sure the money they lend would retain its value in real terms. A precarious balance has to be struck between the interests of borrowers, who want to be sure that their incomes and the market value of their houses rise a bit faster than their repayments, and the interests of lenders, who want to be sure that the value of their savings rises as fast as the cost of living. With the subsidy of tax relief available to help them, it should not be impossible to satisfy both. Several countries – notably Norway and Switzerland – are working on this problem.

The fourth set of problems is related to all the others. It is the apparent surplus of housing now emerging in most of the more affluent European countries. This is due, it is agreed, to a variety of reasons: in some countries, to the high prices and rents of new housing compared with older and more centrally located housing; in others, to the unpopularity of small flats built in tower blocks, or in long slabs with public decks which prevent proper supervision and destroy privacy; and elsewhere, to the unduly tight restriction of the categories of people permitted to rent subsidized housing. Some housing agencies have been reluctant to accept the new kinds of households which are now growing in numbers: teenage householders, communes and collectives, unmarried or previously married couples, couples of the same sex, and so on. Others have accepted anyone prepared to occupy their empty property – but not always with the happiest results. In Sweden and the Netherlands, small but expensive flats intended for single people have been taken by immigrant families who overcrowd them in order to pay the rent. Their crowded conditions and their ethnic distinctiveness advertise to the world at large that theirs has become an unpopular, hard-to-let neighbourhood. We discuss the British version of these problems in Chapter 15. Meanwhile real shortages persist. Young, single people, queuing for cheap and decent housing, have recently been rioting among the 'squats' of Amsterdam and Zurich.

## In Conclusion

If we had to sum up these trends in a sentence, we would say that the housing problems of Europe's market economies are becoming a matter of quality rather than quantity and of distribution rather than production. But since the sizes and quality of Europe's houses are becoming steadily more similar, both within countries and between countries, that assertion poses new questions. The quality of what? The distribution of what?

The housing now regarded as least desirable – some of it being demolished as unlettable and unsaleable – is neither the oldest nor the most poorly equipped. The old measures of housing stress – figures of persons per room and the presence or absence of water-borne sanitation, for example – no longer define the problem. The crucial factors distinguishing desirable from undesirable housing and the well-housed from the ill-housed are now connected either with tenure, price and the financial status of householders (their rights to tax reliefs, to rent controls, to a hedge against inflation, to sell or bequeath their homes, and so on), or they are connected with the layout of housing, its external environment, the character of the neighbourhood, and the access it affords to the rest of the city – its jobs, shops, schools and so on. In brief, tenure and financial status, environment and accessibility, play increasingly important parts in Europe's housing problems.

The constantly evolving demands on Europe's housing policies show that the comprehensive approach can be no more than an approach. A completely comprehensive and wholly consistent set of policies could be found only in a country with an unchanging social and economic character – a country, moreover, which was prepared to give priority to housing over all else. In the more turbulent world in which we live, today's comprehensive policies rapidly become tomorrow's inadequately partial improvisations if they are not constantly developed to cope with new problems. In most of the market economies, the spread of home ownership now compels those who plan housing programmes to rely increasingly on economically based forecasts of demand rather than demographically based estimates of need. As concern shifts from the quantity to the quality of the housing stock, they pay more attention to replacement and improvement and the losses which result from these processes. Meanwhile, recession and the financial crises which it has brought about have led many governments to devote greater efforts to restricting rather than promoting house building.

In future the makers of housing policy must collaborate more closely with those concerned with borrowing and lending, taxation, the tenure of property and related questions, and with those concerned with town and regional planning, the development of the local economy and the character and composition of urban neighbourhoods. All these issues have too often been neglected hitherto. We shall have more to say about them later in this book.

# 6
# Housing in Eastern Europe

## Communist Origins

What have the 'command economies' of eastern Europe achieved in housing during the generation since they were established? Have they kept their socialist faith, or have revolutionaries been corrupted by power? What can the market economies learn from their experience? These are the questions which we explore in this chapter.

In western Europe many governments have assumed increasingly comprehensive responsibilities for the housing of their people. The mechanisms of the market remain important, but these mechanisms work within a framework of controls, subsidies, credit policies and publicly sponsored building operations which produce an outcome very different from that to be expected of a free market. Governments' activities can no longer be regarded as marginal interventions within the market; they go far to determine the supply of housing, the demand for it, and the whole structure of the market. Meanwhile, in eastern Europe, governments which began by trying to control the whole stock of housing are making increasing use of market mechanisms to extend the range of choices they offer. Private saving and spending are being drawn in to bear a growing share of housing investment which would otherwise fall on state budgets. It could be argued that there is a convergence of policies between east and west which shows that certain kinds of housing problem are universal in economies at particular stages of development.

It would be odd if there were no fundamental conflict between the housing policies of the market economies and those of the centrally planned economies. The socialist governments were founded by revolutionaries who were determined to reject the ethics and overthrow the institutions of the market. But in this field they had no deeply pondered doctrine. The founding fathers of Marxist thought had not devoted their most prolonged and rigorous analyses to housing questions. These they tended to regard as a problem created by capitalism and readily, but only, capable of solution once that system was overthrown. In his book *The Housing Question*, Engels assumed the housing 'problem' was simply a product of this system:

> ... one thing is certain; there are already in existence sufficient buildings for dwellings in the big towns to remedy immediately any real 'housing *shortage*', given rational utilization of them. This can naturally only take place by the expropriation of the present owners and by quartering in their houses the homeless or those workers excessively overcrowded in their former houses. Immediately the proletariat has conquered political power, such a measure dictated in the public interests will be just as easy to carry out as other expropriations and billetings are by the existing state.

He attacked proposals for the provision of owner-occupied cottages and a plot of land for working men as a reactionary attempt to defeat the inevitable progress of economic and political evolution:

> ... the ownership of house, garden and field, and security of tenure in the dwelling place, is becoming today, under the rule of large-scale industry, not only the worst hindrance to the worker, but the greatest misfortune for the whole working class, the basis for an unexampled depression of wages below their normal level...

He was equally caustic about socialist proposals for the abolition of rent, lecturing his opponents in a paragraph that our Association of Land and Property Owners might well quote in its next submission to a government committee inquiring into this question:

> Firstly, it is forgotten that the rent must not only pay the interests on the building costs, but must also cover repairs and the average sum of bad debts, unpaid rents, as well as the occasional periods when the house is untenanted, and finally pay off in annual sums the building capital which has been invested in a house which is perishable and which in time becomes uninhabitable and worthless. Secondly, it is forgotten that the rent must also pay interest on the increased value of the land upon which the building is erected and that therefore a part of it consists of ground rent.

As for speculation about the housing policies of a Communist society:

> ... it does not occur to me to try to solve the so-called housing *question* any more than I can occupy myself with the details of the still more important *food question*. I am satisfied if I can prove ... that there are houses enough in existence to provide the working

masses for the time being with roomy and healthy living accommodation. To speculate as to how a future society would organize the
distribution ... of dwellings leads directly to *Utopia*.[1]

In effect, Engels treats housing as a peg upon which to hang his indict-
ments of capitalism and reformist socialism. Yet this was the principal
Marxist text on its subject, and Lenin read and annotated a copy during
the months before he assumed power.

## Centrally Planned Policies

Whether a convergence between east and west is emerging or not, the
housing systems of eastern Europe's centrally planned economies differ
in important ways from those of the west. They differ, for a start, in
their intentions. In the east housing policy is subordinate to economic
policy: it is the handmaiden of industrialization and economic growth.
That does not mean that human values are wholly neglected. But to the
state people are important chiefly for their labour power and for their
capacity to reproduce the next generation of workers. Such values are
not unknown in the west, but governments are not expected or organized
to pursue them in the systematic and explicit east European way.
Timothy Sosnovy calculated that the urban population of the USSR
increased from 21·6 millions in 1923 to 74·5 millions in 1950. Over the
same period urban dwelling space rose from 139 to 297 million square
metres, and space per head fell from 6·4 to 4·0 square metres. The war
must have contributed a great deal to this trend, but the decline in space
per head continued throughout this period with no intervals of improvement.[2] Gregory Grossman, in a foreword to this study, estimates
that the government must in effect have purchased two years of industrial investment by allowing the housing standards of urban workers to
decline by some 40 per cent. In 1952 these policies were dramatically
reversed and the Soviet Union has been rapidly making up for lost time
since then.

Three results follow from the priority given to industrial needs. First,
house building is carried out in close conjunction with other forms of
construction – factories, roads, shops, hospitals, schools and housing
being planned and erected together, often by the same building enterprises – under ministries dominated by engineers and technologists.
Second, housing is allocated in ways which are designed to reinforce
economic incentives to produce. Thus priority for public housing is

given to 'key workers' and undermanned industries, and the distribution of housing is used as a substitute for wage differentials. In some countries – notably Hungary and the Soviet Union – housing is also used as an instrument of demographic policy to reward parents who produce more than the usually small number of children. Third, crèches and other communal services to help the working mother are built into housing schemes on a more generous and systematically integrated scale than they are in the west. Like housing and child-care policies, social security policies are also designed to encourage women to work for most of their lives with only brief interruptions for producing children. That, perhaps, is why there is now growing concern about declining birth rates in several east European countries.

Incentives are a seductive but slippery concept in the hands of revolutionary governments. The centrally planned economies in which housing policies of this kind first took shape were dominated by scarcities. Production was desperately needed, but excessive differences in pay were unacceptable. People were therefore induced to move into defence industries, stay in the coal mines, or whatever was required, by offering them small flats of standard types at low rents. Otherwise they would have to wait for years in the housing queues. But as the queues grow shorter, some of these governments are recognizing that people must in future be offered better housing, housing over which they can gain some control and housing from which they can secure some financial return. And for that it may be proper to charge them a higher price.

Viewed from a thousand miles away, through a curtain of foreign languages from which debates about current developments seldom emerge in English translation, the housing systems of eastern Europe appear very similar. And in comparison with western Europe's they are. Figure 6.1 shows the numbers of dwellings completed per 1,000 inhabitants in eastern countries. The trends move rather more uniformly year by year than those of the western countries shown in Figures 5.1–5.3 (page 86). It is clear, too, from the literature published in English that policies in the eastern countries dealing with tenure, occupiers' rights, allocation, design, prices and rents have evolved in similar ways, often following a lead from the Soviet Union. But that does not mean that their housing systems are identical in practice. Each country is different and each inherited a different pre-revolutionary political tradition and housing stock. The western visitor is struck by the similarities of policy applied to a widely varying urban scene. We begin by describing the general organization of housing, and then turn to a more detailed discussion of selected countries.

**6.1** *Dwellings Completed per 1,000 Inhabitants, 1970–79. Eastern Europe*

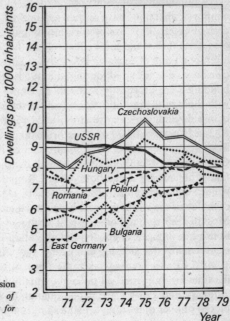

*Source:* UN Economic Commission for Europe, *Annual Bulletins of Housing and Building Statistics for Europe.*

Housing programmes in eastern Europe form an integral part of successive economic plans, prepared in central planning commissions in accordance with the general directives of those in power. Orders are handed down to regional authorities, and mainly carried out by local state building enterprises. The state can readily acquire and redistribute any land or housing it does not already own, and the rights of property owners have been so circumscribed that virtually no commercial profit can be derived from them, except, of course, where illicit markets operate. (In housing, as in other fields, the informal economy is important – but probably no more extensive than in the market economies.) The policies of the past twenty years are clearly visible in the urban landscape. They were designed to house in standard, self-contained units as many families as quickly and as cheaply as possible. Virtually no private open space has been provided. Vast numbers of flats have been built, mainly since the late 1950s, in large suburban estates which frequently house 80,000 people – the size of a large British New Town.

The starting-point for these policies must be remembered. When

Nikita Kruschev said, in an article in *Pravda* in 1957, 'We want to ensure every family an apartment; not a room, but an apartment,'[3] he was aiming at what must have seemed a dauntingly difficult but passionately desired objective. It has been ruthlessly pursued in most of the eastern bloc since then – and most effectively in the Soviet Union itself, where, after long years of declining housing standards, an astounding output of dwellings was achieved during the 1960s. Space standards for new building were drastically reduced, and have remained low compared with those of the rest of Europe. In 1978 the average 'useful floor space' of new dwellings in square metres was 51·1 in the USSR, 62·2 in Poland, 65·3 in Hungary and 70·4 in Czechoslovakia. Comparable figures in the west were much larger: 89·0 square metres in Austria, 102·5 in West Germany and 115·3 in Sweden.[4] Small dwellings must severely restrict family life and the domestic economy. Recent studies suggest that both women and men in the urban areas of the USSR spend at least half of each day of the working week, which often includes Saturdays, at work. Most of their time at home is spent sleeping.[5] As Figure 6·2 shows, new Polish housing, reasonably typical of eastern Europe's, provides an efficient machine for sleeping and eating, but little space for living.

Most of this housing takes the form of flats, system-built at high densities by industrialized methods, usually at least five storeys tall. In Hungary and Poland about one quarter of recently built flats are in blocks of over nine storeys. Estates are run up quickly, taking between six months and a year to build. (In Britain they would take more than twice as long.) To westerners they seem a dreary concrete jungle, but the vandalism so common in British estates of this sort is nowhere to be seen. Their residents are often privileged people who still regard themselves as fortunate to have a self-contained home.

The private landlord and his rents have long been symbols of the exploitation of man by man, and it might have seemed natural for revolutionaries to abolish both of them together. But the first systematic attempt to legislate for rents in the Soviet Union, made in 1927 just before the Five Year Plan, imposed standard levels of payment which were reasonably high in relation to income and not very different from those to be found in capitalist countries at the time, although there were deductions to help families with low incomes. It was the freezing of these rents, coupled with the drastic inflation of the next twenty-five years, which reduced rents to a sum that became negligible. The basic law on rents in the USSR today is still that of 1927, and rent per square metre has remained unchanged since 1928.

The other eastern countries generally began by following the Russian

**6.2** *Polish Flats of the Early 1970s*

### A) For 3 persons

Examples of designs of dwellings to be constructed with a large-panel system, to be erected in the years 1971–5. (a) Dwelling for 3 persons: living space 24·80 sq.m.; usable floor space 42·70 sq.m. (b) Dwelling for 4 persons; living space 35·60 sq.m.; usable floor space 53·00 sq.m. (c) Dwelling for 5 persons; living space 43·70 sq.m.; usable floor space 63·00 sq.m.

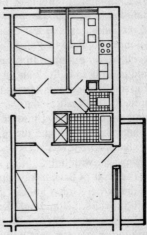

### B) For 4 persons     ### C) For 5 persons

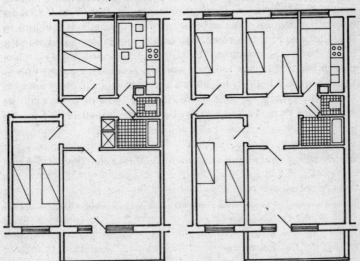

*Source: Housing, Building and Planning in Polish People's Republic*, Warsaw, 1973.

example. In many of them wartime devastation had been appalling, wholesale migrations and frontier changes had taken place, and drastic redistributions of housing were required to provide shelter for the homeless and to eliminate the social injustices of earlier years. The state took over houses which had belonged to municipalities, the larger landlords and the dead and dispossessed – property that had belonged to Jews in Poland and to Germans expelled from the Sudetenland, for example. In rural areas much of this housing was given or sold cheaply to individuals; in towns it was let by the state at low rents. The smaller landlords were in most places left with a formal title to their property, but their tenants were selected by municipal authorities, their rents were frozen and mostly paid into special funds used for meeting maintenance costs, and the principal advantage conferred by their title to the property was the opportunity of getting a flat for themselves somewhere within it.

The rents of flats in state housing today are now very low, averaging in the Soviet Union about 2·5 per cent of the family's income.[6] That sum provides fuel and light as well as housing, although it does not in fact pay for as much as half of the management and repair costs of the housing. Rents for state housing in Poland, Czechoslovakia, Hungary and other countries take similar patterns.

Housing is produced by three main kinds of investor: rented housing built by the state; various forms of cooperative (which in the USSR are not independent investors but managers of housing built for them by the state); and private persons (who usually operate on the biggest scale in the most rural economies). Enterprises, which used to play a major part in building houses for their workers, are now important only in Czechoslovakia; but they still make a big contribution in many countries by lending money for housing to their employees or to cooperatives building for them. Table 6.3 shows the pattern around 1978. Table 6.4

**6.3** *Dwellings Constructed in Eastern Europe by the Type of Investor, 1978*
(Percentages)

| *Czechoslovakia*[1,2] | |
|---|---|
| State | 23 |
| Enterprises | 16 |
| Cooperatives | 31 |
| Private persons[3] | 29 |

*Bulgaria*

| | |
|---|---|
| State and cooperatives | 50 |
| Private persons | 50 |
| *of which:* aided | 34 |
| unaided | 16 |

*East Germany*[4]

| | |
|---|---|
| State | 50 |
| Cooperatives | 40 |
| Private, aided | 11 |

*Hungary*

| | |
|---|---|
| State | 36 |
| Private | 64 |
| *of which:* aided | 57 |
| unaided | 7 |

*Poland*[5]

| | |
|---|---|
| State | 17 |
| Cooperatives | 58 |
| Private persons | 26 |

*Romania* (1977)

| | |
|---|---|
| State, cooperatives and with state aid | 54 |
| Private persons on their own account and with state credit | 46 |

*USSR*

| | |
|---|---|
| State and cooperatives[6] | 82 |
| Employees on their own account and with state aid | 9 |
| Collective farms and rural population | 9 |

*Yugoslavia* (1977)

| | |
|---|---|
| State | 37 |
| Private | 63 |

*Source:* UN, *Annual Bulletin of Housing and Building Statistics for Europe*, 1978.

*Notes:*
1. Dwellings in residential buildings only.
2. New construction only.
3. Mainly in rural areas.
4. Excluding modernizations.
5. Excluding dwellings in houses for institutional households.
6. State institutions and housing cooperatives, excluding collective farms.

**6.4** *House Building in Eastern and Western Europe, 1953–77*
(Dwellings built per 1,000 inhabitants)

|      | USSR | Rest of Eastern Europe | Western Europe | UK  |
|------|------|------------------------|----------------|-----|
| 1953 | 6·6  | 2·6                    | 5·5            | 6·5 |
| 1961 | 11·2 | 5·9                    | 7·0            | 5·9 |
| 1970 | 9·3  | 6·6                    | 8·0            | 6·6 |
| 1971 | 9·2  | 6·4                    | 8·3            | 6·7 |
| 1972 | 9·0  | 6·9                    | 8·8            | 6·1 |
| 1973 | 9·1  | 7·2                    | 8·7            | 5·6 |
| 1974 | 8·9  | 7·6                    | 7·7            | 5·2 |
| 1975 | 8·8  | 8·1                    | 7·5            | 5·9 |
| 1976 | 8·2  | 8·0                    | 6·4            | 6·0 |
| 1977 | 8·2  | 8·2                    | 6·4            | 5·8 |

*Source:* UN, *Major Trends in Housing Policy in ECE Countries*; and UN, *Annual Bulletins of Housing and Building Statistics for Europe.*

compares the numbers of dwellings built in the east (the Soviet bloc and Yugoslavia) and the west (meaning, in this case, all the remaining European countries). Although the USSR's peak years of output are past, she is still producing over 2 million dwellings a year. The rest of the eastern countries have now attained similar rates of production, outpacing western Europe in sheer numbers. Tables 3.6 and 3.8 (pages 48 and 51) show that in standards of space and equipment east and west are slowly converging.


## New Developments

Beneath the orderly surface of these well-established arrangements, the policy-makers of eastern Europe are now in livelier debate and greater uncertainty than for many years past. Centrally planned command economies can achieve massive tasks when the priorities are straightforward – as in wartime. The success of their drive to build and develop cities, heavy industries, strong defence forces and a large supply of trained workers has been achieved by keeping the priorities simple. That success now poses dilemmas which are leading to the reappraisal of earlier doctrines. Housing is one of the fields in which those dilemmas are emerging.

The increasing prosperity of a fully employed population is generating demands for consumer goods to which the central planners have hitherto given low priority. Low rents, coupled with the restriction of foreign travel, private motoring and other expensive pursuits which mop up purchasing power in the west, still further increase these demands. The explosion of birth rates which extended into the 1960s in Poland, the USSR and other war-devastated countries, compelled some of their governments to restrain house building in order to invest in industry to ensure that there would be jobs for the big generations of school leavers entering the labour force in the 1960s and 1970s. Attempts made in Poland to syphon off excess purchasing power by increasing prices were partly responsible for food riots in 1970 and strikes in 1976 and 1980. Here and elsewhere, governments promoted savings schemes which would eventually enable people to buy flats or cars, and these proved very successful. The money invested in Poland's National Savings Bank, and Savings and Loan Cooperatives, doubled between 1970 and 1974. Much of this money went into deposits for cooperative housing. The same thing happened in Czechoslovakia. The housing to be offered in exchange for these savings would have to cost a good deal and be more attractive than ordinary state flats if it was to meet the needs of the economic planners and the savers. And the supply of cheaper alternatives would have to be restricted. The Polish Minister of Municipal Economy put it bluntly: 'The only way to obtain a new or better dwelling is to become a member of a housing cooperative.'[7]

Meanwhile the inflation of building costs has made new housing increasingly expensive, demanding growing subsidies if rents are not to be increased. More recently the rising price of fuel has produced further deficits for housing authorities, whose low rents are often supposed to cover energy costs. The standards of building, static for many years, are also being improved throughout the eastern countries. That costs money too, partly for the building of larger and better-equipped flats, and partly for the improvement of older property, which is a difficult task in countries where industrialized building has gone far to destroy craft skills. The tiny Polish flats shown in Figure 6.2 – little more than half the size of comparable British council housing – were from 1980 to be succeeded by new and larger models providing 60 to 70 (instead of 50) square metres of useful floor space for four people. Poland is also improving its large stock of rural housing: only 15 per cent of it had a supply of running water in the late 1970s, but nearly all should have this by 1990, and 50 per cent should have bathrooms as well.

The growing urban intelligentsia in these countries are generally fairly well housed. But they often live in state flats, which they can be compelled to leave when the departure of their children or the death of elderly relatives reduces the household's size below the norms required to justify the number of rooms occupied. Dissidents can be compelled to leave more abruptly for political reasons – as Czech signatories of Charter 77 discovered. Those who can afford to are therefore prepared to pay a good deal for housing which gives them greater security and independence, and a means of acquiring an asset they can pass on to their heirs.

In countries like Hungary where the growth of urban industries has greatly outpaced the production of rented housing – 'under-urbanization', Szelenyi called it[8] – manual workers have built their own houses in unplanned suburbs outside the city boundaries. They may lack schools, mains water supply and drainage, and other services, but they have houses and gardens instead of flats: houses, moreover, up to 150 square metres in size.

All across eastern Europe governments are responding to these pressures by allowing, or compelling, people to spend more on housing. The Yugoslavs, whose economy is highly decentralized and still mainly rural, had little hesitation about that. From the 1960s they relied increasingly for their new building on publicly subsidized owner-occupation, calling for fairly heavy contributions from the buyers. Other countries followed in various ways. In Czechoslovakia fairly generous mortgage loans are now offered by the state to house buyers, and small enterprises have been set up to produce prefabricated single-family homes. In Bulgaria, Hungary and Romania – all with large rural populations – most of the existing stock of houses is privately owned, and the state has accepted and endorsed this tenure by building housing, subsidized to varying degrees, for sale to owner-occupiers. Other eastern countries are doing this on a smaller scale, or selling older rented housing to sitting tenants – as in Poland, for example. In the more urban economies cooperatives of various kinds play an increasingly important part. They range from 'tenant' cooperatives, for which the payments are fairly modest, to 'owner' cooperatives, which demand higher payments and confer many of the rights of ownership, including the right to sell and bequeath membership. Other forms of cooperative build groups of houses and are then dissolved, transferring ownership to the householders. Cooperatives are now found all over eastern Europe. They play the largest parts in Poland, East Germany and Czechoslovakia – in 1978 they built 58 per cent of Poland's new housing and 40 per cent of East Germany's, as Table 6.3 shows. They call typically for an initial down-payment of 30 per cent of building costs (which is usually a larger sum in relation to incomes than it would be in Britain). In Hungary the deposit for a cooperative dwelling may amount to two years' joint earnings for a husband and wife. The remaining 70 per cent of the price is paid off, with varying degrees of additional subsidy, at low interest rates (2 to 6 per cent, depending on the type of cooperative) over a period of about 30 years – longer in Poland and East Germany, shorter in the USSR. Thus, although the annual repayment is not high by western standards, the initial cost of buying your way into a cooperative may be heavy. Despite that, many people put their children's names down for membership and begin setting aside the necessary savings as soon as the children are born.

In Hungary, which stands roughly midway among the eastern countries in its degree of urbanization, housing is no more 'socialized' than in Britain. But it is distributed in very different ways. Vast urban estates of cheap, densely built flats are occupied by well-established workers and the intelligentsia – engineers, teachers, doctors and officials. Around the fringes of the biggest cities in unserviced suburbs live manual workers in bigger houses which they built for themselves – complete with gardens and in some cases garden gnomes. They pay much more than the flat-dwellers, borrowing up to half the money for their building materials at 6 per cent – a high rate of interest by eastern standards. In the countryside and more distant villages lives another group of workers, half in the urban and half in the rural economy. Konrad and Szelenyi describe them vividly:

> The position of workers from the village would appear as less enviable if we bore in mind that their low earnings from industry and the minimum use they are able to make of the infrastructure are accompanied by doubling their working hours. Following eight hours' work, and long hours spent waiting and travelling, they are often met at the station by their wives, carrying two hoes, and they are off to another four or five hours on land allotted to them as share-croppers by the cooperative, or on their own household plots, which in the course of the years have been turned into extremely intensively cultivated dwarf holdings. A peculiar social class has come into being which lives in two economic systems at the same time, and which shows great sensitivity towards movements that establish equilibrium between the two.[9]

## Conclusion

What are we to make of these trends? There can be no doubt that the east European countries, after a slow start, are making impressive progress towards better housing conditions. The USSR, which began with the lowest standards, was first off the mark and has achieved the most dramatic output. All across eastern Europe housing has taken a growing share of a rising output from the construction industries. (In western Europe the share of construction devoted to housing is simultaneously falling.) The units mass-produced by these central planning machines and their local building enterprises are well equipped but small, uniform and often rather dreary. Quantity was in the early days more important than variety or human scale. But what impact will these colossal building programmes have on the character of the societies concerned?

It seems clear that the proportion of the housing programme financed from the personal contributions of householders is rising in virtually all the eastern countries other than the USSR. That has not yet emerged clearly in the statistics, because there has been a simultaneous decline in the proportion of houses – partly unrecorded but largely private – which are built in rural areas. The trend to private financing has been most marked in some of the richer and more urban economies – Czechoslovakia, Poland, Hungary and Romania in particular. The Soviet Union now diverges increasingly from its neighbours in being the only country still publicly sticking to its aim of providing free housing for all.[10]

The ideal of free housing was not part of Lenin's or Engels's original vision of a Communist society. Does its abandonment matter? To grasp its meaning calls for an understanding of the housing situation of the 1950s when this ideal took shape – particularly in the Soviet Union. When housing is desperately scarce after a devastating war and a long period in which few houses have been built, when whole families count themselves lucky to rent one room and sub-let the corner behind the wardrobe to a lodger, then no one can hope for much and the immediate needs of every household are desperately similar. A small flat which they do not have to share with anyone else is every family's hope and the outermost limit to their aspirations: anything more would be unimaginable. People need privacy and a little living space – the range of consumer goods available to put in that space is very restricted – and once they have secured a decent home few of them will move again.

When everyone wants the same thing and wants it very badly, it is natural to regard housing as a basic and standard necessity which should be provided free. Somewhat similar situations have occurred in Scotland, with similar results.

But what does 'free housing' mean? Rents are already so low in eastern Europe that governments could easily abolish them altogether if they wanted to. It would make very little difference if they did: housing would be 'free', not in the sense that the air we breathe or the sea we swim in is free, but in the sense that a schoolboy's books or a soldier's uniform are free. It would be more accurate to describe it as 'rationed'. Housing, in urban areas at least, is allocated in prescribed amounts to people who qualify for it owing to their needs and owing to their place in the productive system: it is a ration provided along with wages. This is very different from a system in which housing is distributed according to the tenant's capacity to pay, but it does not matter greatly whether the tenant pays very little for it or nothing at all.

While it lasts, that arrangement has considerable advantages. The state, mass-producing whole suburbs at a time, can more easily forecast the number of families and children per hectare, and build in the communal restaurants, the crèches and other services they will need. Housing becomes such a standard product that people can be easily moved to larger or smaller flats as their families change in size. But there are disadvantages too. Cheap housing means small housing; and when people start buying the washing machines and refrigerators which their low rents enable them to acquire, they may have to stand them in the public corridors for lack of space inside their flats. The state views its citizens as workers. It is not interested in the informal and the domestic economies and it provides scant space for their activities: flats often have no separate living room or balcony, and never have a spare room, store room or garden, as Figure 6.2 shows. The state may also be tempted to use its capacity to turn people out of their homes as a way of keeping them politically docile.

The experience of the more advanced of the centrally planned economies suggests that as they grow richer they run into economic and political pressures which ultimately compel them to abandon the ideal of free housing. The USSR may eventually do likewise. Once the heroic days are over, and people gain some scope for choice, material incentives are needed – to get them to work, to save, to move to distant regions, to take on heavier responsibilities at work or to have children. If there is a limit to the financial incentives which society is prepared to use, housing must play some part in the incentive system. That is probably inevitable.

Is it also desirable? For those who want to extend freedom of choice within a society which remains fundamentally equal in its human relationships and in the distribution of life chances, these are the main questions to ask in response to that question.

Are gross inequalities in the quantity and quality of housing emerging, so that the rich and powerful are much better housed than the poor and powerless? So far the answer seems to be a qualified 'no'. In eastern Europe the main privileges in housing are not in physical standards but in the security of tenure and the rights to sell or bequeath property which cooperative members and home owners secure. These benefits are not distributed equally, but manual workers and peasants are well represented among those who get them. Many of the better-off invest their savings in a second home elsewhere in the country. But these second homes, which vary from the glamorous and secret *dachas* of top Soviet bureaucrats to large sheds on a small piece of privately owned land on the outskirts of the major cities, are available to a great many households. In Prague, for example, approximately 60 per cent of households are said to have access to a second home.

Are some neighbourhoods – built for the more exclusive cooperatives, for example, on favoured sites offering good access to the opportunities of urban life – gaining an exclusive 'middle-class' character which may also be reflected in the quality of their schools and in other services? Are other neighbourhoods – more remote, self-built, under-serviced suburbs, for example – inhabited only by the unskilled or the powerless? Are these locational differences then reinforced by an unfair distribution of public services and subsidies which give more help to those who are already privileged in other ways and less help to those who are not? There are signs that something like this is beginning to happen – but, so far, to a less dramatic extent than in the market economies. In several countries the intelligentsia seem to have more than their proportionate share of heavily subsidized state housing. But alongside them there are considerable numbers of people who secured a similar flat because they were skilled manual workers, or had large families, and some of these people have quite low incomes. For them, housing still plays a central part in socialist pricing policies which ensure that the basic essentials of life – housing, fuel, food and public transport – remain very cheap. Whether they can get a larger flat depends more on whether they have another baby than on what they can afford to pay. That has perhaps been the main achievement of eastern housing policies: they have matched their still rather scarce supply of housing very carefully to the sizes of households.

Thus, despite its illogicalities and the new injustices now emerging, the distribution of housing in the centrally planned economies is probably fairer – certainly more equal – than the distributions achieved in most parts of the world.

What about their technological achievements – does central planning 'solve the housing problem'? These countries have shown that, given time and extensive preparation, radical improvements can be achieved in the performance of the building industry. The USSR offers a particularly dramatic example of that. The standardization of dimensions and components, and the assurance of a predictable volume and geographical distribution of demand were the starting-point for this achievement. Building plans had to be prepared as an integral part of plans for the whole economy, and plans for house building had to be systematically related to the maintenance programme and to the work of the construction industry as a whole. In that way, the productivity of the building industry was undoubtedly improved. To do that, effective links had to be forged between the whole network of industries involved. In western Europe the finishing trades of the building industry, and the various branches of the chemical industry which play a vital part in producing materials for joining and sealing large components, are in fact more highly developed than in the east; if properly organized, they could surmount many of the difficulties which have held up the industrialization of building in the east and coarsened the quality of its products.

But such methods cannot be successfully exported *en bloc*. The British construction industry already builds houses very cheaply by eastern standards, and it is particularly efficient when using traditional methods and materials. Further advances in productivity here are therefore likely to be achieved by methods which differ from those which have proved successful in the altogether different circumstances of eastern Europe.

It must also be remembered that the building industry exists to meet human needs. In too many eastern countries its aim seems to have been to produce statistical triumphs of quantitative production. Without systematic and imaginative studies of household routines, domestic equipment, and the standards and patterns of living to be expected in future, it may produce houses which soon become obsolete. Several governments in eastern Europe are in fact building on the assumption that people will make increasing use of public restaurants and public laundries, that wives will always leave their children in nurseries as soon as possible and go out to work, that their sons will continue for ever to do two years' military service, and that travel will be confined almost entirely to public transport. Some of these assumptions may prove valid. But many of the industries now flourishing in the west – those producing washing machines, refrigerators and private cars, for example – are now beginning to develop in the east. If Communist societies were to be permanently deprived of these things, then what is the purpose of their all-consuming drive for economic growth? If their house designs do not soon recognize their inhabitants' aspirations for possessions, space and privacy, a slum-clearance problem of frightening dimensions is being prepared for the next generation.

Finally, it is clear that although central planning can achieve massive output when the priorities are clear and reasonably simple, it cannot work miracles. As in the market economies, what can be done depends on the stage of economic and social development which a country has attained. If population generally, and in cities particularly, is growing fast, if steel is scarce and labour is plentiful, then the improvement of building productivity and housing conditions is bound to remain slow until those conditions change. Thus the Poles, for example, will face a more difficult housing situation than the Czechs for a long time to come.

It is clear that the east European countries will be thinking harder during the next decade about policies for rents, subsidies and housing finance in general, and about the improvement of ill-equipped older housing both in cities and in rural areas. Initiatives of this kind are already under way. Before long it is to be hoped that they will also be more concerned about the contribution which housing can make to the protection of privacy, the development of children, the needs of old people, and the activities of the family. If they can build houses and neighbourhoods which offer more freedom of choice and more scope for the domestic economy without abandoning the attempt to create a more equal society, the whole world will have much to learn from them.[11]

# Part II
# Housing in Britain

Part I of this book explained what housing policy is about. Housing problems differ in countries at different stages of economic and social development and with different political traditions. So, therefore, do housing policies. Within a particular country, problems and policies change as the economy develops and as the nation's perceptions of housing needs and possibilities evolve. Policy is a response to problems – a response constantly relearnt as old issues are settled or reinterpreted and attention turns to new issues.

Part II of this book deals with Britain. It begins, in Chapter 7, with the urban context, looking at houses as a location – a point on the map – which gives or denies access to the rest of the world, and as an integral part of an urban economy. Chapter 8 contrasts the housing resources and problems of the different kinds of town to be found in Britain. Each of these chapters concludes with a discussion of its implications for policy. The next three chapters briefly trace the evolution of housing and town-planning policies which have helped to shape Britain's housing conditions since the Second World War. This part of the book concludes in Chapter 12 with a review of the present situation. It shows the changing character of different sectors of the housing market, the ways in which households move through the housing stock, and the kinds of people who are most likely to be in difficulties.

The purpose of this part of the book is to describe rather than prescribe. Our concerns and values emerge clearly enough in the course of the analysis, and we advocate general strategies from time to time. But we postpone more specific prescriptions for action until the third and last part of the book in which we look to the future.

# 7
# Housing in an Urban Context

## Introduction

Thus far we have discussed housing problems and policies in a national context – housing in France, Poland or the United Kingdom, for example. But a house is fixed to a particular plot of land. What it offers to the people who live in it depends on the surrounding community and on the social and economic opportunities to be found there. Physical differences in housing standards – differences in the size and equipment of houses and the extent of overcrowding, for example – have been greatly reduced throughout Europe over the past generation. Yet differences in the value of houses, measured in the prices which people pay for them, remain very large. As the old criteria decline in importance, differences in location grow more important, and debate about policy deals increasingly with the access which a house affords to everything else that people seek in an urban society.

We must look at houses in this way before we consider them as buildings. That is what we do in this chapter. We start by describing the social and spatial framework in which houses stand, and then pause to consider some of the policy implications of this discussion – a discussion which deals, thus far, with housing within cities or smaller settlements. But in a country as densely populated as Britain, settlements of this size do not function independently. Each plays its part in a larger urban network of inner cities and their suburbs, industrial towns, holiday resorts and other kinds of place, all depending upon each other. In the next chapter we turn to this constantly evolving pattern and consider the influence which it exerts on housing conditions in different places, and the influence which housing exerts in return upon the character of each kind of town.

## The Urban Framework

The long-established cities of mature, urban, industrial economies show common patterns which reflect common features of their social and economic life.[1] Latin American and Indian cities take different but equally well-marked patterns. In the United Kingdom, revealing studies have been made of the economic and social structure of Belfast,[2] Sunderland,[3] Birmingham,[4] Leicester,[5] and other cities, and there is a whole library of books about London.[6] Some of the main findings of this research would be familiar to any perceptive observer of urban life. For just as a palaeontologist can reconstruct a dinosaur from one of its knuckle bones, so observant people can begin to guess the scale and character of a town as they enter its speed limits for the first time. They know from experience what kind of settlement supports homes, cars, street lighting, filling stations and public houses of the sort to be seen at the town's fringes – or at any other point where they may take their stand. A town is an organic whole, its every part related to every other part.

Readers can test this for themselves in any long-established city. Step outside the main entrance of one of Britain's older civic universities, for example: the highway before you probably leads downhill, probably northwards or eastwards, to the centre of the town and the river crossings. The university was built on the more attractive side of town where the views are better and the air is cleaner. The centre is the point from which radiate the medieval rights of way which are the city's most lasting feature – its skeleton. Walk down the road and the prevailing winds will probably be behind you, blowing the smoke of the city away from this neighbourhood. You will probably come before long to the main professional offices and financial institutions – the more successful lawyers, accountants and dentists, and the banks, insurance companies and building societies – conveniently placed near the entry to the town centre which has for hundreds of years been used by the city's more prosperous citizens. The focal point of local politics – the town hall – may stand on this side of the centre too. Around it are the main stores. Beyond, markets and warehouses stand close to rivers and railways – the noisy, polluting heavy-transport routes. On the further side of the centre stand factories and workshops, and recently rebuilt working-class housing. Beyond them again are houses originally built for skilled artisans and the lower middle class, council estates and then the newer suburbs. The predominantly working-class suburbs tend to lie at the fringes of working-class segments of the city, interspersed on either side with new industrial estates, shopping centres and middle-class suburbs.

The highways from the centre on the university's side of town will probably lead past the teaching hospital and medical school, the most famous secondary schools – direct grant or independent – and possibly a technical college. The order in which they come cannot be predicted, because each may have moved several times, selling their increasingly cramped sites as land values in the expanding city centre rose, and building themselves more spacious premises further out on the same side of town. Up the roads which lead away to cleaner air and better views on this side of town stand what were originally the best houses. Those along the inner streets, built perhaps in the eighteenth century, have probably been taken over for commercial and professional offices, if they still stand. City-centre activities and the peak land values they create tend to move gradually outwards towards the more fashionable side of the town. The larger Victorian villas further out may now be subdivided and over-crowded in a rather slummy way, often by students and other migrants. Alternatively they may have been demolished and rebuilt, with expensive flats where the old shrubberies and tennis courts once stood, or replaced by expanding medical and educational institutions. All these patterns may be seen competing with each other. Still further out on this side of town come the leafy middle-class suburbs of interwar and later periods, and beyond them again the 'gin-and-tonic belt' of green fields, commuter villages, country clubs and golf courses.

This is the British 'market city', originally created without much planning by people who went about on foot or on horseback and by their successors who travelled in omnibuses and trams. Usually it is a round city, its main traffic routes leading outwards in radial lines from the centre like the spokes of a wheel. About a third of its total area is filled by houses and their gardens. Each plot of land gives its users a different volume and mix of access to people and activities throughout the city. Land values measuring accessibility rise to a peak in the centre, sloping downwards in a concave gradient which gradually grows flatter. (As the speed of transport increases in less densely occupied territory further from the centre, the difference between neighbouring sites in accessibility, and therefore in price, grows less acute.)

This kind of city was created by investment channelled through par-ticular institutions to borrowers who were regarded as credit-worthy. Since the beginning of this century the building societies, aided by tax privileges, have become the main channel through which funds flow to house buyers. More recently, insurance companies have played an in-creasingly important but smaller part. The local authorities which have built most of the rented housing put up since 1918 look to the central government's lending agencies and to the open market for their funds. These flows of investment have gradually changed. The building societies are now lending steadily growing proportions of their funds to people with average and lower incomes; and they are lending more often than hitherto for the purchase of older housing built before the First World War. The local authorities switched the main focus of their operations, temporarily, in the 1930s and then again in the 1960s, from the expansion of the suburbs to the rebuilding of old, inner-city housing. Since then they have devoted more and more funds to improving older housing rather than replacing it. But at each stage these institutions turn to meet new demands as old ones begin to be satisfied, and they do that in ways which seem likely to minimize costs, risks and political conflicts. That imposes severe constraints on where they invest and for whom they build. Building societies rely on a small staff who have to be given clear and simple rules to help them pick the projects and the people to whom the massive flow of funds to be invested each month can most safely be directed. Local authorities also face much greater demands than they can satisfy: they will generally be reluctant to buy land which seems unnecessarily expensive or to build council houses on sites where they will be resented by large numbers of voters. When interests conflict, they tend to satisfy the big battalions and sacrifice the small ones – building houses for the average, long-established, well-organized worker with a family of average size, while neglecting newcomers and the deviant or eccentric; and building shopping centres for big national chain-stores, while neglecting small family businesses and marginal enterprises.[7] Town planning powers are largely negative: the planning authorities can prohibit development, but they cannot force developers to build in places or in forms which seem unprofitable to them. Thus the patterns of the market city tend to persist even when public investment and planning controls come to play large parts in urban development.[8]

These patterns are not immutable. They vary for geographical reasons, and in response to technical and economic changes. Belfast has been squeezed into odd shapes between the sea and the hills. Geography and transport routes made Adelaide a linear city, quite unlike the fan-shaped amphitheatres of Australia's other coastal cities.[9] The electric suburban railway, followed by the internal combustion engine, led to an explosion of the most crowded big cities into low-density suburbs. More recently, recession, coupled with the rise in fuel prices, seems to be bringing people back from distant suburbs to more accessible inner areas.

Public intervention has also modified the structure of many towns, particularly those which have grown most rapidly in the last two generations. Although council estates are generally built on cheaper land which market forces might have designated for working-class use, they also appear on more expensive inner sites (as in Pimlico, Westminster) and on outer suburban sites, pre-empting what might have been the natural path for middle-class development (as at Wythenshawe, Manchester). New universities have been located in all sorts of places: since they serve a national, not a local, market, they are no longer knitted so predictably into the urban structure. New railways in the past and new highways today, usually driven through working-class areas where the land was cheaper and resistance less effective, have created new arteries of movement and new barriers between the neighbourhoods which they divide. If planned on a large enough scale, they may change the whole structure of the city.

But some patterns of urban activity are very difficult to change. Work and the earnings which it generates are concentrated most heavily in the city centre. Over time, these activities tend to move slowly outwards down the radial routes on which they were first located. Ports and the activities which they generate move down the estuaries in search of broader spaces and better transport routes for the larger containers to be handled. Thus, if older forms of production are not constantly replaced by new ones, the demand for labour will decline in inner areas – as it has done in most of Britain's larger towns.[10] People, too, tend to move outwards from the centre of town in the course of their lives, in search of space, privacy and cleaner air. And they, too, usually move within the same segment of the town.[11] How destructive the losses of activity and people in inner areas become will depend on the relationships between the movements of jobs and workers of different kinds.

What a house offers to those who live in it will depend partly on the capacities and needs of the household, and the access it affords to opportunities they want in the surrounding area. They will probably want to live within reach of friends and relatives; they may want work and earnings for one or more members of the household; they will want to reach shops, medical services and recreation of various kinds; they may need schools; and they will probably be concerned about the status and character of their neighbours and the reputation of the neighbourhood.

Each household will seek the most favourable mix it can get of these resources – a changing mix as their needs change over time. Young childless people who are working or studying value access to jobs, higher education, shops and recreation more highly than space and privacy. That is why households of this sort generally cluster most thickly in the inner parts of cities. But households at a later stage of development, with one earner and several dependants, generally value space, privacy, good schools and access to the countryside more highly, and are less concerned about travel costs. They usually cluster most thickly on the fringes of the city. Middle-aged and older people do not want to make such long journeys as the heads of young families are prepared to tolerate, but they need more space than young childless householders for possessions they have accumulated over the years. They generally cluster most thickly midway between the inner city and the suburbs.[12] This may have been where new houses were being built in their younger days, when they were looking for their first homes: they may have stayed in the same neighbourhoods ever since as the city grew around them.

The city means different things to different kinds of people. They use different parts and different amounts of it. Working-class households and the poor travel much shorter distances than middle-class households and the rich. The areas of the city used by different social classes generally take similar patterns, typically shaped like a long cigar which starts a little further out of town than their homes and reaches inwards to the centre astride the nearest radial traffic routes. But this strip of the city is larger for the rich than the poor.[13] Women generally have access to smaller areas than men, and young children cover still smaller areas.[14]

Most of the people who move house feel that they have secured something better than they had before. But what they have got is rarely just a better house: it is an improvement in their general living standards, which may include a better or wider choice of jobs, shops or schools, more congenial neighbours, or an address which confers a higher status on them. Housing is embedded in these patterns both as cause and as effect. By enabling them to increase their incomes or reduce their travelling costs, it may help them to pay more for shelter and improve their housing standards still further. And that may extend their children's opportunities in the next generation. When other influences have been discounted, children in crowded homes tend to do less well at school than those with plenty of space; children who use public libraries tend to do better than other children.[15] Children who take their education furthest tend ultimately to earn more and are likely in their turn to acquire better housing.


## Policy Implications

Those who plan the development of cities should therefore beware of allowing major disjunctions to emerge between the opportunities offered by different sectors of the urban economy. Housing placed where its users cannot reach the kinds of jobs, schools and shops they want, or jobs placed where house types and prices do not match the earnings and aspirations of the workers, will restrict improvements in all sectors of the economy including housing.

Discontinuities within sectors of the local economy may also have destructive effects. A housing market which offers housing of one type and price only (as for a while many New Towns did) or of two widely separate standards (cheap and nasty or dear and luxurious, with few houses between these extremes) must either prevent some people from improving their standards or compel them to move elsewhere in order to do so. Discontinuities in other sectors may have similar effects: a local labour market which offers one kind of job at one level of income, or two widely separated kinds of job (low paid and unskilled or highly paid and highly qualified) with few falling between these extremes, will prevent a lot of people from improving their housing standards or compel them to move elsewhere in order to do so.

All these constraints will be particularly important for the least skilled people, the largest families, elderly people, one-parent families, and the more vulnerable ethnic minorities. They are confined to a small urban space because they cannot spend much on transport, or because they must stay close to other people upon whom they depend for support: for example, the grandmother who minds the baby while her daughter goes to work, the daughter who goes shopping for her elderly mother, and the neighbours who cannot speak much English but share the same native language and attend the same mosque. For such people the social and economic costs of moving house may be very high.[16] A major slum-clearance scheme or a new urban motorway built alongside them may drastically transform or restrict the world to which they have access.[17] Major projects of this kind have in fact been conducted on the biggest scale in the old, industrial, working-class neighbourhoods, where poverty, low skill, large families and one-parent families are most common.

People find it easiest to improve their housing conditions in places where they have a considerable range of houses to choose from at standards around and slightly above those of the house they currently occupy. They also need easy access to a matching range of opportunities in other sectors of the economy – opportunities for education and training, for work and earning, and for social interaction of various kinds. Disjunctions between the supply of housing and the range of opportunities available in other sectors of the local economy, and discontinuities within any of these sectors, make it harder for people to improve their standards – both in housing and in other matters. These destructive disjunctions and discontinuities may be economic in character (compelling people in search of better housing to pay far more than they have been accustomed to, for example); they may be spatial (compelling them to travel long distances to their work or to adequate schools, for example); or they may be social (compelling a move to a neighbourhood with a social class, age structure, ethnic or religious character, which they find unattractive.)

Most people who move house go to one which was previously occupied by someone else: their movements form a chain as householders succeed each other along well-marked routes through the housing market – from privately rented housing to council housing or owner-occupation, and from inner city to outer suburbs, for example (see pages 178–83). It follows that any major interruption of these flows, whether brought about by discontinuities in the housing market or elsewhere, is likely to frustrate demands at earlier stages of the flow. Green belts and rugged terrain on the western side of Belfast, which restrict the outward flow of Catholic families who are also excluded from neighbouring Protestant segments, must restrict opportunities of all sorts throughout the western segment of the city. Conversely, the building of New Towns beyond the northern and western fringes of London, which drew much of their population from adjacent outer fringes of the city,[18] must have helped to open up opportunities all the way through the northern and western segments of the city.

Movement and growth are not necessarily benign. Left to itself, the unplanned 'market city' will gradually tend to differentiate its neighbourhoods and segregate different kinds of people as industries and residents move out down radial routes from the centre, as people search for neighbourhoods populated by others of their own kind,[19] and as the centre of gravity of the city's most prosperous and prestigious central activities shifts slowly away from poorer neighbourhoods towards the more attractive residential districts, where the city's political, professional and commercial leaders live. These things have been happening in London, Glasgow, Dublin and many other places for generations.

In round cities with radial communications, this process of differentiation can be particularly destructive. The centre, engrossing the main generators of wealth and power, tends repeatedly to become so congested that expensive, large-scale redevelopment is needed, destroying familiar meeting-places and landmarks, evicting less profitable land uses and with them many of the people who live in poorer neigh-

bourhoods and earn their living in low-cost work places. James Simmie
has documented that process in Oxford.[20]

In Dublin the city's political, commercial and professional centre of
gravity is shifting south-eastwards towards the more attractive and predominantly middle-class suburbs along the coast,[21] while cheaper suburbs are thrust out in the opposite direction into less attractive inland
areas. Dublin's main expansion of housing is in effect being extruded
inland between the airport to the north and the Wicklow Hills to the
south, while the richest opportunities are moving out from the centre in
the opposite direction. Alternative patterns of development would have
been conceivable – a linear city extending northwards up the coast, for
example – but the building of massively expensive water and sewage
mains to sustain westward growth means that Dublin is now probably
committed to its present strategy for many years to come. The poverty
and social disorder of inner areas on the north side of the river, which
have constantly lost jobs without gaining any compensating economic
*raison d'être* or any escape routes to better things elsewhere, are predictable results of these trends. Thus a city has built itself a poverty trap
which comes to be perceived not as a disaster area created by urban
policies – or the lack of them – but as a problem of law and order.
Massive investment in expensive but much vandalized housing estates
does little to correct the fundamental deprivations of this inner area.
Somewhat similar patterns are to be seen in Glasgow, Liverpool, Sydney,
Melbourne and many other cities.

Housing policy-makers must remember that people do not only have
housing needs. Some of Britain's most ambitious redevelopment schemes
have left the people who were rehoused poorer than they were before,
when account is taken of the earnings of all members of the family, their
journeys to work, and the costs imposed on them by the search for new
jobs. Their housing then has to be more heavily subsidized than would
otherwise be necessary. People's wishes must be carefully studied and
respected. Studies in Glasgow showed that people who were rehoused
after putting their names on the waiting-lists tended to do better than
those who were picked up by clearance schemes without asking to be
rehoused[22] – which suggests that they knew pretty well whether they
and their families were capable of coping with the move to new estates,
often built on distant and rather desolate fringes of the town.

Programmes designed to improve housing conditions will be more
successful if they are closely coordinated with programmes to improve
opportunities for work, education, transport services, shopping facilities,
medical care and so on. People will pay more to improve their own

housing standards if they and their families thereby gain access to better jobs and other advantages. The scope for achieving these things will depend partly on the whole structure of a city, the health of its economy and the pattern of its development. This is not a plea for or against public or private enterprise. An unregulated free market and clumsy public intervention can both too easily create poverty traps for vulnerable people starved of opportunities in neighbourhoods from which there is little chance of escape to more prosperous areas.

Town planners and 'housers' should not rest content with ensuring that houses and jobs in the formal economy are located conveniently near to each other. Growing proportions of British households – particularly in the most deprived neighbourhoods[23] – are headed by retired people or single parents who are permanently or temporarily outside the formal economy. Meanwhile, with unemployment rapidly rising to 3 million or more and industrial investment collapsing, the formal labour market will for many people be of declining importance, particularly in the more depressed towns of northern Britain and Ulster. Some towns, like Clydebank and Corby, have lost, perhaps forever, their major sources of employment. They will henceforth contain more and more old people and ex-workers with time on their hands. For them, life at home will inevitably assume greater importance. For a while some of them will have redundancy payments which give them a little capital. Whether such places remain alive and active will depend on the vigour of their informal and domestic economies. The character of their housing will go a long way to determine whether men and women with the necessary skills can improve their houses and gardens, repair their cars, exchange services with their neighbours and start backyard enterprises. In places where such housing is scarce – often the very places where unemployment is most severe – the scope for the development of such an economy is unnecessarily limited. Those who build mass housing in future must create environments which allow for this kind of small-scale and communal response to the enormous problems of a decaying economy. That was always a humane and sensible policy; it is now also an urgent necessity.

These warnings do not mean that nothing can be done to improve housing conditions until a town's economy grows prosperous enough to make that easy. If housing is unfit for human habitation, those who live in it must be offered something better: Parliament promised them that. But to raise housing standards in advance of creating a more prosperous industrial framework in which people can develop their own skills and earnings will inevitably cost more in subsidies than would otherwise be necessary. Above all, we should remember that when building for the poor and the vulnerable it is not less but more important to understand people's behaviour, to consult them, to respect their capacity for survival in a precarious world, and to intervene in that world with the greatest care and sensitivity.

# 8
# Different Kinds of Towns

## The Urban Pattern

Thus far we have considered one town at a time. But in a country as densely populated as Britain, every town is part of a larger pattern of neighbouring settlements. In this chapter we consider the whole pattern and the parts played by different kinds of town within it, concluding once more with a discussion of policy implications.

Since houses are built and replaced very slowly, a town's housing conditions are the outcome of a long history. Different histories produce different conditions. Three main trends in urban settlement are now to be seen at work among British towns.[1] First, beginning about the turn of the century and gathering speed since the First World War, there is the decline, still proceeding rapidly, of old industrial Britain – the old coal, steel and textile towns, mainly in Scotland and the north of England – and the growth of public and commercial services and new forms of light engineering, mainly in the Midlands and the south. In the folklore of television, the world of *Coronation Street* is giving way to the world of *Crossroads*. This trend has brought about shifts of activities and people from north to south, and from peripheral to more central regions.

Second, beginning early in the century and accelerating since then, there is the decentralization of the great conurbations as their inner areas have lost, first, much of their resident populations to the suburbs, and then a growing proportion of their jobs as well. Meanwhile the suburbs and the middle-sized towns standing between the conurbations have grown. These trends have been carried forward by the building of suburban electric railways, the spread of the motor car and the telephone, and the replacement of steam power, which works best in very large plants, by more efficient and flexible small power units.[2]

Together these developments are transforming Britain's urban structure. What used to be a pattern of large towns surrounded by smaller satellites on a predominantly green backcloth is becoming a less dense but more continuous interlocking urban network interspersed with a few large patches of green – the Highlands, the Pennines, mid Wales and the Yorkshire moors, for example. The biggest cities and the predominantly green areas are both losing population to suburbs and middle-sized towns.

The third major trend, beginning in the nineteenth century and still going on, is the growth of tourist and retirement centres along the coasts, particularly in the south and west. These resorts are a new form of settlement, sheltering growing numbers of retired people, and depending heavily on service industries and self-employed workers, with large seasonal fluctuations in employment and demands for housing.

For twenty years after the Second World War the housing conditions of these different kinds of town could be contrasted fairly simply. To caricature them slightly: old, industrial Britain was housed in slate-roofed brick terraces (or stone-walled tenements in Scotland) originally built for private landlords. These houses were ill equipped, and in the biggest cities still rebuilding after the blitz, they were often overcrowded too. The new, expanding Britain of commuter suburbs, light engineering and service industries was housed in the kind of buildings which had been produced since the First World War – detached or semi-detached with between four and six rooms and a garden, built for owner-occupiers and council tenants. The owner-occupied and council houses of the new Britain were both well equipped, but the latter, filled with working-class ex-servicemen and their young families, were sometimes rather crowded.

Since then the picture has been complicated by several developments. First came slum clearance, launched throughout the country in the 1960s to replace older privately rented property with council houses and flats – flats built in increasingly massive blocks. These projects transformed housing conditions for working-class people in all the older cities. Next there was the steady loss of older privately rented housing, first to owner-occupation, beginning in the 1950s and still proceeding, and, on a smaller scale more recently, to municipal ownership and housing associations.

Meanwhile the local authorities have rehoused far more elderly people, and the tenants they rehoused in earlier years have grown older too. Pensioners, who used to be most heavily concentrated in privately rented housing, are now most often found in council or owner-occupied houses.

We will summarize the present complicated pattern, using 13 categories of towns devised in a recent study of 154 British towns.[3] These towns were compared in a cluster analysis based on 40 variables derived largely from the census of 1971. The areas examined were defined by parliamentary constituencies which, singly or in groups, matched municipal boundaries as nearly as possible. The towns' industrial structure and the occupations of their workers were the central features of the analysis. Demographic structure, housing conditions, education, transport and ethnic origin – the other factors examined – were all related to these central features. The clusters (a statistical term, indicating similarity, not necessarily proximity) have been labelled with descriptive names such as 'textile towns' or 'resorts', but for each we also give the names of the two towns most typical of the cluster. (For those who know these towns, their names will give a fuller and more objective description of the character of the cluster than the labels we use. The towns studied, grouped in their clusters, are shown in the Appendix.)

We particularly noted the distribution of potentially vulnerable groups amongst these towns: unskilled workers, large families (two adults with five or more dependent children), young workers in the unemployment-prone age group under 25, and one-parent families with two or more dependent children. These are classic indicators of working-class poverty, and all four tend to be most heavily concentrated in the more deprived towns of old, industrial Britain. Two other indicators of potential vulnerability which we examined – the proportions of older people, and the proportions born in New Commonwealth countries – were not concentrated especially heavily in these towns.

Some of the main features of the towns we describe are summarized in Tables 8.1 and 8.2 on pages 130–32, and the map opposite. *Greater London* dominates the first small cluster of 2 cities. The other is Cambridge. (Oxford and Edinburgh are rather similar, but ended up in the neighbouring cluster of Regional Service Centres.) Government and service industries play a large part in these towns, which have correspondingly large proportions of the more routine white-collar jobs and the women and younger single people who often do these jobs. In comparison with other towns, London has large proportions of people from the New Commonwealth countries, but skilled manual workers are under-represented. The housing of these towns is their most distinctive characteristic: it includes larger proportions of privately rented furnished accommodation and shared accommodation than are found anywhere else.

Next come four clusters of towns with many similarities. All are relatively prosperous places with high proportions of white-collar workers and low proportions of the more vulnerable social groups. Their housing conditions are generally good, and all four clusters depend heavily on private housing – the newer and better owner-occupied housing and, in

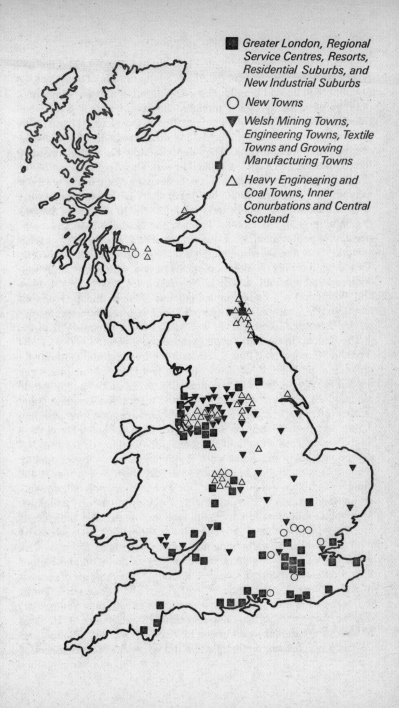

■ Greater London, Regional Service Centres, Resorts, Residential Suburbs, and New Industrial Suburbs

○ New Towns

▼ Welsh Mining Towns, Engineering Towns, Textile Towns and Growing Manufacturing Towns

△ Heavy Engineering and Coal Towns, Inner Conurbations and Central Scotland

the first two cases, privately rented housing too. The four clusters are:
**1.** The 16 *Regional Service Centres* (e.g., Bristol and Cardiff). Like
London, they depend heavily on service industries and have high proportions of privately rented furnished housing, but they have more
elderly people. **2.** The 10 *Resorts* (e.g., Bournemouth and Thanet) with
many elderly and small households, and many professional, managerial
and self-employed workers. They depend fairly heavily on privately
rented housing, and have few council houses. Their large proportions of
childless middle-aged and elderly people mean that these towns generally
have very few crowded homes, but demands for labour and for housing
show marked seasonal peaks and troughs. **3.** The 10 *Residential Suburbs*
(e.g., Chertsey and Walton-on-Thames, and Solihull) have large proportions of professional and managerial workers, relatively few women
at work, many families with children and high proportions of car owners.
They depend mainly on owner-occupied housing, which is generally well
equipped and spacious. **4.** The 12 *New Industrial Suburbs* (e.g., Pudsey
and Worcester) are rather similar but less affluent, and they depend
more heavily on the more prosperous forms of manufacturing, less on
service industries. These too are well-housed owner-occupiers' towns.

The 10 areas in the next cluster each include a *New Town* (e.g., Hertford and Stevenage, and East Kilbride). They are the cluster most rapidly
growing in population – followed by the two kinds of Suburbs. They
depend heavily on newer forms of manufacturing which employ a wide
range of the more skilled white-collar and manual workers and many
women (often part-timers). Housing conditions are good, overcrowding
is rare, and most of their homes are rented from public authorities.

Then come four clusters of predominantly working-class towns, all
depending heavily on manual work in manufacturing industries (and, in
the first case, mining). The last two have fairly high proportions of the
more vulnerable social groups. All four depend heavily on older owner-
occupied housing which is reasonably spacious but poorly equipped.
Many of these houses must originally have been rented. The four clusters
are: **1.** A small group of 3 *Welsh Mining Towns* (e.g., Rhondda and
Aberdare) which have declining populations, high unemployment, few
women at work, many elderly people and high sickness rates. Much of
their predominantly owner-occupied housing is badly in need of renewal
or replacement. **2.** Next comes a large group of 19 *Engineering Towns*
(e.g., Doncaster and Stockport) also with low growth rates and similar,
if less extreme, labour market and housing characteristics. **3.** Housing
conditions are similar again in the 16 *Textile Towns* (e.g., Bolton and
Oldham) which have declining populations, considerable numbers of

the more vulnerable groups and high proportions of women in full-time work, mainly of semi-skilled manual kinds. **4.** Housing – much of it owner-occupied – is newer and better equipped in a cluster of 14 *Growing Manufacturing Towns*[4] (e.g., Swindon and Gloucester) with fairly high proportions of vulnerable groups and many semi-skilled workers.

This leaves three clusters which have varied housing problems. All depend heavily on council housing. They rely mainly on manual work in manufacturing (and in two cases in mining too). **1.** There are 22 *Heavy Engineering and Coal Towns* (e.g., Walsall and Farnworth). They are fairly prosperous places, full of skilled manual workers but with few women at work. **2.** The 14 *Inner Conurbations* (e.g., Nottingham and Manchester) lie at the centre of the big urban concentrations of the Midlands and the north of England. They rely fairly heavily on semi-skilled and unskilled work, and their populations are declining. Unlike London, their housing densities are low and there is relatively little sharing or overcrowding. But much of their housing is old and poorly equipped. They have many of the vulnerable social groups, and a lot of unemployment, particularly among men. **3.** The 6 towns of *Central Scotland* (e.g., Glasgow and Paisley) are in many ways similar, but with more extreme needs: they have even more unskilled workers, fewer professional and managerial workers, worse unemployment and more of the potentially vulnerable groups. They depend to an even greater extent on council housing. Since this housing – much of it built as flats – is well equipped, it has transformed the housing conditions of these towns. Their main problems arise no longer from the prevalence of old and poorly equipped housing but from crowding – due partly to the large numbers of big families in the council estates of these cities. Anyone familiar with those estates would add that they are often forbiddingly isolated and dreary.

Some of the evidence which we have summarized in words is presented in Tables 8.1 and 8.2. The four main groupings of these clusters are shown on the map on page 127. These urban areas, being assembled from data based on parliamentary constituencies, often do not match municipal areas of the same name: only 27 per cent of the 154 towns in the analysis were the same as the local authorities of 1971 or very similar to them (that is to say, their populations differed by less than 5 per cent). Three years later the reorganization of local government changed many of these boundaries.

The picture we have presented is one in which a town's industrial base, because it helps to shape the town's rate of growth and social character, is the main determinant of housing conditions. Commuter

**8.1** *Social and Economic Characteristics of Towns of Different Kinds, Great Britain, 1971* (Percentages of the averages for all towns)

| Types of towns | Number of towns | Occupational groupings | | | | | Households of: | | Age 65 and over | Born in New Commonwealth |
|---|---|---|---|---|---|---|---|---|---|---|
| | | Professional and managerial | Other non-manual | Skilled | Semi-skilled | Unskilled | 2 adults 5 or more children | 1 adult 2 or more children | | |
| Greater London | 2 | 119 | 126 | 83 | 89 | 88 | 73 | 88 | 101 | 206 |
| Regional service centres | 16 | 102 | 114 | 93 | 95 | 101 | 83 | 97 | 111 | 35 |
| Resorts | 10 | 139 | 122 | 83 | 88 | 60 | 41 | 72 | 184 | 13 |
| Residential suburbs | 10 | 213 | 99 | 98 | 89 | 35 | 69 | 65 | 97 | 20 |
| New industrial suburbs | 12 | 131 | 119 | 70 | 58 | 70 | 61 | 47 | 89 | 17 |
| New towns | 10 | 138 | 105 | 97 | 85 | 56 | 89 | 82 | 64 | 19 |
| Welsh mining towns | 3 | 53 | 61 | 134 | 117 | 113 | 76 | 72 | 109 | 2 |
| Engineering towns | 19 | 85 | 88 | 114 | 111 | 104 | 79 | 86 | 104 | 40 |

| Types of towns | Number of towns | Occupational groupings | | | | | Households of: | | Age 65 and over | Born in New Commonwealth |
|---|---|---|---|---|---|---|---|---|---|---|
| | | Professional and managerial | Other non-manual | Skilled | Semi-skilled | Unskilled | 2 adults 5 or more children | 1 adult 2 or more children | | |
| Textile towns | 16 | 81 | 77 | 111 | 118 | 115 | 112 | 124 | 107 | 154 |
| Growing manufacturing towns | 14 | 85 | 87 | 105 | 120 | 101 | 130 | 116 | 79 | 84 |
| Heavy engineering and coal towns | 22 | 72 | 64 | 131 | 105 | 107 | 108 | 83 | 88 | 83 |
| Inner conurbations | 14 | 70 | 86 | 107 | 117 | 130 | 146 | 139 | 98 | 100 |
| Central Scotland | 6 | 63 | 92 | 106 | 108 | 154 | 202 | 151 | 89 | 20 |
| TOTAL | 154 | 100 | 100 | 100 | 100 | 100 | 100 | 100 | 100 | 100 |

Source: David Donnison with Paul Soto, The Good City, Heinemann, 1980.

Note:
Here and in Tables 8.2 and 8.4 the figures show each variable as a percentage of the average for all 154 towns included in the analysis. Thus a figure of 100 represents the average frequency for all towns.

**8.2** *Housing Conditions, Tenure and Demographic Growth in Towns of Different Kinds, Great Britain, 1971*
(Percentages of the averages for all towns)

| Types of towns | Housing | | Tenure | | | | Rate of demographic growth[4] |
|---|---|---|---|---|---|---|---|
| | Severely crowded[1] | Poorly equipped[2] | Private | | | Publicly owned[3] | |
| | | | Owner-occupied | Rented furnished | Rented unfurnished | | |
| Greater London | 117 | 90 | 92 | 189 | 134 | 77 | 90 |
| Regional service centres | 83 | 90 | 106 | 127 | 94 | 90 | 99 |
| Resorts | 40 | 46 | 136 | 142 | 114 | 36 | 107 |
| Residential suburbs | 32 | 62 | 134 | 53 | 67 | 79 | 130 |
| New industrial suburbs | 23 | 30 | 155 | 52 | 71 | 48 | 116 |
| New towns | 46 | 25 | 87 | 31 | 40 | 161 | 160 |
| Welsh mining towns | 33 | 282 | 137 | 12 | 89 | 69 | 86 |
| Engineering towns | 45 | 121 | 105 | 60 | 90 | 105 | 96 |
| Textile towns | 75 | 151 | 128 | 57 | 77 | 80 | 92 |
| Growing manufacturing towns | 69 | 83 | 118 | 70 | 68 | 97 | 116 |
| Heavy engineering and coal towns | 68 | 111 | 96 | 25 | 75 | 132 | 104 |
| Inner conurbations | 97 | 131 | 78 | 86 | 120 | 122 | 90 |
| Central Scotland | 487 | 117 | 43 | 45 | 97 | 189 | 96 |
| TOTAL | 100 | 100 | 100 | 100 | 100 | 100 | 100 |

*Source:* David Donnison with Paul Soto, *The Good City.*

*Notes:* 1. ¹Households living at more than 1·5 persons per room. 2. Households lacking unshared use of standard amenities (see Chapter 11, note 27). 3. Houses belonging to local authorities and New Towns. 4. Growth of the population aged 18 and over, 1955–70.

suburbs and towns full of new, prosperous service industries and light engineering have built the largest numbers of good, modern houses for owner-occupiers. The New Towns have done likewise for tenants through public enterprise. London and the Regional Service Centres depend more heavily on privately rented housing, much of it furnished. That is to be expected: on the demand side of the market they have more young, mobile households who want this kind of housing; and throughout the country the private landlords, who built most of the houses put up until the First World War, still retain a larger holding in the older cities and inner urban areas. Elsewhere their property has been more quickly bought up for owner-occupation.

It is the predominantly working-class manufacturing communities, which constitute most of Britain's towns, where people have gone furthest in acquiring rented housing for owner-occupation, either because industry is reasonably prosperous (as in the Engineering and Growing Manufacturing Towns) or because population and house prices have been falling (as in the Welsh Mining Towns) or because women have added to the earnings of the household (as in the Textile Towns) or for some combination of these reasons. In these towns overcrowding is rare, but many houses are ill equipped and some badly need repair. The gaps left in their supply of housing have generally been filled by the local authorities.

But it is in the old industrial Britain of the Heavy Engineering and Coal Towns, the Inner Conurbations and Central Scotland that local authorities play the biggest part. Many of these towns still have a lot of obsolete, poorly equipped housing, much of it in the hands of private landlords. That is being cleared away in public redevelopment schemes. Central Scotland has other housing problems too, particularly of overcrowding.

While a town's industrial structure and the labour market based on it go far to determine its housing resources and problems, the causal relationships do not run in one direction only. Housing plays an independent, though secondary, part in urban development by attracting and retaining particular kinds of people who in turn help to create particular kinds of community. Skilled and semi-skilled manual workers, along with others now retired from such work, hold the great majority of council houses, as we show in Table 11.13 on page 182. Towns which provide a lot of this housing attract and retain these workers, and elect councils determined to build more council housing.

Meanwhile, towns providing a lot of new housing built for owner-occupiers attract and retain the more highly qualified white-collar workers and tend to exclude people with low earning capacity, poor credit and no cars – the unskilled, the chronically sick, one-parent families, and the largest families, for example. Pensioners are their main dependent group. Not surprisingly, the councils they elect are less enthusiastic about building council housing and more enthusiastic about selling what they have.

Big old cities with a lot of privately rented housing, standing close to centres of service industry, government and higher education, tend to attract single people, women, and households with several earners and no children – people who value access to this kind of labour market and to recreational resources more highly than the space and gardens which they will want if they marry and have children. Furnished rented housing – fairly well equipped but often shared and crowded – particularly attracts well-educated young people, who tend to leave their parents' homes earlier than most but marry later. Unfurnished rented housing – often poorly equipped but generally uncrowded – serves a wider range of people, including some of the most vulnerable and deprived.

The local authorities have now succeeded in housing a large proportion of more vulnerable groups such as the large families, lone parents, the aged and the unskilled. This sometimes produces local problems of crowding and vandalism, but their tenants' main difficulties lie more often in the labour market than in the housing market. There are high unemployment and low proportions of women at work in towns with large proportions of council housing. These towns also depend heavily on bus transport. That suggests that council tenants tend either to live in the centre of town, but may no longer find there the kinds of jobs which they, their wives and children can do; or they live on the fringes where poor or expensive transport services confine them to too small a labour market. It may also be that reasonably good and modestly priced council housing, coupled with the difficulty of arranging exchanges between council tenants, has tied many of them to areas where prospects of work are poor.

Table 8.3 enlarges the picture presented in this chapter by looking within cities to enumeration districts. These are the smallest areas used in the census, with an average of 163 households or 470 people in them. It shows the districts in which the three main forms of housing stress are most heavily concentrated; and it relates these to two of the main conditions which prevent people from buying a solution to their housing problems – unemployment and retirement. Unemployment, which is related to all the main deprivations afflicting the less skilled working class, is most heavily concentrated in Scotland, the north of England,

**8.3** *Geographical Distribution of the Worst Conditions, 1971*
(The 5 per cent of worst enumeration districts in Britain as percentage of all EDs in each area)

| | Over-crowding[1] | Shared housing[2] | Poorly equipped housing[3] | Unemployment[4] | Pensioners[5] |
|---|---|---|---|---|---|
| *Country* | | | | | |
| England | 2·8 | 5·8 | 4·5 | 3·6 | 4·8 |
| Wales | 0·4 | 2·5 | 3·6 | 6·0 | 3·9 |
| Scotland | 24·7 | 0·3 | 9·8 | 15·6 | 7·5 |
| *Region* | | | | | |
| North | 1·8 | 1·0 | 7·7 | 12·7 | 4·1 |
| Yorks. and Humberside | 1·8 | 0·8 | 5·0 | 4·9 | 5·4 |
| North West | 1·5 | 1·4 | 6·8 | 7·2 | 3·9 |
| East Midlands | 1·0 | 1·1 | 4·9 | 2·3 | 3·5 |
| West Midlands | 3·5 | 1·5 | 3·5 | 2·0 | 1·2 |
| East Anglia | 0·3 | 1·9 | 1·1 | 3·3 | 6·8 |
| South East | 4·4 | 11·7 | 3·7 | 0·9 | 5·5 |
| South West | 0·3 | 6·4 | 0·6 | 1·7 | 8·5 |
| *Conurbation* | | | | | |
| Inner London[6] | 12·9 | 32·4 | 12·6 | 1·7 | 2·5 |
| Outer London[7] | 2·7 | 8·5 | 0·9 | 0·2 | 1·6 |
| Tyneside | 3·3 | 0·8 | 10·6 | 16·6 | 3·5 |
| West Yorkshire | 3·6 | 1·1 | 3·0 | 4·9 | 6·2 |
| Merseyside | 2·8 | 2·1 | 10·0 | 16·7 | 1·8 |
| S.E. Lancashire | 1·7 | 1·3 | 8·2 | 5·2 | 3·3 |
| West Midlands | 6·0 | 2·4 | 4·9 | 2·9 | 1·5 |
| Clydeside | 43·9 | 0·5 | 15·6 | 26·6 | 5·0 |
| *Great Britain* | 5 | 5 | 5 | 5 | 5 |

*Source: Census Indicators of Urban Deprivation, Working Note No. 6, Department of the Environment, February 1975. Appendix D.*

*Notes:*
1. Per cent of households living at more than 1·5 persons per room.
2. Per cent of households sharing dwellings.
3. Per cent of households without unshared use of hot water supply, bath and indoor WC.
4. Per cent of economically active males unemployed but seeking work or sick.
5. Pensioner households as per cent of all households.
6. Inner London Education Authority area, plus Haringey and Newham, minus Greenwich.
7. Remainder of Greater London Council area.

and their conurbations. Retirement takes different and much less concentrated patterns. Each form of housing stress has different causes and is therefore distributed in different ways.

**1.** *Overcrowding* is due to a complex mixture of factors: large families, small dwellings, and competition for space which is often keenest in relatively prosperous areas. It is most heavily concentrated on Clydeside, in inner London, and (to a smaller extent) in the west Midlands conurbation. **2.** *Shared housing* is most often found among the poorer and younger people in furnished, subdivided property in towns attracting students and young clerical workers. It is most heavily concentrated in inner and (to a smaller extent) outer London, and it is very rare in Scotland and the north of England. **3.** *Poorly equipped housing* tends to be old, or shared, or both. For these rather different reasons it tends to be most common in Scotland, the north of England and some of their conurbations, and in inner London.

## Policy Implications

In conclusion we note some of the practical implications of these findings. Different kinds of place have different kinds of housing problem. Regional comparisons are much too coarse to reveal these patterns. For that we must get down to urban scale. A town's housing conditions reflect its economic history and the social structure and political culture derived from that experience. Housing is both an effect and a cause of these patterns.

Every housing market has its particular strengths and weaknesses. Many people assume that owner-occupied housing must be good, probably standing in leafy suburbs. But much of it was built long ago for renting, and stands in working-class manufacturing and mining towns. Of the 643,000 houses in England classified as unfit in 1976, 33 per cent were owner-occupied.[5] Many of these unfit houses were occupied by pensioners who could not afford to improve or repair them. The spread of owner-occupation among the growing numbers of elderly people means that these figures will grow. There is no magic about home ownership. Without generous help, people with low incomes cannot afford to secure good houses or to keep them in good condition, whether they be owners or tenants.

The local authorities have solved many people's most urgent housing problems. But they may be the only problems they solve. Indeed, their housing policies sometimes exacerbate other problems. Council tenants and their families may find it harder than other people to reach the jobs they want, and the narrow range of dwelling sizes in this sector of the market leaves many of them seriously overcrowded. Single people and larger families may be excluded, or confined to the few places where the smallest and largest council houses have been built. Meanwhile, by excluding from council housing certain kinds of people who get low priority on the waiting-lists – newcomers, and young, single people, for example – local authorities may contribute to the sharing and crowding still to be seen in other parts of the market.

Privately rented housing still plays an important part in the housing market by offering people first footholds in it, often within easy reach of city centres and the opportunities to be found there. Authorities which demolish the remainder of this housing, or allow it to be taken over for owner-occupation, must find other ways of meeting these needs in their own stock or elsewhere, and in similar locations. Otherwise serious problems will arise, both for the displaced people and for cities which need their labour. For some of these people it will not be enough to provide small units in the right places. They may also need furnished housing, or help with the hire purchase of domestic equipment – both of which the local authorities are empowered to provide but rarely offer.

It is in the expanding, prosperous centres of service industries, government and light engineering which we described as the 'new Britain' that housing conditions are generally best. These towns also appear to distribute their opportunities more equally than the old industrial centres do, for it is their manual workers (and particularly the less skilled among them) who gain most from the lower unemployment rates, the higher car ownership, and the greater opportunities for travelling to work by car which distinguish the new from the old Britain. Table 8.4 compares unemployment rates for different occupational groups in the two most impoverished and the three most prosperous clusters of towns. It shows that while all classes benefit from growth and prosperity it is manual workers in general, and the unskilled in particular, who benefit most. The educational attainment of children also appears to be better in expanding, prosperous towns than elsewhere. In these towns, too, mothers with young children seem to have more opportunities for getting the part-time work which often suits them best. Better and more equal opportunities are likely to produce better and more equal housing conditions too. All that looks like good news. It is not every pattern of urban growth which has these benign effects, or every pattern of contraction which is destructive. But it is in general the more prosperous and equal Britain which is growing, while the old Britain – the world of

**8.4** *Unemployment Rates by Occupational Group for Selected Clusters of Towns, 1971*

(Percentages of the average for each group in all towns[1])

| Clusters | 1 Professional and managerial | 2 Other non-manual | 3 Skilled manual | 4 Semi-skilled | 5 Un-skilled | Professional ÷ Unskilled $\left(\dfrac{1}{5}\right)$ | Non-manual ÷ Manual $\left(\dfrac{1+2}{3+4+5}\right)$ |
|---|---|---|---|---|---|---|---|
| *Most impoverished* | | | | | | | |
| Central Scotland | 157 | 161 | 210 | 209 | 228 | 0·69 | 0·74 |
| Inner Conurbations | 118 | 121 | 132 | 130 | 133 | 0·89 | 0·91 |
| *Most prosperous* | | | | | | | |
| New Industrial Suburbs | 93 | 79 | 63 | 61 | 64 | 1·45 | 1·37 |
| Residential Suburbs | 64 | 67 | 53 | 64 | 60 | 1·07 | 1·11 |
| New Towns | 75 | 62 | 52 | 52 | 48 | 1·56 | 1·34 |
| *All towns in cluster analysis* | 100 | 100 | 100 | 100 | 100 | 1·00 | 1·00 |

*Source:* David Donnison with Paul Soto, *The Good City.*

*Note:*

1. A figure of 100 means that the occupational group in the cluster of towns shown has the same incidence of unemployment as the average for all members of this group in the 154 towns included in the thirteen clusters analysed.

*Coronation Street* – is dying. Or it was in 1971, when the evidence for that generalization was assembled.[6]

But each kind of town plays a part in the wider urban pattern. Many of the most prosperous and best-housed places have grown by attracting people from less prosperous places, while in effect excluding less fortunate and successful people. For every Residential Suburb and New Town which grows more prosperous and more equal, there are likely to be Inner Conurbations and towns in Central Scotland which grow relatively less prosperous and less equal, losing economic activities and skilled workers while retaining their largest families, their poorest, their oldest and their more disabled people – all those who find it hardest to move away, to find a new home and to start a new life elsewhere.

This does not mean that nothing can be done to improve matters. With hard work, a reasonably fortunate location, and a lot of investment, declining towns with fairly poor housing conditions can be turned within a generation into prosperous, expanding places with better housing than the average town – and that can be done not only in places with large proportions of highly skilled people such as the New Towns, but also in places with more than their share of the vulnerable social groups. Swindon[7] is an example, as are others in the category we described as Growing Manufacturing Towns. There is no reason to assume that economic and social development have to be a zero-sum game – every local advance towards better conditions being achieved by robbing other communities of exactly equivalent opportunities. National economic revival does not start in some non-spatial limbo: it begins on the ground, in towns. But, from the evidence presented here, we can only say that development at urban scale must make some net contribution to national resources and opportunities if it is to do more than shift an unchanged total of good and bad things around the map. Some patterns of urban development probably achieve this; others, ineptly or wastefully conducted, probably operate at a loss, nationally speaking. The London town expansion schemes, for example, probably benefited more people for every pound spent on them, and benefited more people with housing needs, than the more prestigious New Town schemes.[8]

How much can government do about these problems? Can it bring about more constructive urban development, and ensure that local housing programmes match and sustain the growth of the rest of a town's economy? These questions demand a review of housing and planning policies to which we turn in the next chapters.

# 9
# Housing Policy:
# The Issues Formulated

## Politics is a Learning Process

In housing, more than in most fields of government, nothing can be done without the collaboration of a lot of independent institutions and individuals subject to no common authority. Land owners and developers, builders and building societies, local authorities and private landlords, Whitehall and town hall, must all be induced to work together. They will not do that unless they share some common expectations and compatible objectives. Politicians play important parts in creating that consensus and shifting it forwards (or backwards) from time to time. They never achieve a final solution to *the* housing problem, but as some problems grow less important and new ones become more important the issues are reformulated and policy evolves. Politics is a learning process for the whole nation.

In the next chapters we consider what Britain has learnt about housing policy since the Second World War, and try to identify which issues have been settled during these years and which are now the more important ones that remain unresolved. We break the story into two parts in the 1960s; then, in Chapter 11, we review the progress made. Finally, in Chapter 12, we identify the issues which have been settled and the new issues now on the policy-makers' agenda. This treatment of the subject will be more controversial and less authoritative than a straightforward history of housing in Britain. But it may be more helpful to readers who want to think about priorities for the future. There are excellent histories of housing policy which can be found elsewhere.[1]

## Aftermath of War

A generation and more after the Second World War, much of the debate about housing policy is still couched in terms formulated at the time of the Labour Party's first majority government, elected in 1945. Distant though they are, these years are therefore worth careful study.

Britain emerged from the war with 200,000 houses destroyed, another 250,000 so badly knocked about that they could not be lived in and a similar number severely damaged. Millions of men and women were about to come home, and the marriage and birth rates were rising fast. The pre-war building labour force of a million men had fallen to a third of this number, mainly concentrated in south-east England in the path of the flying bomb and rocket attacks. The rents of privately owned houses had been frozen at their 1939 levels, and in England and Wales 71,000 houses had been requisitioned by local authorities.

But amidst the confusion there was determination and high confidence, fortified by an underestimate of long-term needs, a war-won capacity for bold decisions and a strong sense of social priorities. Procedures for compulsory purchase were temporarily simplified to enable the Minister to confirm orders 'without public local inquiry or hearing'. Pre-war subsidies, which in 1933 had been restricted to slum clearance, were extended to cover housing built to meet 'general needs', and were later increased. Three quarters of the subsidy (instead of the pre-war two thirds) was to be paid by the central government. Orders were issued for the production of prefabricated temporary houses, and local authorities were empowered to erect them on public open spaces where no other land was available. 'Housing,' said Mr Tomlinson, introducing the first post-war Housing Bill, 'should be tackled as one would tackle a military operation.' The previous 'caretaker' government had adopted a new principle – 'to afford a separate dwelling for every family desiring to have one' – and it expected that between three and four million houses would be built in the next ten or twelve years. (It took six years for the first million, three more for the second, and another three years for the third.)

The dimensions of the standard three-bedroom council house were enlarged. Local authorities were given still wider powers to requisition property 'to ensure as far as possible that all houses are reasonably fully occupied' and 'for the purpose of preventing a situation where people become or are likely to become homeless' (i.e. to protect tenants from eviction). They built four fifths of the houses put up, and were responsible for controlling and rationing work on repairs and the small amount of new private building permitted. But their designs, layouts, methods and materials were tightly controlled by the central government, and the Ministry directed a continuous flow of instruction and exhortation at them – an average of five circulars a week in 1946. Their status was tersely explained by the Minister, Aneurin Bevan: 'If we are to plan, we have to plan with plannable instruments, and the speculative builder, by his very nature, is not a plannable instrument . . . We rest the full weight of the housing programme upon the local authorities, because their programmes can be planned, and because in fact we can check them if we desire to . . .' Builders could be forced into less profitable areas by restricting building quotas in the most profitable centres.

Although the 'housing drive' was mounted quickly and pretty successfully in this way, it did not call for any fundamental reappraisal of pre-war thinking. The twin pillars of the whole programme – rent control and subsidized council housing – were devices which had been employed since the First World War. The 'prefabs', Europe's first post-war experiment in industrialized building, were designed to produce rapid results during the inevitable delay while men were released from the forces and conventional building resources were mobilized. They were produced by workers employed in defence industries – particularly aircraft manufacture – caught over-extended by the unexpectedly sudden defeat of Japan. They proved very expensive, gave prefabrication a bad name and were dropped as soon as possible. (Later, however, their popularity increased when urban housing authorities turned increasingly to the building of flats.) Requisitioning was an avowedly temporary procedure, cut down after 1948 and finally brought to a close in 1960, provoking no fresh thought about government's responsibility for acquiring or assisting privately rented housing. Proposals for municipalizing private property, advanced in the debate on the 1949 Housing Bill, were dismissed by Aneurin Bevan in characteristically forceful fashion: 'It cannot and would not be done at the present time . . . if we tried to do that through the 1,700-odd local authorities, it would be an operation compared with which the Italian campaign was one of the most simple ever carried out.'

Taken as a whole, the provisions made were bold and expensive by pre-war standards; but they bore the marks of a 'crash' programme. They were designed to meet essentially temporary needs (for housing requirements were gravely underestimated) with instruments many of which were also avowedly temporary. Little more could be expected in the chaotic months between VE Day and the economic crisis of 1947, when this system was being created. But housing policies would some day demand the kind of probing and radical reappraisal which the Beveridge Committee had recently given to social security policies, the Curtis Committee had given to policies for deprived children, and two long series of committees had given to policies for town and country planning and the health services. Housing never got that treatment. The nearest attempt came later in the Housing Finance – renamed Housing Policy – Review which reported in 1977. But that was neither deeply probing nor radical. The last Royal Commission to study the subject on a national scale was – and still is – the Commission on the Housing of the Working Classes. It reported in 1885.

By the end of 1946 this country was well ahead of the field in getting its housing programme going, and the government announced a further increase which would have taken output to 240,000 during the following year. But the building industry was already running short of materials; and then came a hard winter and the fuel crisis, followed by a first-class crisis in the balance of payments. The export drive became the government's all-consuming concern, and, with it, the restraint of inflation, the control of imports, the rationing of building materials, and the restriction of building. Despite occasional increases in the programme, notably in 1953 and 1964, house building has generally been overshadowed by anxieties about the balance of payments and has been employed as one of the principal regulators of the economy ever since. Today, as a new government makes swingeing cuts in public expenditure, it has again been housing which is to provide much the biggest contribution to them: £1,500 million out of a total cut in public expenditure of £4,100 million for the financial year 1980–81 [2] (see Table 10.1 on page 162). For the five years after the crisis of 1947 – while most local authorities, regardless of Party colouring, were determined to build as many houses as possible – the main task of central government was to restrict the building programme to the level permitted by those responsible for the balance of payments.

Ambitious schemes devised at the end of the war to recruit and train more building workers were thrown out of gear; the recruitment of apprentices fell off sharply and the training scheme for adults was abandoned. The average floor area of three-bedroom council houses in England and Wales, raised at first from its pre-war figure of 800 square feet to a post-war peak of 1,050 square feet in 1951, fell to a low point of under 900 square feet in 1959 and 1960. (Later it rose again to about 960 in 1969, since when the size of council houses with five bed-spaces has fluctuated around a gently falling trend.) [3]

Unlike housing, British town planning policies were transformed during these first post-war years. The whole planning system is still largely based on five Acts of Parliament passed at this time. These were the Distribution of Industry Act of 1945, giving powers to restrain the growth of industry in some places and to attract it to others; the New

Towns Act of 1946, providing for the building of New Towns by centrally funded development corporations to be set up for the purpose; the Town and Country Planning Act of 1947 (the most important of all), giving counties and county boroughs the duty of preparing development plans and extensive powers for controlling all forms of development; the National Parks and Access to the Countryside Act of 1949, enabling planning authorities to create and manage countryside parks with advice from a central Countryside Commission; and the Town Development Act of 1952, which enabled the big cities to transfer some of their population to smaller towns wanting to expand.

Lewis Silkin, the Minister of Town and Country Planning, told Parliament when introducing the Town and Country Planning Act of 1947 that planners should create environments which would be humane in scale, moderate in density, interspersed with green spaces, and likely to foster neighbourly relations in socially mixed communities. These priorities were confirmed by successive governments. They were much concerned with housing. We described in the last chapter how densities have been reduced in the biggest cities as people, and then jobs too, moved out to the suburbs and smaller towns. This planning philosophy carried those trends forward. Indeed, the philosophy itself was a public governmental expression of individual desires and market forces working on a worldwide scale at this time in most urban, industrial countries. People wanted to live and work at lower densities, in smaller places and in cleaner, greener settings. With cheap fuel and improving means of communication, more and more of them could do so. Planners devoted much of their work to helping them to achieve these aims.

The elite of the profession were generally architect planners, concentrated in local authorities and consultancies where they were mainly concerned with physical design and the use of land. The New Towns, and later the great new hospitals, universities and city-centre redevelopments, are their monuments. Planning on a regional and national scale and planning for the enlargement of economic opportunities gained less recognition – partly because these forms of planning were less well understood and less successfully handled, and partly because it was assumed that Keynesian policies of economic management would assure economic progress without calling for any intervention by town planners. Town planning was not entirely innocent of economics: the Distribution of Industry Act, the first of the five post-war measures on which the system was founded, was designed to steer economic growth into some towns and regions and out of others. But planners' powers were almost entirely negative, giving them no independent driving force

– only a set of reins to steer whatever investment the economy generated. Neither did they have much scope for redistributing economic opportunities amongst citizens. Although it was repeatedly stressed that planned communities would be 'socially mixed', no one asked whether 'mixed', to become a social reality, must also mean 'more equal'.

The one device introduced by the 1947 Act for redistributing the wealth generated by economic growth was its provision for a development charge which would acquire for the community the increase in land values brought about by development. The Act enabled the community, through its town planners, to nationalize development rights by controlling land uses without paying any compensation to land owners to whom permission for development was refused. It followed (argued the wartime Uthwatt Report)[4] that the community was entitled to acquire for itself the gains brought about by its own development – gains allocated to particular plots of land by its own planners. What proportion of this increase in land values would be acquired by the state for the community was still being debated when the Bill was introduced. The decision to go the whole hog and impose a 100 per cent development charge arose not from socialist principles or public debate – these complex problems were a mystery to most people – but from the Treasury's insistence that government revenues be maximized.[5] This proved to be only the beginning of a much longer story, still unfinished.

The weakness of planners in dealing with economic forces was less obvious then than it later became. Profitable commercial development was tightly restricted and the state's local housing authorities were building the great majority of new houses. Government licensing of all construction meant that the private sector could be treated as the flexible margin of investment which would be used when necessary to regulate and manage the economy.

## How the Issues were Perceived

Thus there developed a housing system, regarded by its creators as one of the pillars of socialism, which was in fact little more than the extension into peacetime of various features of a wartime economy. This system was widely accepted while wartime scarcities and a sense of national solidarity in the face of crisis persisted; but it was to become as irksome as a 'demob' suit once those pressures began to lift. Spokesmen of the socialist movement, originally founded to give ordinary people a collective defence against oppression and exploitation of every kind, came to sanctify some of the nation's less sensitive bureaucracies – the big city housing departments – as symbols of their collective creed. Small-scale local centres of power of all kinds were suspect at this time. Since the turn of the century, progressives had battled to replace the poor law, the local charities, and the local friendly societies with nationwide services which would give everyone, wherever they lived, a right to the same basic standards of income, education, medical care and housing.

The Labour movement was hostile towards private landlords and unwilling to subsidize them or to relax rent controls (as Scandinavian social democrats had done), yet also reluctant to take over their housing or to provide public housing for many kinds of people who lived in the landlords' steadily decaying property. House buyers, too, were often regarded with the kind of suspicion that is reserved for the class enemy, as were the developers and builders who put up houses for them – despite the fact that more and more working-class people were buying their own homes, and some of Europe's highest proportions of housing for owner-occupation were to be found in centrally planned economies to the east, as we showed in Chapter 6.

Meanwhile many Conservatives adopted a contrary ideology. Some called as passionately for the freeing of private landlords and developers, the reduction of housing subsidies and the abolition of the local housing authority itself, as for the abolition of food rationing and identity cards. They seemed unaware how odd this attack on planning and the public sector would seem to some of the world's more successful Conservative régimes – in France and Germany, for example.

The potentially crucial significance of the powers contained in planning law to harvest and redeploy the windfall profits of urban development was not widely grasped by the Labour movement and never became a central article of socialist faith. Like nearly everyone else at this time, the movement tended to assume that the problems of maintaining full employment with sustained, if rather slow, economic growth had been solved by Keynes and his followers. Town planning therefore seemed largely a matter of tidying up the urban estate, protecting the rural landscape, and building new towns.

The lack of close collaboration between planners and 'housers' was symbolized and reinforced by giving planning powers to the Minister of Town and Country Planning and housing powers to the Minister of Health (who was much busier at this time creating the National Health Service). At local level the professions involved in housing and planning were (and still are) recruited and trained in quite different ways and usually employed in different tiers of local government. Most of the local housing authorities were urban and rural districts and municipal boroughs. Most of the planners were based in the counties. Even in the county boroughs, which were all-purpose authorities, collaboration between planning and housing was often poor. Housing responsibilities at this time were usually divided between different departments – borough engineers, surveyors, treasurers, and medical officers might all play a part. They were not (and often are still not) concentrated in a single housing department. Although the housing committee was often regarded as the most important in the council calendar, its administrative and political communications linked its members most closely to interests other than those concerned with planning. Thanks to building sites cleared by bombing or acquired before the war, the main bottlenecks in the housing programme at this time arose not from shortage of land, but from shortages of labour and materials. Only in the New Towns, still at a very early stage in their development, were responsibilities for housing, planning, economic development and community development brought more closely together under a general manager and a development corporation, each well aware that the whole enterprise might founder if the growth of jobs, housing, social services and public confidence in the town did not advance together.

## Back to a Residual Role

Gradually the role of the state was diminished. Controls over the use and prices of building materials and restrictions on private building were already being relaxed before the Conservatives returned to power in 1951. They took the process further with conviction. The licensing of house building was first relaxed, and then abolished altogether in 1954. Controls on local authorities' building plans were simplified, and they were sent out to borrow their money in the open market instead of getting it from the Public Works Loan Board. The proportion of houses built for private owners rose from 15 per cent in 1952 to 63 per cent in 1961 (see Table 9.1). By then the last requisitioned houses had been handed back to their owners or acquired outright. The 1957 Rent Act removed rent restrictions for the most expensive houses and raised rents for the remainder to higher levels. Whenever existing tenants moved or died, rents were freed from all control. House purchase and the sale of council houses were encouraged, and more generous grants for the improvement of older housing were introduced which gave home owners a right to claim standard sums of money, whether their local authorities

**9.1** *Dwellings Completed in the United Kingdom, 1945–80*
(Annual averages in thousands)

|  | Public sector | Housing associations | Private sector | Total |
|---|---|---|---|---|
| 1945–50 | 113 | * | 28 | 141 |
| 1951–5 | 224 | * | 67 | 291 |
| 1956–9 | 159 | * | 135 | 294 |
| 1960–64 | 137 | * | 186 | 322 |
| 1965–9 | 193 | * | 208 | 401 |
| 1970–74 | 138 | 9 | 182 | 328 |
| 1975–9 | 131 | 19 | 150 | 300 |
| 1980 | 89 | 21 | 129 | 239 |

*Source:* Department of the Environment, *Housing and Construction Statistics.*

*Note:*
* Included in Public sector.

approved the policy or not. A boom in office building began. But a whole-hearted attempt to revive private enterprise in the housing market was postponed till after the second Conservative victory in 1955.

Many believed that the election of 1951 had been won partly by Harold Macmillan's promise to build 300,000 houses a year. To achieve that the council building programme had first to be increased, along with a rising output of houses for owner-occupation. That was made possible by a favourable turn in the terms of trade, which reduced pressure on the balance of payments and made a massive increase in housing subsidies easier to sustain. Standards of council housing were cut down sharply, with results which now contribute to the problems of unlettable housing which we discuss in Chapter 15. By 1954 Macmillan's target was handsomely surpassed with an output of 357,000 houses, and the stage was set for a major change of direction.

Already, with private building released from controls, it was the local authorities which had to provide the flexible element in the programme when the managers of the economy needed to cut back investment and reduce housing subsidies. The new order began to take shape between 1954 and 1957. Its principal objectives were first explained in a White Paper, *Houses: The Next Step*,[6] and implemented through a succession of measures, the most important of which were the Housing Repairs and Rents Act of 1954, the Housing Subsidies Act of 1956, and the Rent

Act of 1957. Council housing programmes were reduced and switched to slum clearance and – to a lesser extent – to the housing of old people. Local authorities, the Minister told parliament, 'should subsidize only those tenants who require subsidizing, and only to the extent of their need'. Private investment in housing grew dramatically, supported by increasingly generous improvement grants.

For a while it looked as if the government was extricating itself from its extensive, though never comprehensively planned, involvement in the housing market and reverting to a residual role. The local authorities would clear the slums – still regarded as a finite, public health problem for which a final solution would soon be found. Thereafter they would administer their inheritance of some three and a half million houses as a form of social service, adding a few to bring about the expansion of selected towns and to meet the special needs of selected groups in the population. The 'free market' would meet all normal requirements.

Meanwhile 'planning' had become a dirty word. Reference to it, which had played a major part in the 1945 election (the Labour Party's manifesto had bravely promised 'a radical solution for the crippling problems of land acquisition and use in the service of the national plan'), disappeared almost entirely from Labour manifestoes for the elections of 1950 and 1951.[7] When the Conservatives returned to power in 1951, the word 'planning' was dropped from the title of the central department responsible for it, which became instead the Ministry of Housing and Local Government. Fourteen New Towns had been designated since the war, ending with Corby in 1950. No more were designated till Cumbernauld in 1955 and Skelmersdale in 1961. The Town Development Act of 1952, giving powers to expand smaller towns which would take people from the big cities, provided much less generous financial support from the Exchequer than had been given to the New Towns.

Town planning nevertheless survived, partly because its central themes accorded with individual desires and market trends. The profession adopted conservationist priorities, dear to the hearts of the rural and suburban interests which were in the ascendant. For Duncan Sandys, Minister of Housing and Local Government from 1954 till 1957, green belts became a consuming and successful preoccupation. Indeed, for some years they were probably the main thing which the public thought town planning was for. Economic planning became unfashionable too. Economists tended to leave the planning profession and the public services. A boom in consumer goods developed. Marriage rates rose, and in 1956 the birth rate, which had been falling for eight years, began to rise too. The revival of free enterprise seemed to be working rather well. Town planners were still needed, no longer to create a new world, but as estate managers to a capitalist society.

The attempt made under the 1947 Act to nationalize the increase in land values brought about by development had not been successful. People were reluctant to sell land for development, or they simply added to its price the development charge levied on the land. Thus new development was, in effect, delayed or taxed. As scarcities of labour and materials eased and restrictions on non-essential building were lifted, the prospect of more profitable commercial development lay ahead, whetting the appetite of powerful interests for a return to a free market. The Town and Country Planning Acts of 1953 and 1954 abolished development charges and reduced the number of cases in which claims could be made to compensate people for the loss of development rights. For a while there were two markets in land: one in which private transactions took place freely, and another in which public authorities acquired land at lower prices – an arrangement which soon became indefensible. The Town and Country Planning Act of 1959 retained the power of the planning authorities to confer or withhold development rights, but restored a 'fair market price' for land compulsorily purchased. This price, intended to reflect the values ruling in the market, was fairer to sellers but more expensive for taxpayers, the tenants of council houses, and others who had to foot the bill for land acquired by public authorities.

The experience of the first decade after the war had reinforced the ideologies both of the left and of the right. It dramatized public debate about housing as a contest between Labour, who saw themselves as the party concerned with needs, fair shares and the public sector, and the Conservatives, who saw themselves as the party concerned with demands, growth and private enterprise. The latter expected to eliminate housing scarcities before long. They would then resume slum clearance, originally undertaken by Arthur Greenwood in 1930 and interrupted by the war. Thereafter, it was assumed, the public sector could be confined to a residual role, helping only those few people who could not cope unaided in the open market.

## Government Resumes an Active Role

Government was not to be let off the hook so easily. Economic and social changes were already at work, increasing needs and demands, distorting and restricting the capacity of the market to meet these demands, and sharpening political tensions which would in due course drag the state back into a deeper involvement in the housing field. The principal factors making it difficult for government to restrict itself to a residual, 'social' policy can be briefly outlined.

The relatively slow growth of the United Kingdom's population had throughout the century distracted attention from underlying changes in demographic structure. These changes called for an increase in housing which had to proceed much faster than the increase in population if headship rates were not to fall – that is to say, if people of any given age, sex and marital status were to have as good a chance of finding a home as their predecessors had. Between 1931 and 1951 the population of England and Wales had increased by less than 10 per cent, but households had increased by over 28 per cent. Although it was nearly three times as large as the increase in population, this increase in households probably occurred without any appreciable rise in the headship rates for particular groups within the population: single men aged twenty, married couples aged forty, or widows aged sixty, for example, probably had about the same chance of forming separate households as their predecessors in the same demographic groups had twenty years earlier. (If some had a better chance, then others had worse: census data do not permit a more precise conclusion.) The fall in family size, the growing numbers of old people and the increasing popularity of marriage meant that one- and two-person households had increased from 29 to 39 per cent of all those in the country, while households of six or more people fell from 16 to 8 per cent of the total. There were 300 instead of 256 households for every thousand people. But these changes occurred without any improvement in the privacy and independence actually afforded to individuals by the housing available. The dynamics of these changes in demographic structure – which are still continuing, though now at a slower rate – were not widely understood in this country until the publication of J. B. Cullingworth's book, *Housing Needs and Planning Policy*, in 1960 (although demographers working on the 1951 census had pointed it out somewhat earlier[8]). This partly explains why housing needs were continually underestimated, even by radical prophets, from the time when Sidney Webb, Ramsay Mac-Donald, J. R. Clynes and others published a pamphlet[9] in 1917 estimating that when a million houses had been built, only 100,000 a year would be required for replacement and further growth of the population, to the time when the Economics Committee of the Royal Commission on Population predicted there would be so sharp a fall in household formation during the 1950s that a major programme of slum clearance would be required to prevent a slump in the building industry.[10]

In 1951, national income per head barely surpassed the level attained in 1939; but in the years which followed it began to rise – at a modest rate by European standards, but a faster rate sustained over a much longer period than ever before in living memory. One of the first things to which the British devoted their extra income was the bearing and raising of children. From the mid fifties the birth rate began to rise, steadily and quite unexpectedly. It would be another twenty years before this change could affect the numbers of households to be sheltered, but already it was clear that earlier estimates of housing need and demand would have to be increased. Many people on modest incomes still depended on rent control and council housing to enable them to secure living space for their growing families, and they would be seriously threatened by a reduction in council building, by a reorientation of municipal priorities which prevented the rehousing of families from the waiting lists, or by the elimination of rent controls.

Many of the poorest and most vulnerable people in Britain had in the past depended mainly upon the private landlord for shelter. But private rented property, as will be shown in the next chapter, had been dwindling for years. The growing slum-clearance programme, the encouragement of owner-occupation through more generous loans and improvement grants, and the workings of a tax system which favoured the owner-occupier and penalized the private landlord all hastened this process. Private rented property was demolished or converted to owner-occupation, and new investment was concentrated in other sectors of the market. Those who could not gain a foothold in the expanding sectors of the market were thus compelled to compete for a dwindling supply of poor-quality rented housing.

The 1957 Rent Act did nothing to improve things. It was passed with the applause of politicians rallying to the colours of 'free enterprise' and economists in search of a problem to which their ready-made academic solutions could be applied. Both were unaware of the massive shortages building up as the uncontrolled growth of employment increased the demand for housing space in areas where town planning controls and slum clearance restricted the supply. Neither understood the long history of government policies (in which rent controls played a relatively small part) which had weighted the scales so heavily against private landlords that they were going out of business.

It took several years for the stresses resulting from these developments to break surface. But after a time, problems arising at opposite ends of the social processes now at work demanded growing attention. Newspaper readers were repeatedly reminded of the decaying and underemployed cities of Scotland, the north of England and (more faintly) Ulster, and of the increasingly ruthless battle for space going on in the booming inner areas of London. In the summer of 1961 homeless London families, who had been growing in numbers since the last quarter of 1957, began to appear on the television screens. Thereafter every editor made a regular feature of 'human stories' about housing. Then in 1963 a public scandal blew up, involving the Secretary of State for War and a notorious London landlord who had died the year before. The uproar which followed succeeded – where researchers, social workers and local authorities had failed – in securing action on London's housing problems. A Committee of Inquiry was appointed – the Milner Holland Committee[11] – which proceeded to make a more thorough investigation than may have been expected.

Rising concern about the failure of the British economy to keep pace with its competitors, and about the decay of industries and towns in the northern regions, led to the establishment of the National Economic Development Council and the launching of a series of regional studies by the Town and Country Planning Division of the Ministry of Housing and Local Government. Reports published by these bodies contained national and regional forecasts of population, housing requirements and the output of the building industry – *total* requirements and *total* output, not just the residual programmes to be left to the public sector. Before long, new government initiatives of all sorts were being taken: to promote housing associations which would fill the gap being left by the disappearing private landlord; to compel owners of the worst housing to make repairs under threat of direct public action paid for by confiscation of their rents; to set up a National Building Agency to promote the industrialization of building methods; and to form consortia of local authorities which would pool their orders, share technical resources and build housing on a larger and more efficient scale.

During the general election which followed in 1964 much of the debate centred on housing, rents, the rights of tenants, the rising price of land, the building of offices – many of them still standing embarrassingly empty – the needs of the homeless, and the plight of decaying and depressed areas. The outcome of the election was widely attributed to public disquiet about these issues. Government was being drawn ineluctably back into deeper involvement in the housing and town planning fields.

# 10
# New Times, New Policies

## Hopes Frustrated

For a few years the British seemed to regain confidence in their capacity to transform their country by purposeful collective action. The Labour governments elected in 1964 and again, with a larger majority, in 1966 were as much a result as a cause of that mood. A National Plan was prepared which was to incorporate an output of 500,000 houses a year. With declining rates of demographic growth or change, about half that production would have had to be devoted to replacing unfit housing.[1] Since that would have called for a tripling of the rate of slum clearance then being achieved, it was going to be very difficult to maintain so high an output. Nevertheless the government asked local authorities to reassess their clearance programmes and aim for a faster rate of progress. These programmes had always recorded the councils' cautiously realistic aspirations rather than the larger numbers of houses actually unfit to live in. Henceforth they were to list every house which ought to be improved or replaced, not just those which they expected to be able to deal with in the near future. These ambitious building programmes were described as a 'campaign'; that was the mood of the times. Meanwhile the sizes of new council houses were to be enlarged and their standards improved, following the recommendations of the Parker Morris Committee,[2] and a Rent Act setting up a new system of fair rents was passed in 1965. Later the option mortgage scheme was introduced to extend benefits equivalent to tax relief to house buyers who had incomes too low to pay the standard rate of tax. Rate rebates were introduced, which for the first time made Britain's exceedingly regressive system of local taxation slightly less onerous for the poor.

In the planning field this was a more innovative period than any since the late forties. The town planning 'interest' played a leading part in campaigns to reform the whole system of local government. The Planning Advisory Group, set up by the Ministry of Housing and Local Government, proposed a complete overhaul of the planning system[3] which led eventually to the Town and Country Planning Act of 1968. This Act replaced the cumbrous development plans of the 1947 Act with more flexible structure plans designed to focus attention on longer-term strategies of social and economic development, while local plans, action area plans, subject plans and other more detailed proposals dealt with particular neighbourhoods and issues demanding more intensive attention. The report of the Skeffington Committee the next year led to more systematic attempts to inform and involve people in debate about town planning.[4] Planning authorities were henceforth obliged by law to show that they had taken some account of public opinion in preparing the new structure plans.

In the Finance Act and the Land Commission Act of 1967 a second attack was made on the old problems of land pricing, compensation and betterment. The former levied a capital gains tax on increases in the current use values of land. The latter levied a betterment levy (of 40 per cent initially – no longer 100 per cent) on increases in development value. It also set up a Land Commission with wide powers to acquire land and encourage development, particularly for housing purposes.

To the clearance programme was added an expanded programme for house improvement, carried forward by the more generous grants which followed from the Denington Report,[5] and the 1969 Housing Act. Grant-aided improvements in Great Britain rose to 180,000 in 1970 and eventually to a peak of 454,000 in 1973. Meanwhile, city-centre re-development had been gathering speed, and so had the increasingly contentious road-building programme. The urban middle class, financed partly by the stock market boom, invaded (or re-invaded) once-fashionable but decayed inner London neighbourhoods to buy up houses previously rented to working-class people and improve them with the help of grants from the government. 'Gentrification', the term coined for this process, became part of the vocabulary of an angrier public debate about urban policies. Coloured immigrants, who came crowding into Britain just before the barriers imposed by the Commonwealth Immigration Act of 1962 and subsequent legislation came down, competed for space in many of the same neighbourhoods.

Planning, in short, was becoming 'politicized'. Previously, most of the new building had been done in green fields or on blitzed urban sites for people whose identity was unknown when decisions to develop were taken. These decisions could therefore be made privately in the back rooms of town halls in consultations between developers, planners, politicians and their advisers. But as the bulldozers bit into densely built areas, it became increasingly obvious who gained from the process, who lost, and who was taking the decisions. People in run-down neighbourhoods learnt that a slum-clearance scheme would mainly benefit the long-established local working class, who would be rehoused by the council in new flats. A scheme for rehabilitating houses and improving the environment would probably benefit the invading gentry, buying their way in with the help of improvement grants and tax reliefs. Leaving things alone would often benefit poorer immigrants from Ireland, the New Commonwealth and Mediterranean countries, who fended for themselves at the bottom end of the market. Building new offices, shopping centres and urban motorways would benefit commuters, motorists, tourists and others coming from further afield. In rural areas similar choices had to be made between the interests of local people, commuters and passing motorists. Arguments about housing, planning, transport and community became increasingly heated and inextricably entangled with each other.

Writing an earlier book, when these ambitious programmes and the contentions they provoked were in the air, we pointed out that the government's plan for housing – *The Housing Programme, 1965–70*[6] – was

> not, strictly speaking, a programme at all ... It is an outline of national building targets and a check list of the problems to be confronted on the route leading to them ... There is nothing surprising or abnormal about this state of affairs.

The big problems of government are resolved not just by rational analysis but when they *have* to be – under pressure.

> The experience of other countries suggests that a government intent on achieving an appreciable improvement in housing conditions can seldom mobilize the material, technical and administrative resources required for this unless it raises its sights sufficiently sharply to compel a reappraisal of many accepted practices and assumptions. Planning of the sort that changes things – not just urban estate management – only begins when people are determined to attain objectives that cannot be reached under existing arrangements.

We concluded with a warning:

> Any major programme for the rebuilding of Britain will founder in a welter of political rhetoric at the first unfavourable turn in the balance of payments unless we first build a more robust domestic economy.[7]

That was to be the fate which befell these high hopes.

The economic setback of 1966, leading to the July measures of that year and a doubling of the numbers unemployed – they rose to what then seemed the intolerable level of 600,000 for the whole of the United Kingdom – proved to be a turning-point in British history. With two brief and slight remissions, unemployment has risen since then to its present level of 3 million, with more inevitably on the way. The abandonment of the National Plan and the half million housing programme followed. Twelve more New Towns were designated in the 1960s, but there have been none since. The problems which had for a while challenged government to formulate more comprehensive housing policies were not resolved, because they no longer seemed to require solutions. Before long, politicians, professionals and administrators who had been seeking ways of increasing output without commensurate increases in resources were instead defending existing establishments and enterprises which had too little work to do. In the early seventies Britain's biggest cities were still contending with severe scarcities of land for their building programmes. By the late seventies they had a different problem: finding people who might do something with land, amounting to between 6 and 12 per cent of their inner areas, which was unused and unwanted.[8] The decay of Britain's economy was becoming her dominant and unsolved problem.

A great deal was nevertheless achieved during the late 1960s and early 1970s. The Conservative government elected in 1970 placed a reforming Secretary of State in the Department of the Environment who pressed on with studies of inner cities and urban problems which helped to focus attention on areas of special need and the people living in them – not just the property standing there – and to break down barriers between the different services which could be brought to bear on these communities. 'The total approach' was the phrase that Peter Walker coined for these policies. As the worst housing was demolished, people began to recognize the destructive effects of wholesale clearance schemes. More and more of the houses in the remaining areas which needed attention were owner-occupied – often owned, too, by immigrants for whom rehousing in council flats might be less welcome, both for them and to local electorates. Richard Crossman, Minister of Housing and Local Government in the Labour administration of 1964, had originally been committed to big clearance schemes, but he turned increasingly to rehabilitation which seemed to produce more attractive environments at lower costs.[9] His Conservative successors were even more determined to transfer resources from redevelopment to improvement. But in the private sector, improvement did more for the affluent and the young than for the poor and the old.[10] When 'general improvement areas' were first introduced in 1969, local authorities were quick to take advantage of them to improve their own ageing estates. 'Housing action areas', introduced by the 1974 Act, were intended to steer grants towards more difficult areas – decaying, disorganized and impoverished – but hopes for more rapid progress were soon blighted by public expenditure cuts.[11] Some progress was nevertheless achieved, and these policies were carried forward by the Labour government which took over in 1974.

Other developments under the Conservatives were of a less bipartisan kind. The Land Commission was abolished: it had been slow to start work and never took root. The reform of local government brought about in 1974 brushed aside the proposals of the Redcliffe-Maud Commission[12] which, over most of the country, would have placed planning and housing together at the centre of powerful, all-purpose authorities. These functions were again divided between two tiers of government, each rather ill matched to the economic and social realities of the settlements to be served. A bold attempt to redistribute the widely varying burdens of local authorities' housing debts, to rationalize rents, to reduce total housing subsidies and concentrate them more effectively on those in greatest need, was made in the Housing Finance Act of 1972. It proved a failure. The Act provoked great bitterness in local government, it failed to prevent the burden of housing subsidies growing still further, and it was repealed by the next government. Nevertheless, it created a system of housing allowances for private tenants which – despite obstinately poor take-up – may eventually lead to some more effective system of subsidies for this sector of the housing market. (We have more to say about that in Chapters 13 and 14.)

The Labour government of 1974 never had a reliable majority and lost its nerve in the face of growing economic difficulties. Anthony Crosland was for a while Secretary of State for the Environment. His assertion that, so far as public expenditure was concerned, 'the party's over', and the angry response that it provoked, characterized the political climate of the times. The government's principal achievement in the 'urban' field for a while seemed likely to be the Community Land Act of 1975. This gave the counties and districts of England, the regions and districts of Scotland and the newly created Land Authority in Wales enhanced powers to acquire at market values land which was due to be developed; and then, if they did not undertake the task themselves, to dispose of it to developers. A development land tax was imposed on private transactions which, in effect, conferred a profit on local authorities because their own transactions escaped this tax. It was intended that the number of authorities using these powers and the range of land uses to which they were applied would gradually be extended until eventually all land for development would be acquired at its current use value and pass through, or remain in, public ownership. Previous reforms had concentrated on the distribution of the gains to be made from development without paying much attention to the process of development itself. This Act accepted that there must be motives for development and a living to be made from it. It therefore gave developers a recognized role as professionals providing a service rather than as speculators in land values. While asserting the need for public ownership of land at the point when sites were assembled and allocated for development and the gains to be made from the process were apportioned, it recognized that once development had taken place land might usefully revert to private ownership: the capital recouped from selling it could then be redeployed to bring about further development in future. Debate had previously been focused mainly on the question of whether development should be privately or publicly financed. But as local authorities had gained more experience of working in partnership with private capital in commercial projects such as the rebuilding of city centres, that issue seemed less important.

Housing associations, which had been given a new lease of life in the early sixties, were still treated with some suspicion by Labour authorities. But they gained bipartisan support under the Housing Act of 1974 and generous grants through the Housing Corporation. Soon they took on more work, both as builders of new houses and as renewers of old ones. (Table 9.1 on page 148 provides a glimpse of their success.) The growing flow of public funds channelled through them brought closer control by the central government, posing questions about their future role to which we will return in the next chapter.

The biggest issues in the housing field examined by the Labour government of 1974 concerned finance. What began hopefully as the Housing Finance Review was spun out for years, renamed the Housing Policy Review, and eventually published in 1977 when the credibility of a minority government was running out. It provided an immensely valuable set of working papers attached to a Green Paper which proposed no major new departure.[13] Aspirations for more 'comprehensive' national policies in housing, as in other fields, faded during these years. At local level, however, an attempt was made to give the housing authorities broader scope to develop their own response to local needs. If central government could not operate more comprehensive policies, perhaps local government could. Councils were asked to prepare 'housing investment programmes' – in Scotland, 'housing plans' of a rather more ambitious kind – in which they outlined their housing needs, their plans for meeting them, and their proposals for investment of various kinds. The central authorities then struck bargains year by year with each of them. It is too early to say how these procedures have worked out in practice. They probably gave central government more power over total expenditure, while allowing local authorities greater freedom to distribute their money between different projects within overall cash limits.

The wheeling and dealing – reminiscent of the eighteenth century – which went on in a parliament without any clear majority gave birth to some interesting reforms. One which emerged in the housing field was the Housing (Homeless Persons) Act of 1977. We discuss that in Chapter 16. It extends the responsibilities of local housing authorities for the prevention of homelessness, and may prove to be a significant step towards the goal with which we concluded an earlier book: the hope 'that homeless families, overcrowding and the more squalid housing conditions . . . become as intolerable as untreated illness, hunger and', we over-optimistically added, 'lasting unemployment'.[14]

## A New Régime

The government which took over in 1979 will test the durability of many of these policies, no matter whether they originated under Labour or Conservative administrations. It is attempting to bring about more radical changes than any government since Attlee's came to power in 1945. Instead of managing the decline of the economy with as little hardship as possible – which was roughly the programme of previous régimes – it is seeking to transform it by a return to the values and practices of the free market. Inflation is to be brought under control at all costs. Taxes on income are to be reduced, and so is the whole scale of the public sector of the economy. In the private sector and the nationalized industries, productivity and the return on capital are to be increased by the more rigorous climate of a free market created by withdrawing subsidies, scrapping uneconomic plants and large-scale shedding of labour. Cutbacks in public expenditure, coupled with rising indirect taxes, are producing as their first result a sharp rise in inflation and unemployment. It is too soon to say whether the new medicine will eventually exert any therapeutic influence. Its side effects are so drastic that only a patient already completely fit seems likely to survive them.

The local authorities' housing programmes are being sharply reduced, and building for the private sector has slumped. The Community Land Act has been repealed, although the Land Authority in Wales will be left in being and may keep alive some of the compromises which were worked into Labour's third attempt to resolve the problems of betterment and compensation. (The local authorities had in fact made little use of the Act.) Research funded internally and externally by the Department of the Environment is being cut back. The more controversial clauses of the 1980 Housing Act are to provide massive encouragement for council and housing association tenants who want to buy their own homes. Council rents are expected to rise fairly sharply. Rates are already rising. Private landlords are to be given more scope for raising rents and getting their tenants out. In clauses supported by the opposition, the Act will also give council tenants more firmly entrenched rights in dealing with their landlords, and will extend improvement grants still further.

It is much too early to say how far these changes will go. The main changes in public expenditure are summarized in Table 10.1. Past experience in the housing field – with the Rent Act 1957, the half-million housing programme of 1966 and the Housing Finance Act 1972, for example – suggests that the impact of new policies is rarely as dramatic as their advocates hope or their critics fear. The local authorities have been increasingly successful in housing the poor and the elderly – 44 per cent of their tenants now get rent rebates or an income of some kind from the social security schemes of the Department of Health and Social Security[15] – and this is bound to restrict sales of council houses to a minority of tenants. More important than the details of legislation is the new climate of opinion from which these proposals emerge.

For a generation after the Second World War, a broad spectrum of influential people, strongly represented in the media, the civil service, the academic community and all the main political parties, shared a number of basic expectations. They expected a modest rate of economic growth which would ensure, year by year, that living standards would rise. Production would expand and industry – the horse between the shafts of the economy – would keep pulling. The job of government was to tend that horse from time to time and steer it in socially acceptable directions. Hardship, squalor and poverty, being unacceptable to a civilized nation, would gradually be eliminated, partly by the general advance in living standards, and partly by raising the standards of the poorest closer to the steadily advancing levels attained by average people. Unemployment would remain very low, for to 'go back to the thirties'

**10.1** *A Summary of Differences between Planned Government Expenditure on Various Programmes in January 1979 and March 1980* (Changes expressed in £ million at 1979 survey prices)

|  | 1980–81 | 1981–2 | 1982–3 |
|---|---|---|---|
| Defence | − 178 | + 20 | + 260 |
| Overseas aid and services | + 29 | + 90 | + 70 |
| Agriculture, fisheries, food and forestry | − 105 | − 40 | − 50 |
| Industry, energy, trade and employment | − 460 | − 1,010 | − 1,490 |
| Lending to nationalized industries | − 100 | − 400 | − 1,150 |
| Roads and transport | − 279 | − 390 | − 470 |
| Housing | − 1,576 | − 2,580 | − 3,290 |
| Other environmental services | − 317 | − 470 | − 590 |
| Law and order services | + 10 | + 20 | + 30 |
| Education, science, arts and libraries | − 530 | − 800 | − 970 |
| Health and personal social services | − 237 | − 380 | − 400 |
| Social security | − 186 | — | − 500 |
| Other public services | − 50 | − 80 | − 90 |
| Common services | − 101 | − 130 | − 150 |
| Northern Ireland | − 101 | − 150 | − 210 |
| TOTAL | − 4,180 | − 6,300 | − 9,000 |

*Source: The Government's Expenditure Plans, 1980–81 to 1983–84, Cmnd 7841, March 1980, p. 179.*

would be intolerable. Families with young children were thought to deserve special priority. Wherever possible, public services and benefits should be provided as of right: since the depression of the 1930s everyone aimed to get people off means tests. Economic growth would in time make all these things possible without reducing anyone's real income. The reports produced by liberal-minded researchers, journalists and civil servants would keep opinion moving in humane directions. Thus democratic politicians could rely on continuing popular support for equalizing policies. Government, funded increasingly by progressive, nationwide taxes on income, was regarded as the natural instrument for making progress in these directions. For that purpose it would have to employ growing numbers of teachers, doctors, social workers, planners, housing managers and other public servants. Progressive governments would – and did – recruit more and more of them.

Over-simplified and slightly caricatured though they are, these beliefs were the basis of the 'Butskellite' consensus which occupied the dominant middle ground of British opinion and politics for many years. Some of these beliefs were no more than aspirations. What actually happened was often very different. Britain did not in fact grow significantly more equal. Families with children have suffered in various ways from recent trends in economic development and social policy. The numbers of people depending on means-tested benefits did not decline: indeed, they grew steadily. Unemployment rose to what would not long ago have been regarded as intolerable levels. But, at least in their rhetoric, governments and their spokesmen still held to these doctrines.

Those who adopted these assumptions did not ask what would happen if the economy failed, unemployment rose, and falling living standards destroyed people's faith in growth. They did not foresee that as the real costs of labour-intensive public services rose by comparison with the cost of consumer goods, these services would seem a less attractive 'buy' to hard-pressed wage earners paying tax on lower and lower levels of real income. No one asked what would happen if a government, unimpressed by the Butskellite consensus, were brought to power by a swing of votes among manual workers in the more prosperous southern half of England, disillusioned by these trends. That is roughly what has happened.

The government believes that economic recovery calls for a restoration of incentives for work and enterprise, which they interpret as larger rewards for success. But they face a declining national income. Thus they can only make rich people richer by making poor people poorer. The poorest of all – nearly one tenth of the population living partly or wholly on supplementary benefit – have so far been protected. The larger number of families living on low wages are bearing the brunt of the redistribution of resources which has been set in train. These are the people whose child benefits are falling in real value, whose rents, rates and mortgage charges are rising, and who will pay more for school meals and other services. More and more of them are dropping into the ranks of the unemployed.

The budget of 1980 and its related measures have made it clear that for the first time since the war Britain has a government for which reducing unemployment, improving the living standards of families with children, getting people off means-tested benefits and helping the worst-housed to get decent homes are not urgent priorities. This may be a temporary turn of events, but it would be rash to rely on that. Housing, along with other fields of policy, must in time show the effects of this régime.

# 11
# Progress and Prospects

### Introduction

In this chapter we review Britain's housing progress and prospects. We look first at the stock of houses, their character, condition, age and equipment. Then we look at the people passing through the stock. We ask who gets what, and how satisfied they are with it. That helps us to identify, in the next section of the chapter, who comes off worst and where they are likely to live. Finally we look ahead and consider the implications of these trends for the future. Next, in a chapter which concludes this part of the book, we consider what Britain has learnt about housing policy since the Second World War, and identify the issues which now demand attention. The third part of this book deals with some of these issues and discusses proposals for resolving them.

When writing *The Government of Housing* some fifteen years ago, we had to rely on our own surveys for most of our information about housing conditions. Apart from the census, there were few other sources to draw on. That has all changed. Excellent government studies have been made since then, and it is from these that we derive the figures presented here. They enable us to go much further in tracing changes taking place in recent years. But they have one drawback. Responsibility for housing policy is divided between the different departments of government responsible for the different countries of the United Kingdom, and each assembles different information for its own purposes. Thus some of our evidence is for England only, some is for England and Wales, some is for Great Britain, and some – but very little – is for the whole United Kingdom. In this chapter we have always taken the largest unit for which information is available, and have clearly shown which area we are dealing with. In the next section of this chapter we present a brief comparison of housing conditions in the different countries of the United Kingdom (see Table 11.9 on page 173). That may help to clarify the main biases which are likely to arise when one or more countries are excluded from the figures.

Another feature of the analysis should also help to avoid confusion. Much of the service which a house provides for its users depends on their tenure of the property. The rights and obligations of owner-occupiers, local authority tenants, and the tenants of privately rented furnished and unfurnished housing differ in important ways. They gain access to their housing in different ways, and the houses themselves are apt to be different in character. Movement between them is restricted as we shall show: most existing households who move house stay within the same tenure, as Table 11.12 shows. For many purposes these tenures amount, in effect, to different markets. Thus we shall repeatedly distinguish housing and people in these different sectors: tenure will be the most important heading in our tables of figures. And since housing of any particular tenure varies much less between one part of the United Kingdom and another than the total housing stock does, that helps to reduce the biases which arise from tables which deal with different areas.

## Changing Housing Conditions

In Britain, as in most countries, housing is getting better. For a long time the quantity of houses has been increasing at a rate which has outpaced the growth in households. Since 1960 there have been more dwellings [1] than households,[2] as Figure 11.1 shows. That surplus may not mean there are too many houses: some are empty because they are to be sold, reconditioned or demolished; some are second homes occupied only at the weekends; and some are unwanted because they stand in places where no one wants to live. Meanwhile, people who are unable to form separate households might do so if only they could afford to. Nevertheless, the steadily growing excess of houses over households must make it easier to satisfy demands and meet needs as time goes by.

The increase in the stock of dwellings in the United Kingdom since 1950 is shown in Figure 11.2, which distinguishes their tenures. The total number of rented houses has scarcely changed for a generation, but within the rented sectors of the market local authorities have steadily taken over from private landlords as the main providers.

In the 1960s the loss of privately rented housing was due about equally to slum clearance and to sales of rented houses for owner-occupation. More recently, as the supply of rented housing attractive to owner-occupiers has begun to dry up, clearance and acquisition by local

**11.1** *Dwellings and Households, 1951–78. Great Britain*

**11.2** *Stock of Dwellings: By Tenure. United Kingdom*

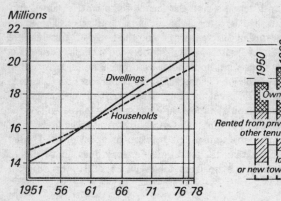

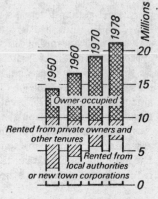

*Source:* Central Statistical Office, *Social Trends, 10*, HMSO, 1980, p. 193.

*Source:* Central Statistical Office, *Social Trends, 10*, p. 193.

**11.3** *Stock of Dwellings by Tenure, United Kingdom, 1951–78* (Numbers in millions)

|  | Owner-occupied | Rented from local authority or new town | Rented privately | TOTAL |
|---|---|---|---|---|
| **1960** |  |  |  |  |
| Number | 6·97 | 4·40 | 5·24 | 16·6 |
| Per cent | 42 | 27 | 32 | 100 |
| **1970** |  |  |  |  |
| Number | 9·57 | 5·85 | 3·77 | 19·18 |
| Per cent | 50 | 31 | 20 | 100 |
| **1975** |  |  |  |  |
| Number | 10·76 | 6·40 | 3·19 | 20·35 |
| Per cent | 53 | 31 | 16 | 100 |
| **1978** |  |  |  |  |
| Number | 11·39 | 6·79 | 2·93 | 21·11 |
| Per cent | 54 | 32 | 14 | 100 |

*Source:* Department of the Environment, *Housing and Construction Statistics.*

authorities and housing associations have accounted for a larger share of the private landlords' losses – losses which have amounted each year throughout this period to between 2 and 3 per cent of their remaining stock. Meanwhile, owner-occupied housing has been growing about as fast as council housing. The growth in the total stock of houses has in fact been roughly equivalent in numbers to the growth in owner-occupied houses. These by 1978 accounted for 54 per cent of all the dwellings in the United Kingdom, as Table 11.3 shows.

What are the houses like? Table 11.4 shows, for a more detailed breakdown of tenures in Great Britain, what they were in 1971. Owner-occupiers nearly always lived in houses, not flats – houses divided rather equally between detached, semi-detached, and terraced buildings. Most council tenants lived in semi-detached and terraced houses, but over a quarter of them lived in purpose-built flats. Nearly half the tenants of private unfurnished housing lived in terraced houses, and the rest were scattered in every kind of building. The small number of furnished tenants lived mainly in flats and rooms. The slightly larger number of people whose housing went with their jobs were a more varied group, living in every kind of building from farm cottages to janitors' flats to Buckingham Palace.

How big are these houses? Table 11.5 shows, for different tenures in England and Wales in 1971, the numbers of rooms available to each household. More than half of them lived in five or six rooms and 85 per cent lived in between three and six rooms. Council housing was even more tightly confined to this narrow range of sizes, having few smaller units and virtually no larger ones. Owner-occupiers had a better chance of occupying more than six rooms – 14 per cent did so – but virtually none had less than three. Only private furnished tenancies offered a large proportion of smaller units – half with one or two rooms – but there were few of them in total. The range of dwelling sizes available is much more restricted than the sizes of the households which have to fit into them – particularly for households confined, as many are, to one tenure. Moreover, households change in size more frequently than they move house. Thus many people are bound to have too much or too little space for much of their lives. Overcrowding and 'under-occupation' depend more on the sizes of households – and thus on the stage of family formation they have reached – than on the sizes of their houses. Tables 11.6 and 11.7 throw some light on this.

What is the condition of these houses? By 1976 only 5 per cent of the dwellings in England and Wales were classed as unfit for human habitation.[3] In England the numbers unfit had fallen from 1,147,000 to

11.4 *Households by Tenure and Type of Accommodation, Great Britain, 1971* (Percentages)

| Tenure | Type of accommodation | | | | | | | Base (= 100 per cent) |
|---|---|---|---|---|---|---|---|---|
| | Detached house | Semi-detached house | Terraced house | Flat or maisonette – purpose built | Other flat or rooms | With business premises | Other | |
| Owner-occupied – owned outright | 30·4 | 28·9 | 30·3 | 3·6 | 3·6 | 2·8 | 0·4 | 2,633 |
| Owner-occupied – mortgage | 25·1 | 45·4 | 24·0 | 2·5 | 2·2 | 0·7 | 0·1 | 3,185 |
| Rented with job or business | 22·6 | 27·1 | 15·7 | 8·0 | 6·8 | 17·9 | 2·1 | 575 |
| Rented from local authority or new town | 1·0 | 36·2 | 33·8 | 27·5 | 1·3 | Nil | 0·2 | 3,661 |
| Rented from housing association | (3) | (10) | (17) | (32) | (7) | (Nil) | (Nil) | 68 |
| Rented privately unfurnished | 6·3 | 13·5 | 44·3 | 15·5 | 19·9 | 0·5 | 0·2 | 1,385 |
| Rented privately furnished | 5·7 | 5·7 | 11·4 | 7·3 | 69·0 | 0·6 | 0·6 | 316 |
| TOTAL | 15·9 | 33·0 | 30·0 | 12·6 | 6·3 | 1·8 | 0·3 | 11,823 |

*Source:* OPCS, *The General Household Survey, Introductory Report*, HMSO, 1973, p. 99.

*Note:* Figures in brackets derived from small sample.

794,000 dwellings[4] – a decline of 31 per cent in five years. Of these, 68 per cent were terraced houses, and most of the rest were detached or semi-detached houses.

Equally dramatic improvements have been achieved in the equipment of houses. In Britain the percentages of households without a bath or shower, and without an internal flush lavatory, were roughly halved between 1971 and 1978, as Table 11.6 shows. The proportion with central heating grew from a third to just over a half. The extent of overcrowding, as measured by bedroom deficiencies, had also declined dramatically. Table 11.7 throws further light on this measure of crowding over the longer period from 1960 to 1975. It confirms that standards have steadily improved. The numbers of households in housing which was below this standard fell by more than half. The numbers of households with two bedrooms or more above the standard nearly doubled.

Now that so few houses are legally unfit for habitation, a more sensitive measure of their condition can be derived by showing what it would cost to bring them up to a proper state of repair. Table 11.8 shows that the answer depends largely on the age of the house. In

**11.5** *Size of Household Spaces by Number of Rooms, England and Wales, 1971*

(Percentages)

| Number of rooms | Owner-occupied | Rented from local authority or new town | Rented unfurnished from private landlord | Rented furnished from private landlord | All tenures |
|---|---|---|---|---|---|
| One or two | 0·6 | 6·4 | 7·8 | 50·4 | 5·8 |
| Three or four | 22·2 | 39·4 | 41·0 | 29·7 | 30·6 |
| Five or six | 63·2 | 52·4 | 44·1 | 16·0 | 54·7 |
| Seven to nine | 12·6 | 1·7 | 6·2 | 3·4 | 8·0 |
| Ten or more | 1·4 | 0·0 | 0·8 | 0·5 | 0·8 |
| All sizes | 100·0 | 100·0 | 100·0 | 100·0 | 100·0 |
| TOTAL (thousands) | 8,288 | 4,628 | 2,792 | 754 | 16,434 |

*Source: Housing Policy*, Technical Volume, Part I, p. 54.

*Note:*

Accommodation occupied with job or business is included under 'rented unfurnished from private landlord' or 'rented furnished from private landlord' as the case may be.

11.6 *Housing Standards by Tenure, Great Britain, 1971 and 1978*
(Percentages)

| Percentage of households: | Below bedroom standard [1] | | Lacking sole use of | | | | With central heating | | Total sample size (= 100 per cent) | |
| | | | bath or shower | | WC inside building | | | | | |
| | 1971 | 1978 | 1971 | 1978 | 1971 | 1978 | 1971 | 1978 | 1971 | 1978 |
| Owned outright | 3 | 2 | 12 | 5 | 13 | 6 | 39 | 52 | 2,654 | 2,634 |
| Owned with mortgage or loan | 4 | 3 | 4 | 2 | 5 | 2 | 57 | 73 | 3,206 | 3,478 |
| All owner-occupiers | 4 | 3 | 7 | 3 | 9 | 3 | 49 | 64 | 5,860 | 6,109 |
| Rented from local authority or New Town | 10 | 6 | 3 | 2 | 5 | 2 | 24 | 43 | 3,691 | 3,999 |
| Rented privately unfurnished [2] | 8 | 4 | 33 | 19 | 37 | 18 | 15 | 28 | 2,043 | 1,309 |
| Rented privately furnished | 19 | 14 | 58 | 52 | 57 | 51 | 17 | 27 | 320 | 283 |
| All tenures | 7 | 4 | 12 | 6 | 13 | 6 | 34 | 52 | 11,914 | 11,700 |

*Source*: Central Statistical Office, *Social Trends, 10*, 1980, p. 200.

*Notes*:
1. The standard number of bedrooms used in this concept is: one for each married couple; one each for other men and women aged 21 or over; one for each of two people of the same sex aged 10–20, or for anyone aged 10–20 together with a child of the same sex under 10; one for anyone aged 10–20 not covered by the above; one for each two remaining children; and one for any child remaining.
2. Includes those renting from a housing association and those renting with a job or business.

**11.7** *Households and Bedroom Standard by Tenure, England and Wales* (Thousands)

|  | 1960 | 1971 | 1975 |
|---|---|---|---|
| *Below standard* | | | |
| Owner-occupiers | 360 | 290 | 220 |
| Local authority tenants | 470 | 380 | 270 |
| Other tenants | 770 | 320 | 220 |
| TOTAL | 1,600 | 990 | 710 |
| *Equal or one above* | | | |
| Owner-occupiers | 4,320 | 5,680 | 5,850 |
| Local authority tenants | 2,860 | 3,600 | 3,950 |
| Other tenants | 3,470 | 2,560 | 2,440 |
| TOTAL | 10,650 | 11,840 | 12,240 |
| *Two or more above* | | | |
| Owner-occupiers | 1,310 | 2,260 | 2,870 |
| Local authority tenants | 200 | 650 | 660 |
| Other tenants | 660 | 700 | 610 |
| TOTAL | 2,170 | 3,610 | 4,140 |

*Source: Housing Policy*, Technical Volume, Part I, p. 67.

*Notes:*

'Other tenants' comprise households renting accommodation with job or business, tenants renting unfurnished accommodation from private landlords and housing associations; and households renting furnished accommodation.

The number of households by tenure in 1975 is an approximate estimate only. The housing stock is estimated to have increased by 845,000 between 1971 census date and mid 1975, whereas the projected increase in households was 670,000. The 670,000 was apportioned *pro rata* to the changes in number of dwellings in each tenure, and added to the 1971 figures used in this chapter.

1971 figures are of households enumerated at their dwellings. The 1975 figures are consistent with those for 1971, and therefore differ from projected figures that are based on totals that include households absent from home at the time of the census.

England in 1976, 43 per cent of all houses built before the First World War needed repairs costing at least £500. These included 35 per cent of owner-occupied houses of this age. Among houses built between the wars, only 12 per cent needed repairs on this scale, and among still newer houses virtually none.

**11.8** *Dwellings in England in 1976; Analysed by Amount of Repairs Needed, Tenure, and When Built*

(Percentages, except for totals which are in thousands)

| | Owner-occupied | Rented from local authority | Other tenures | All tenures [1] |
|---|---|---|---|---|
| *Pre-First World War* | | | | |
| Under £250 | 33 | * | 21 | 29 |
| £250–499 | 32 | * | 23 | 28 |
| £500 or over | 35 | * | 56 | 43 |
| All ranges | 100 | | 100 | 100 |
| TOTAL (thousands) | 2,870 | 180 | 1,570 | 4,960 |
| *Inter-war* | | | | |
| Under £250 | 62 | 56 | 42 | 58 |
| £250–499 | 32 | 27 | 31 | 30 |
| £500 or over | 6 | 17 | 27 | 12 |
| All ranges | 100 | 100 | 100 | 100 |
| TOTAL (thousands) | 2,610 | 1,240 | 380 | 4,310 |
| *Post-war* | | | | |
| Under £250 | 97 | 89 | 93 | 93 |
| £250–499 | 3 | 9 | 4 | 6 |
| £500 or over | — | 2 | 3 | 1 |
| All ranges | 100 | 100 | 100 | 100 |
| TOTAL (thousands) | 4,070 | 3,370 | 340 | 7,850 |

*Source: Housing Policy*, Technical Volume, Part I, p. 58.

*Notes:*
1. Includes vacant dwellings.
* Sample too small to analyse.

This is one of the very few housing statistics measuring a problem which is now increasing in size. While the numbers of overcrowded, unfit and ill-equipped houses are steadily falling, the numbers needing repairs at various levels of cost have been growing. In England there were in 1971 about 636,000 dwellings needing repairs costing over £1,000 at the prices of that year. By 1976 the number had risen to about 911,000, an increase of 43 per cent.[5]

**11.9** *Some Comparisons between the Countries of the United Kingdom*

|  | England | Scotland | Wales | N. Ireland |
|---|---|---|---|---|
| Gross domestic product per head (UK = 100) | | | | |
| 1966 | 103 | 89 | 86 | 63 |
| 1977 | 102 | 96 | 88 | 76 |
| Weekly earnings[1] (UK = 100) | | | | |
| 1961 | 100 | 93 | 99 | 78 |
| 1976 | 100 | 101 | 101 | 93 |
| Infant mortality[2] (UK = 100) | | | | |
| 1951 | 95 | 120 | 117 | 133 |
| 1976 | 98 | 102 | 94 | 126 |
| Per cent of housing – owner-occupied | | | | |
| 1961 | 42 | 25 | 47 | 42 |
| 1978 | 56 | 35 | 59 | 49 |
| – publicly rented from local authority or New Town | | | | |
| 1961 | 24 | 23 | 38 | 35 |
| 1978 | 30 | 54 | 29 | 40 |
| – other tenures, including housing associations | | | | |
| 1961 | 34 | 37 | 30 | 37 |
| 1978 | 14 | 11 | 12 | 11 |
| – with a bathroom[3] | | | | |
| 1951 | 64 | 57 | 51 | 51[4] |
| 1971 | 92 | 88 | 87 | 73 |
| Public expenditure per head (Great Britain = 100) | | | | |
| 1964–5 | 99 | 109 | 106 | 127[5] |
| 1976–7 | 96 | 120 | 111 | 141 |

*Source:* Ian McAllister *et al.*, *United Kingdom Rankings*, Studies in Public Policy No. 44, Centre for the Study of Public Policy, University of Strathclyde, 1979; and Central Statistical Office, *Regional Statistics, No. 15, 1980*, HMSO, 1980.

*Notes:*
1. Earnings of full-time, adult, male, manual workers.
2. Deaths under one year per 1,000 live births.
3. Households with a bathroom.
4. 1961.                    5. 1972–3.

There are important differences in housing conditions between the various countries of the United Kingdom. Table 11.9 shows some of them. The physical quality of housing tends to be best in England, followed closely by Scotland and Wales, with Northern Ireland some way behind. The distribution of tenures is much the same in England and in Wales, but owner-occupation is less common in Northern Ireland, and much less common in Scotland. Public rented housing is correspondingly more common in Northern Ireland and Scotland. Most of these differences have steadily diminished over the last twenty-five years. Northern Ireland alone now stands out as an exception to the generally converging patterns of these countries (Table 11.16 confirms this). These trends reflect a more fundamental equalization of living standards between England, Scotland and Wales: infant mortality rates, average weekly earnings, gross domestic product per head, and the proportions of households with cars and telephones have each improved and converged, for it is among the laggards that the greatest advances have been made. Unemployment rates have deteriorated, but again the differences between the countries are smaller than they used to be – or they were until the late seventies. (These patterns may now be changing.) That has not happened by accident. Public expenditure separately attributable to the different countries has grown increasingly unequal since the 1960s, rising fastest in Northern Ireland and, somewhat less dramatically, in Scotland and Wales too. Just how much of the equalization has been brought about by public policy it would be harder to say. It is often said that, despite years of egalitarian rhetoric, the United Kingdom remains as unequal a society as ever. In many respects that is true. But if the different countries of the Kingdom are compared, a large measure of equalization has been brought about. Given the necessary political will, redistribution can be achieved.

The picture presented by this brief review of the housing situation is encouraging. Despite the disappointment of some of the most ambitious hopes, such as the Conservatives' attempt in the 1950s to revive a free market in rented housing and the Wilson government's promise in the 1960s of a building programme of 500,000 houses a year, housing conditions have dramatically improved. The deteriorating general state of repair of older houses is the only major problem which, on a national scale, seems to be growing worse and might eventually get out of hand. The quantity of housing has grown larger and its quality better. Sharing[6] and crowding have declined, although they remain heavily concentrated in Greater London. Differences in housing conditions between the more affluent and the less affluent parts of the United Kingdom have also

**11.10** *Headship Rates,*[1] *England and Wales, 1966 and 1971*

| Age, marital status | Men | | Women | |
|---|---|---|---|---|
| | 1966 | 1971 | 1966 | 1971 |
| **15–19** | | | | |
| Single | 4·8 | 5·2 | 3·0 | 3·3 |
| Married | 58·1 | 64·9 | 0·7 | 1·1 |
| Widowed | — | — | 31·3 | 15·0 |
| Divorced | — | — | 33·3 | 20·0 |
| **20–24** | | | | |
| Single | 13·4 | 16·4 | 10·4 | 13·6 |
| Married | 82·7 | 87·0 | 1·4 | 2·7 |
| Widowed | 43·5 | 32·5 | 43·8 | 48·7 |
| Divorced | 33·3 | 37·7 | 31·7 | 47·3 |
| **25–29** | | | | |
| Single | 27·2 | 35·2 | 22·1 | 28·7 |
| Married | 91·7 | 95·2 | 1·7 | 2·6 |
| Widowed | 48·0 | 82·5 | 64·4 | 63·6 |
| Divorced | 40·1 | 57·0 | 47·1 | 60·0 |
| **30–34** | | | | |
| Single | 40·9 | 46·7 | 33·3 | 42·8 |
| Married | 95·4 | 96·0 | 1·7 | 2·6 |
| Widowed | 62·7 | 97·3 | 77·3 | 66·7 |
| Divorced | 56·4 | 55·1 | 60·0 | 89·6 |
| **35–39** | | | | |
| Single | 53·2 | 59·1 | 44·5 | 54·8 |
| Married | 96·9 | 97·8 | 1·6 | 2·2 |
| Widowed | 79·7 | 83·6 | 72·1 | 81·4 |
| Divorced | 67·0 | 75·6 | 62·2 | 58·6 |
| **40–44** | | | | |
| Single | 58·8 | 69·7 | 49·9 | 57·8 |
| Married | 97·4 | 97·6 | 1·5 | 2·0 |
| Widowed | 86·2 | 78·1 | 64·1 | 68·0 |
| Divorced | 69·1 | 74·2 | 63·5 | 68·1 |
| **45–49** | | | | |
| Single | 58·8 | 65·8 | 51·0 | 58·3 |
| Married | 97·2 | 97·6 | 1·8 | 2·3 |
| Widowed | 84·4 | 78·3 | 59·9 | 65·2 |
| Divorced | 68·5 | 72·5 | 62·8 | 65·3 |

**11.10**—*Continued*

| Age, marital status | Men | | Women | |
|---|---|---|---|---|
| | 1966 | 1971 | 1966 | 1971 |
| **50–54** | | | | |
| Single | 58·1 | 64·5 | 52·7 | 58·4 |
| Married | 96·8 | 96·3 | 2·5 | 3·1 |
| Widowed | 82·4 | 88·6 | 57·2 | 65·6 |
| Divorced | 64·8 | 74·6 | 62·4 | 69·3 |
| **55–59** | | | | |
| Single | 59·0 | 64·3 | 55·5 | 61·0 |
| Married | 95·7 | 97·6 | 3·5 | 5·0 |
| Widowed | 79·0 | 81·0 | 57·5 | 62·8 |
| Divorced | 65·7 | 80·6 | 62·7 | 69·6 |
| **60–64** | | | | |
| Single | 58·7 | 68·1 | 50·4 | 55·8 |
| Married | 93·4 | 94·8 | 4·5 | 6·0 |
| Widowed | 72·2 | 81·1 | 57·7 | 68·2 |
| Divorced | 63·1 | 66·8 | 58·7 | 67·5 |
| **65–69** | | | | |
| Single | 50·3 | 57·4 | 50·9 | 60·2 |
| Married | 77·3 | 77·8 | 4·8 | 5·6 |
| Widowed | 57·1 | 66·8 | 58·2 | 68·8 |
| Divorced | 57·9 | 69·4 | 58·9 | 70·4 |
| **70–74** | | | | |
| Single | 50·1 | 61·4 | 53·7 | 61·0 |
| Married | 77·4 | 81·9 | 3·5 | 4·2 |
| Widowed | 53·3 | 61·4 | 55·9 | 66·0 |
| Divorced | 53·3 | 54·2 | 59·6 | 66·9 |
| **75 plus** | | | | |
| Single | 48·2 | 54·5 | 52·1 | 57·9 |
| Married | 76·3 | 80·4 | 3·4 | 4·0 |
| Widowed | 43·5 | 50·0 | 46·1 | 54·2 |
| Divorced | 46·8 | 55·8 | 46·2 | 75·5 |

*Source:* 1966 sample census and 1971 census, *Summary Tables and Household Composition Tables.*

*Notes:*

1. The rate applies to 'chief economic supporters' for both census years.

The chief economic supporter of a household (CES) was selected from those members of diminished. It is difficult to be sure how many 'concealed' households live reluctantly with others when they would prefer to set up on their own, but the numbers of married couples and lone parents living in other people's households fell from nearly 400,000 in 1971 to about 250,000 in 1977.[7] The probability that people of any given type (defined by age, sex and marital status) succeed in setting up a separate household has increased. Table 11.10 shows that married men over the age of 25 had by 1971 nearly all become heads of households. (Married women were hardly ever defined as 'head of household' or 'chief economic supporter' according to the definitions used in the 1971 census.) The headship rates for women on their own – be they single, widowed or divorced – were still low in 1971, although these rates slightly increased between 1966 and 1971 for most women. More encouraging were the increases in headship rates achieved over this short period by divorced women – particularly between the ages of 25 and 35 – and by single, widowed and divorced people over the age of 60. But this picture has been painted with a broad brush of average and total figures which tell nothing about smaller groups and areas. We need a more detailed picture.

## Who Gets What?

Before examining the experience of different kinds of households, we should note the main kinds of households for whom space must be found. Table 11.11 summarizes the essential patterns and trends. It shows that a

---

the household who were 15 years of age and over and were either the head of the household or related to the head, by applying the following rules.

(a) Employment status is considered first. Those in full-time employment (that is who worked more than 30 hours in the week before the census) or out of employment were selected before those in part-time employment, who in turn were selected before those retired, who in turn were selected before any others.

(b) Among those selected by rule (a) above, position in family was considered next, married men or widowed or divorced persons in families being considered before other members of families or persons not in families.

(c) Among those selected by rules (a) and (b), sex was considered next, males being selected before females.

(d) Among those selected by rules (a), (b) and (c), age was considered next, older persons being selected before younger.

If these rules finally select two or more persons, the person whose name appears first on the form was selected as CES. In the rare cases where the head of household and all related persons were aged under 15, the head was selected as CES.

**11.11** *Types of Households, Great Britain, 1961–78*
(Percentages)

|  | 1961 | 1971 | 1978 |
|---|---|---|---|
| *No family* | | | |
| One person – under retirement age | 4 | 6 | 7 |
| One person – over retirement age | 7 | 12 | 15 |
| Two or more people – one or more over retirement age | 3 | 2 | 2 |
| Two or more people – all under retirement age | 2 | 2 | 1 |
| *One family* | | | |
| Married couple only | 26 | 27 | 27 |
| Married couple with 1 or 2 dependent children | 30 | 26 | 26 |
| Married couple with 3 or more dependent children | 8 | 9 | 7 |
| Married couple with independent child(ren) only | 10 | 8 | 7 |
| Lone parent with at least 1 dependent child | 2 | 3 | 4 |
| Lone parent with independent child(ren) only | 4 | 4 | 3 |
| *Two or more families* | 3 | 1 | 1 |
| Total households (thousands) | 16,189 | 18,317 | 19,650[1] |
| Total households (per cent) | 100 | 100 | 100 |
| Average household size (persons) | 3·09 | 2·89 | 2·71 |

*Source: Social Trends, 10*, p. 78.

*Note:*
1. Estimated.

declining number of households – now only one third – consist of parents with dependent children. A steadily rising 15 per cent consist of one person over retirement age. Households consisting of one younger person are also growing in numbers. So are lone parents with dependent children – now amounting to 4 per cent of all households, caring for 12 per cent of all children under 16.[8] The average size of households has fallen from 3·09 persons in 1961 to 2·71 in 1978. One-person households have grown from 11 to 22 per cent of all households during this time.

If they want the best housing, most of these people will have to get into the growing sectors of the market where the newest and best-equipped property is to be found. Those sectors, as Figure 11.2 and Tables 11.6–11.8 clearly show, are owner-occupied and council housing.

**11.12** *Tenure of Housewives Who Had Moved in the Previous 12 Months, by Type of Household,[1] England, 1978*
(Percentages)

| | Individual aged 16–59 | Small adult household | Small family | Large family | Large adult household | Older small household | Individual aged 60+ | All households |
|---|---|---|---|---|---|---|---|---|
| *Present owner-occupier, previously* | | | | | | | | |
| Owner-occupier | 12 | 21 | 37 | 35 | 36 | 42 | 23 | 30 |
| Local authority/New Town tenant | 1 | 3 | 3 | 4 | 2 | 1 | 0 | 3 |
| Privately rented – furnished | 5 | 6 | 3 | 2 | 3 | 0 | 0 | 3 |
| – unfurnished | 5 | 7 | 5 | 4 | 6 | 3 | 3 | 5 |
| New household – married couples | 0 | 24 | 4 | 1 | 2 | 1 | 0 | 7 |
| – other | 17 | 1 | – | 0 | 2 | – | 1 | 2 |
| TOTAL | 41 | 63 | 53 | 46 | 52 | 48 | 27 | 51 |
| *Local authority/New Town tenant, previously* | | | | | | | | |
| Owner-occupier | 1 | 1 | 2 | 4 | 1 | 4 | 6 | 2 |
| Local authority/New Town tenant | 5 | 6 | 14 | 27 | 20 | 25 | 30 | 15 |
| Privately rented – furnished | 4 | 1 | 3 | 2 | 2 | 1 | 1 | 2 |
| – unfurnished | 2 | 3 | 7 | 8 | 6 | 11 | 14 | 6 |
| New household – married couples | 0 | 3 | 5 | 1 | – | 0 | 0 | 3 |
| – other | 5 | – | 2 | – | – | – | 6 | 2 |
| TOTAL | 17 | 14 | 34 | 43 | 31 | 42 | 58 | 31 |
| *Privately rented furnished, previously* | | | | | | | | |
| Privately rented – furnished | 9 | 1 | 1 | 1 | 3 | 0 | 0 | 2 |
| New household – married couples | 0 | 3 | 1 | 0 | 0 | 0 | 0 | 1 |
| – other | 17 | 1 | – | 0 | 4 | 0 | 0 | 2 |
| TOTAL | 27 | 5 | 2 | 1 | 7 | 0 | 0 | 5 |
| *Privately rented unfurnished, previously* | | | | | | | | |
| Owner-occupier | 1 | 1 | 2 | 1 | 2 | 1 | 4 | 1 |
| Local authority/New Town tenant | 1 | 1 | 1 | 1 | 1 | 3 | 0 | 1 |
| Privately rented – furnished | 3 | 2 | 1 | 0 | 0 | 0 | 0 | 1 |
| – unfurnished | 5 | 3 | 4 | 3 | 1 | 2 | 1 | 3 |

**11.12** *Continued.*

| | Indi-vidual aged 16–59 | Small adult house-hold | Small family | Large family | Large adult house-hold | Older small house-hold | Indi-vidual aged 60+ | All house-holds |
|---|---|---|---|---|---|---|---|---|
| New household – married couples | 0 | 7 | 1 | 1 | 0 | 0 | 0 | 2 |
| – other | 4 | 1 | – | 0 | 1 | 1 | 5 | 1 |
| TOTAL | 14 | 15 | 9 | 6 | 5 | 8 | 11 | 9 |
| *Other moves across tenures* | *1* | *3* | *2* | *4* | *5* | *2* | *4* | *4* |
| *TOTAL* (percentages) | 100 | 100 | 100 | 100 | 100 | 100 | 100 | 100 |
| (sample sizes) | 348 | 993 | 1,542 | 451 | 431 | 306 | 277 | 4,348 |

*Source: Social Trends, 10*, p. 203.

*Note:*

1. See text for definitions of household types.

People confined to privately rented property have to compete for space in a dwindling submarket in which the houses are older and often poorly equipped and poorly maintained. Thus, to discover who gets what we must first ask who gains access to the growing sectors.

In England, at the end of the 1970s, about half the people moving house were buying a home of their own. Of these house buyers, about 60 per cent were already owner-occupiers with a house to sell. Most of the rest were divided in equal proportions between newly formed house-holds who had not been householders before they moved, and private tenants, mainly from unfurnished tenancies. Very few were council ten-ants. The newly formed households setting up a home for the first time were mainly young single people and married couples who did not yet have children. People moving from privately rented housing were drawn from a wider range of ages and household types.

About one third of all the movers were going to local authority hous-ing. Half of these were council tenants moving from another council house. About half the remainder came from privately rented housing, and most of the rest were newly formed households. Very few had been owner-occupiers. The newly formed households had mostly started their families already. Many had probably been living with their children in their parents' homes before the move. In our research during the 1960s,[9] we found that people moving for the first time into council houses were on average five years older than those buying a house for the first time. This pattern still persists.

The great majority of the people rehoused for the first time by local authorities came from the waiting-lists which have long given priority to those who are sharing or overcrowded, to people with children, to people with illnesses which would respond to rehousing, and – in all these groups – to people who have been waiting in the queue for a long time.[10] In England and Wales, by 1977, 70 per cent of the tenancies allocated by local authorities to new tenants went to the waiting-list. The numbers rehoused because their homes were pulled down in slum-clearance schemes had fallen from over 20 per cent in the mid seventies to 10 per cent. The 10 per cent rehoused on the ground that they were homeless took half the remaining tenancies allocated.[11]

Table 11.12 shows the main flows of movement. The household types listed across the top of this Table represent very approximately a typical progression through the life cycle. Many people first appear in the housing market when they leave their parents' homes to live on their own for a while as 'individual small households'. They become 'small adult (i.e. two-person non-pensioner) households' when they marry. They then have one or two children and become 'small families' – 'large' ones later if they have more than two dependent children. As their children grow up and go to work from home, they become 'large adult households' for a while, and probably then revert to the group of 'small adult households' when their children leave home. Later they become 'older small households' when one or both partners reach pensionable age, and finally 'individuals aged 60 or more'. The first three groups bulk larger in these statistics of movement than they do in the population as a whole because younger people are more likely to move than older ones. Their battle for the housing they want is often won or lost for good before they are 40. After that age, movement becomes much less frequent. Our own research, reported in *The Government of Housing*,[12] showed that the proportions of people who say they are dissatisfied with their housing and want to move remain fairly high through middle age to retirement. But the urgency of their needs seems to diminish: perhaps they have more to lose and less to gain from a move as time goes by. And their opportunities dwindle: local authorities give priority to younger and more crowded families, and building societies rarely lend money to people for the first time when they are in their forties. In the United Kingdom in 1978, only 8 per cent of first-time buyers were over the age of 44.[13] That is not surprising, because 63 per cent of mortgages in 1975 were for repayment over periods of 25 years or more.[14]

**11.13** *Tenure of Households by Socio-Economic Group, by Income of Head of Household, and by Number of Earners, Great Britain, 1978*
(Percentages)

| | Owner-occupiers | | Tenants | | | All tenures (total sample size = 100 per cent) |
|---|---|---|---|---|---|---|
| | Outright owners | Mort- gagors | Local authority | Unfurnished private[1] | Fur- nished private | |
| *Socio-economic group*[2] | | | | | | |
| Economically active heads | | | | | | |
| Professional and managerial | 19 | 63 | 7 | 9 | 2 | 1,762 |
| Intermediate and junior non-manual | 15 | 46 | 22 | 12 | 4 | 1,574 |
| Skilled manual, etc | 12 | 39 | 38 | 9 | 2 | 2,832 |
| Semi-skilled manual, etc | 14 | 23 | 49 | 12 | 2 | 1,209 |
| Unskilled | 12 | 14 | 61 | 12 | 2 | 338 |
| Economically inactive heads | | | | | | |
| men | 43 | 5 | 38 | 11 | 2 | 1,806 |
| women | 36 | 3 | 46 | 14 | 2 | 1,950 |
| *Head of household's income per annum* | | | | | | |
| Economically active heads | | | | | | |
| Up to £2,000 | 17 | 8 | 49 | 19 | 7 | 467 |
| £2,000 but under £3,000 | 14 | 21 | 46 | 15 | 4 | 1,085 |
| £3,000 but under £4,000 | 13 | 37 | 38 | 10 | 2 | 1,767 |
| £4,000 but under £5,000 | 11 | 52 | 28 | 8 | 2 | 1,376 |
| £5,000 and over | 15 | 66 | 12 | 6 | 1 | 1,483 |
| Economically inactive heads | | | | | | |
| Up to £1,000 | 38 | 2 | 43 | 16 | 2 | 640 |
| £1,000 but under £2,000 | 31 | 2 | 52 | 13 | 3 | 1,715 |
| £2,000 and over | 54 | 9 | 26 | 8 | 2 | 536 |
| *Number of earners in household* | | | | | | |
| None | 40 | 2 | 43 | 13 | 1 | 2,749 |
| One | 20 | 30 | 33 | 12 | 4 | 3,141 |
| Two | 12 | 48 | 28 | 10 | 2 | 3,443 |
| Three or more | 14 | 40 | 38 | 7 | 1 | 1,005 |
| *All households* | 23 | 30 | 34 | 11 | 2 | 11,700 |

*Source: Social Trends, 10, p. 199.*

Most people who move get a second-hand home: someone else had to move out of it before they could move in. In the late seventies, 76 per cent of the council tenancies allocated were 're-lets', and only 24 per cent were in new property;[15] 85 per cent of the houses sold for owner-occupation were second-hand, and only 15 per cent were new or newly converted.[16] Thus households succeed each other, pursuing well-beaten paths through the housing market. New households used to gain their first footholds in this market in the declining privately rented sector, but about half of them now buy their way straight into owner-occupation, as Table 11.12 shows. More, too, start in council housing, but many of the new households appearing there are lone parents making not a first start but a fresh start after the breakdown of an earlier family. From the dwindling stock of privately rented housing people still move, if they can, into one or other of the growing sectors. Once there they usually move on again to better housing within these sectors. Rarely do they move between owner-occupied and council housing or back into privately rented housing.

Our own earlier research showed that the great majority of movers want to move, and most of them get a more satisfactory home by doing so. But their satisfactions may be due to advantages other than the size and quality of their homes.[17] Most of those questioned in the government's National Movers Surveys said that they wanted a better or a larger or more convenient house. Second in importance came personal reasons – a move to bring them closer to relatives and friends, or a move following from bereavement, for example. Many said they simply wanted to buy a home of their own or to get a council house, and some of those entering council housing moved because their previous homes were demolished in redevelopment schemes. People buying a home of their own were more likely than others to give reasons for their move which were related to their jobs, and more likely to move longer distances. But in all sectors of the market these job-related moves were only a small proportion of the total. Whatever their tenure, most people move to a house which stands within less than thirty minutes' travelling distance from their previous homes.[18] These patterns have continued with little change for many years.

So who gets what? Table 11.14 summarizes the social and economic

---

*Notes:*
1. Including those renting from a housing association and those renting with a job or business.
2. Excluding armed forces, full-time students, and those who have never worked.

**11.14**  *Households by Tenure[1] and Gross Income, Great Britain, 1978*
  (£ per annum)

| | Income of household | | Income of head of household | | Sample size |
|---|---|---|---|---|---|
| | Mean | Median | Mean | Median | |
| *Households with economically active heads* | | | | | |
| Tenants of | | | | | |
| – local authority housing | 5,560 | 5,102 | 3,786 | 3,661 | 1,412 |
| – privately rented unfurnished housing | 4,952 | 4,900 | 3,661 | 3,537 | 293 |
| Owner-occupiers | | | | | |
| – mortgagors | 7,286 | 6,659 | 5,333 | 4,855 | 2,048 |
| – outright owners | 6,545 | 5,759 | 4,642 | 3,857 | 687 |
| *Households with retired or economically inactive heads* | | | | | |
| Tenants of | | | | | |
| – local authority housing | 2,423 | 1,752 | 1,538 | 1,397 | 860 |
| – privately rented unfurnished housing | 2,109 | 1,744 | 1,555 | 1,356 | 229 |
| Owner-occupiers | | | | | |
| – mortgagors | 4,582 | 3,600 | 3,134 | 2,100 | 73 |
| – outright owners | 3,034 | 2,200 | 2,006 | 1,452 | 751 |
| *All households* | | | | | |
| Tenants of | | | | | |
| – local authority housing | 4,372 | 3,846 | 2,935 | 2,711 | 2,272 |
| – privately rented unfurnished housing | 3,704 | 3,174 | 2,738 | 2,377 | 522 |
| Owner-occupiers | | | | | |
| – mortgagors | 7,193 | 6,585 | 5,257 | 3,794 | 2,121 |
| – outright owners | 4,712 | 3,673 | 3,265 | 2,540 | 1,438 |

*Source:* Department of the Environment, *Housing and Construction Statistics, Quarterly*, HMSO. Derived from Family Expenditure Survey, 1978.

*Note:*
1. Excluding tenancies held rent-free or by virtue of employment.

character of the people in each sector of the housing market. With figures derived from the government's General Household Survey, it shows – reading horizontally – the percentages of various groups in each tenure. Owner-occupiers tend to divide into two very different groups. Those who own their homes outright (having paid off the mortgage, or perhaps inherited the house or acquired it on favourable terms as sitting tenants) tend to be retired, and have modest or low incomes. Those who are still buying their homes tend to work in the more skilled manual jobs or in white-collar jobs. Many of them have more than one earner in the family.

The majority of council tenants are manual workers, but large and growing proportions of them are retired or for other reasons have no earner in the household – some are lone parents, for example.

We have picked out the dominant patterns in these comparisons. But the class distinctions we have therefore emphasized should not be exaggerated. Nearly two fifths of the 'intermediate and junior non-manual' workers – the lower middle class, roughly speaking – are tenants, and 22 per cent of them are council tenants. Only among the small fraction of household heads who are unskilled workers do council tenants account for more than half; and even among these, 26 per cent are owner-occupiers.

Meanwhile, private tenants, furnished and unfurnished, are more representative of all social groups. Other evidence suggests that they, too, tend to divide into two kinds: young people, with modest incomes and no dependants, who are working their way up through the labour market and the housing market and unlikely to remain private tenants for long; and older people, some still with dependent children but many in retirement – people who have missed their chance of getting into the expanding sectors of the market unless they are rehoused in the now dwindling programmes of redevelopment and improvement.

A useful comparison of the incomes of those in different sectors of the market can only be made if we first distinguish the economically active from the inactive, and the mortgagors from those who own their houses outright. They are very different. That is clear from Table 11.14 which shows, for each of the groups distinguished, mean or 'average' incomes, and median incomes (a median divides those concerned into two equal parts: half are richer and half are poorer than the median. This measure of the central tendency of a group is the more revealing because it is less liable than the mean to be distorted by a few extremely high or low figures). The economically active have consistently higher incomes. Even in the poorest tenure group (private tenants), the active are better off than the most affluent group of the inactive (the mortgagors). When comparisons are made between those in different tenures, the mortgagors who are still buying their houses stand out as the richest group in terms both of mean and median incomes. People in the other three tenures – public tenants, private tenants, and people who own their homes outright – have very similar median incomes. The outright owners tend to be slightly richer, the private unfurnished tenants slightly poorer, than the others. The differences between these three groups are somewhat greater if mean incomes are compared, but the pattern is much the same. Had we compared incomes per person, rather than the incomes of households or their heads, then council tenants would be the poorest group because they have larger households than any of the other groups.[19]

The comparative affluence of the mortgagor does not arise simply from the fact that richer people can afford a mortgage. As Chapter 13 will show, Britain's system of lending and borrowing for house purchase provides money at an interest rate which is generally smaller than the annual rate of inflation. In the struggle to maintain their real living standards borrowers generally win and lenders lose. The borrowers' advantages have then been redoubled by giving them various kinds of tax relief which help to reduce the cost of buying a house. People who can afford to do so therefore have the strongest incentives to get a mortgage, whether they need one or not. Mortgagors were repaying at this time a median of 8 per cent of their gross household incomes in interest and principal, before taking account of tax relief. Those who owned their houses outright were paying much less. Meanwhile, council tenants were paying a median of 6 per cent of their gross household incomes in rent.[20] Although home owners would have to add to these payments expenditure on repairs and maintenance from which council tenants were at this time largely protected, it is clear that they were generally getting better value for their money, particularly in old age.

What conclusions can be drawn from this brief review of the distribution of housing? When Charles Booth and Seebohm Rowntree made their first surveys of London and York at the end of the nineteenth century,[21] their investigators could form a pretty reliable estimate of the social composition of each street and neighbourhood by looking at the houses which stood there. Housing, income and class were directly related to each other. That has changed. The opening up of owner-occupation to more than half the population – many in houses originally built for renting – has enormously diversified the range of people who buy their own homes, and the quality of the houses in this sector of the market. As many houses as before are rented, but most of them are now well equipped and modern, and were built or rebuilt by the local authorities. By allocating them according to need, rather than ability to pay, these authorities have brought a lot of the poorest people into good housing. In 1975, 25 per cent of their tenants depended partly or wholly on supplementary benefit for their incomes,[22] which puts them roughly in the poorest tenth of the population; 44 per cent were receiving a rent rebate or supplementary benefit.[23] The growth of elderly households and of one-parent families, shown proceeding so rapidly in Table 11.11, and the growth of unemployment, rising from about 300,000 in 1966 to nearly 3 million in 1981, means there are more and more households without an earner. Meanwhile the growing number of women employed – amounting for Great Britain between 1961 and 1976 to an increase of 2·3 million[24] – means that there must also be more households with several earners. These trends, coupled with progressive taxation of high earnings, mean that the biggest differences in the incomes of households are now due not to the head of household's earnings but to the balance between earners and dependants in the household. Meanwhile the biggest slum-clearance and grant-aided improvement programmes to be attempted anywhere in the world have gone far to eliminate the worst conditions: unfit, ill-equipped and overcrowded housing are all getting steadily rarer, and most of those whom they afflicted have been rehoused. They may still have housing problems, as we shall see, but these problems are no longer a matter of leaking roofs and shared toilets. Nor are they a simple reflection of social stratification and poverty.

## Who Gets Left Out?

Old-fashioned physical squalor is still to be found. Who are the people who suffer from it? For England in 1976 the Department of the Environment has provided a more precise statistical answer to this question than we have ever had before.[25] Houses may be in poor condition because they lack essential equipment such as baths and a hot water supply, because they need repair or because they are legally unfit for human habitation. The government's survey, conducted by environmental health officers from the local authorities, distinguished about 2·6 million houses – 15·6 per cent of the total in England – which needed rehabilitation. These consisted of three overlapping groups: 3·6 per cent of the total stock which were unfit for human habitation;[26] 8 per cent which lacked one or more of five 'basic amenities';[27] and 12·2 per cent which needed essential repairs.[28]

Five main characteristics distinguished the people who lived in this bad housing. These were: low income, old age, non-married status, duration of residence in the house, and having been born outside Europe. (Age and duration of residence each had a 'U-shaped' relationship to housing conditions: the probability of living in bad housing was highest of all among old people who had lived a long time in the same house, and next highest among young people who had recently arrived in their houses. People in their forties who had spent 5 to 10 years at the same address did best.) Those most likely to live in poor housing had at least three of the following four characteristics: they were aged 55 or over; they had an income in the lower half of the income distribution; they were single, widowed or divorced; and they had lived for more than 17 years in the same house. Equally likely to live in poor housing were households with heads born outside Europe. Those born in the West Indies did worst of all.

The extent of householders' dissatisfaction with their homes clearly reflected the conditions in which they lived: the worse the housing, the larger the proportions dissatisfied. But even among those who lived in homes classed as unfit for human habitation nearly half said they were satisfied with their housing. Less than half the people in houses without bathrooms and indoor lavatories said they would like these things installed.[29] Various influences help to explain this. For many the costs of improving their homes were far beyond their reach, even with the help of government grants which tend to be used, as a result, by more affluent people to improve better houses. In housing of equally poor standards, owner-occupiers, who have to pay for improvements, were much more satisfied than tenants, who may not have to do so. But, having discussed these explanations for the acceptance of poor housing, the authors of this study conclude that the main reasons for it are 'that, as householders grow older and become settled in their homes, they become less willing to recognize their defects or to tolerate the disturbance caused by repairs or improvements'.[30]

Housing problems are concentrated in certain kinds of area as we showed in Chapter 8.[31] The inner parts of some of the biggest cities are particularly afflicted, as Figure 11.15 shows. Inner Birmingham, London, Liverpool and Manchester have heavy concentrations of old, crowded and shared housing, and their people are more dissatisfied with their housing than people elsewhere in England. Glasgow would show still higher concentrations of overcrowding, but – thanks to massive

**11.15** *Housing Conditions in Selected Inner Areas, 1977*

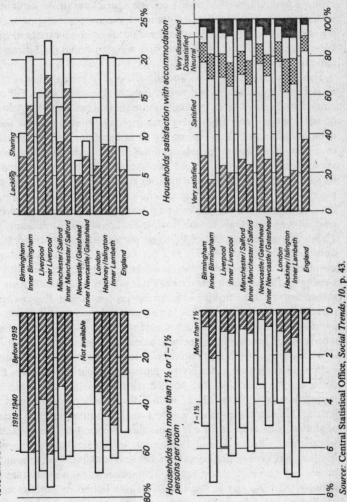

*Source:* Central Statistical Office, *Social Trends, 10*, p. 43.

rebuilding – less shared housing. These areas are not catching up with the rest of the country: on the contrary, despite their falling populations, housing conditions are improving more slowly here than elsewhere. In 1966 the percentages of inner-city households lacking an indoor lavatory or living at a density of more than one person per room were, respectively, about 1·85 and just under 2·00 times the national average. Eleven years later in 1977, both had risen to about 2·15 times the national average.[32]

The most extreme form of housing stress is to have no home at all. How many suffer homelessness can only be measured when the community is prepared to do something for them. Until then they do not declare their existence; they share with friends and relatives, seek shelter in empty buildings, sleep out, or abandon their families and set off on their own. Now that more is being done for the homeless, some figures are available, but they reflect the priorities for action: they tell us more, for example, about mothers with young children, who are given high priority, than about young people in 'squats' or elderly alcoholics sleeping in the parks, who are given low priority. Homeless families in England for whom local authorities accepted a responsibility increased from 17,380 during the first half of 1976 (1·1 per 1,000 households) to 26,510 during the second half of 1978 (1·7 per 1,000).[33] But that increase may owe more to growing recognition of their needs, associated with the passing of the Housing (Homeless Persons) Act of 1977, than to any real change in the numbers of homeless people. About 70 per cent of those accepted as homeless had dependent children – usually with one parent only – and 10 per cent more were pregnant. Most of the rest were elderly, or physically or mentally handicapped.

What emerges from this summary of the evidence about those at the bottom of the housing market? A great deal could be said about the details of a complex picture, but the main conclusion to be drawn is simpler and more important. In Britain, as in many other countries, the greatest advance achieved during the twentieth century in the standards of new housing came at the end of the First World War. That was when a house with between four and six rooms, a hot water supply, an indoor lavatory and a bit of garden at the front and back became the standard product of the building industry. The specifications for this kind of housing were laid out in the Tudor Walters Report.[34] But the results can be seen more clearly by anyone walking outwards from the centre of a British town at the point where the buildings of the pre-war period give way in an outburst of trees, garden gates and little hedges to the building of the 1920s. There are exceptions to this generalization. Scottish cities abandoned tenements much later – indeed they are still building them. English cities built outdoor lavatories and even some bathless houses for a while, and have reverted from time to time to flats – recently on a disastrous scale. Building has too often been shoddy. But the general standards of the houses built for ordinary people never went back to those of earlier days. Useful though they have been, the improvements in standards achieved since then have been less important: the provision of central heating and parking space for a car have been the most significant – both starting on a widespread scale for working-class families in the 1960s, following the Parker Morris Report.[35]

Since the First World War the central purpose of housing policy has been to get everyone into housing, new or improved, of the post-war standard. During the 1920s working-class people were housed, and often grossly overcrowded, in older buildings. Campaigners for better housing were therefore campaigning on behalf of the whole working class. That tradition was still running strongly after the Second World War. Every party entered the elections with housing targets on its banners, and every ambitious local councillor wanted to get on to the housing committee.

After two generations, thanks to public and private building, slum clearance, subsidized improvement campaigns and the German bombers, the attainment of this objective is within reach. As demographic growth and immigration have slowed to a halt in the late 1970s, the British can complete the task of getting everyone into decent housing if they organize themselves to take the final steps.

The small numbers of people who now remain in physically bad housing are a diverse mixture. The largest group are elderly, living alone or with one other person – frequently owner-occupiers, and many of them reasonably content with what they have. Others are more dissatisfied, particularly if they are tenants. The decay of their homes presents a problem to those who will follow after, and to the taxpayers who may eventually have to subsidize their repair and improvement. Poor insulation and antiquated heating arrangements make a lot of these homes miserably cold in winter,[36] and burden their occupiers with unnecessarily heavy fuel bills. These are serious problems, but they have as much to do with poverty, old age and the rising price of energy as with housing.

Others suffer more dramatic hardships: lone parents with young children and recently arrived black immigrants frequently appear among them. Many other homeless people do not appear in the statistics at all. Some of these people will eventually find their own solutions. In 1977 no less than 26 per cent of the households headed by someone from

India, Pakistan or Bangladesh (and 17 per cent of those headed by West Indians) had six or more people in them.[37] Many of these large households suffer severe overcrowding. In England as a whole, only 4 per cent of households were of this size. But nearly 70 per cent of the Asian householders were owner-occupiers, and over 45 per cent of the West Indian group were council tenants.[38] Both figures are well ahead of the national averages, but they do not necessarily mean that the housing problems of these people have been solved. Many of them are housed in their own small and badly maintained houses or in the worst and least popular council houses.

Harrowing though the plight of these people can be, their numbers are trivial by comparison with those who have already been rehoused. When official statistics begin to focus not, as they used to, on the millions still living in slums or overcrowded housing, but on some 50,000 a year now accepted as homeless (and in most cases rehoused[39]), the whole scale of the housing problem has changed. It has changed in character too. For the statistics of stress are not only smaller in number; those afflicted no longer represent the mass of average working people.

The worst-housed people are now drawn mainly from groups who cannot or do not work (such as pensioners, the mentally or physically handicapped, and single parents with young children) and from groups on the margins of the labour force (such as the mobile and unskilled who have accumulated no credit on the waiting-lists, and recently arrived black immigrants who may have a poor command of English). Pat Niner and others have summarized the factors which get people a council house: high amongst them come time spent on the waiting-list, a family of the right size to fit the narrow range of council houses available, acceptance by a local authority that a family is homeless, and occupation of unfurnished, rented housing which is due to be demolished in a clearance scheme.[40] If some of these criteria tend to discriminate against those on the margins of the labour force, that is because such people also tend to be excluded from the core of its political system. Many studies have been made of the communities where they cluster most thickly. They include Cynthia Cockburn's account of the struggles of West Indian families in Lambeth,[41] Jan O'Malley's account of the struggles of furnished tenants and squatters (many of them Irish) in North Kensington,[42] Desmond McConaghy's study of a cosmopolitan overcrowded neighbourhood of Liverpool,[43] the reports of various community development projects, and – abroad – José Olives's study of immigrant workers fighting to retain a foothold in dilapidated hostels and hotels threatened by urban renewal in Paris.[44] Broken families, women, foreigners and mobile inner-city residents often play leading parts in these stories, and it is rarely the traditional, capitalist landlord they fight against. Usually it is government – and most often a Labour government. Such people have not been well served by the bureaucracies which have been so successful in solving the housing problems of the well-organized, long-established, local working class.

As the character of housing problems and of their main victims changed in the 1960s, it was no accident that new kinds of pressure group and advice centre were set up to tackle these problems. Shelter, founded in 1967, is the best known of these, but there are many others. The work of several of them is discussed in Chapter 16 of this book. Some were led by middle-class activists; others, like the Campaign for the Homeless and Rootless, gave the victims themselves a larger role in their work. All were independent of traditional political parties and movements for the good reason that they often had to do battle with them, both at central and at local levels.

Some progress is being made towards the solution of these problems. The plight of the homeless is no longer as harrowing as it was when *Cathy Come Home*, the television programme which launched Shelter, stirred the conscience of the nation. The rapid decline of population in inner-city areas has helped by giving more space for those who remain there. So has the Housing (Homeless Persons) Act of 1977. But hardship and insecurity are still to be found at the bottom of the housing market. These problems are now essentially political, rather than economic or technical: they have more to do with the allocation than with the creation of resources.

## Looking Ahead

What are the broader implications for policy of this review of the housing situation? We could now ensure that everyone has a reasonably well-equipped and uncrowded home. Whether we shall, and how soon, depends on the state of the economy, the level and distribution of incomes, and the will of government and the electorate. What that achievement will demand of housing policy depends on how successful we are in reducing unemployment and providing adequate incomes for larger families, lone parents, the retired, and others who are unable to support themselves from their earnings. The more successful we are, the less will government have to intervene in the housing market. Estimates of the numbers of houses which we must in future build to

**11.16** *Numbers of Households in Selected European Countries*

| | Census date | Number of households (Thousands) | | Column 1 as percentage of Column 2 |
|---|---|---|---|---|
| | | Actual 1 | At England and Wales 1971 headship rates 2 | |
| Austria | 1971 | 2,536 | 2,547 | 99·6 |
| Belgium | 1970 | 3,234 | 3,293 | 98·2 |
| Czechoslovakia | 1970 | 4,632 | 4,823 | 96·1 |
| Finland | 1970 | 1,519 | 1,495 | 101·6 |
| France | 1968 | 15,763 | 16,553 | 95·2 |
| East Germany | 1971 | 6,404 | 5,934 | 107·9 |
| West Germany | 1970 | 21,991 | 21,344 | 103·0 |
| Hungary | 1970 | 3,378 | 3,614 | 93·5 |
| Ireland | 1971 | 726 | 867 | 83·8 |
| Italy | 1971 | 15,981 | 17,928 | 89·1 |
| Poland | 1972 | 9,376 | 11,115 | 84·4 |
| Spain | 1970 | 8,854 | 10,476 | 84·5 |
| Sweden | 1970 | 3,050 | 2,843 | 107·3 |
| Switzerland | 1970 | 2,052 | 2,125 | 96·5 |
| Yugoslavia | 1971 | 5,375 | 6,306 | 85·2 |
| Northern Ireland | 1966 | 399 | 450 | 88·8 |
| Scotland | 1971 | 1,686 | 1,719 | 98·1 |

*Source:* Census, 1971, General Summary Tables (1% sample) and Household Tables (10% sample).

*Notes:*

The chief difficulty with data of this kind is the definition of the term 'household'. In the case of these selected countries, the problem is not very great and the notes below explain the differences.

The demographic and household data are all taken from the *United Nations Demographic Yearbook, 1976*, Tables 41 and 42. The following notes appear in the introduction to these two tables:

'The definition recommended by the UN has been characterized as the *housekeeping* concept. According to the UN definition, the general criterion used in identifying a multi-person household is that its members have common housekeeping arrangements, that is, common arrangements for supplying basic living needs such as principal meals.

'Some countries or areas, instead of using the housekeeping concept recommended by the UN have simply defined a household as the entire group of persons jointly occupying a housing unit, or a person living alone in a separate unit. For convenience, this is referred to as the *housing unit* concept' (p. 52).

The following countries use the United Nations *housekeeping* concept: Austria (including all lodgers under 21 years of age); Belgium (limited to persons within a single housing unit);

satisfy the needs and demands of a more or less static population vary. But all agree that output need not be larger than the modest programmes of recent years, and the investment required to produce it is likely to be a falling proportion of the gross domestic product.[45]

Table 11.16 shows there is still some scope for increasing the number of households in Britain even if this country's population remains unchanged in size and structure. To construct this table we divided the population of each of the countries listed into groups distinguished by age, sex and marital status. We then estimated how many households there would be in each country if members of each group had the same probability of becoming the head of a separate household as they would have in Britain. The actual number of households in each country was then expressed as a percentage of this figure. Thus if people in another country, after taking account of differences in its demographic structure in this way, had a 10 per cent better chance of forming separate households than the British, its score would be 110.

The Table shows that some European countries – the two Germanies, Finland, and Sweden, all of which have for many years had big building programmes in relation to their rates of population growth – score higher in this respect than England and Wales. To that extent their people have greater independence and privacy. That was a decade ago. The drastic reduction in this country's more recent rate of building means that several other countries may already have overhauled her by now. The Table shows that Northern Ireland falls well behind the rest of the United Kingdom, but Scotland differs little from England and Wales. Headship rates in Britain are near 100 per cent for married couples, as Table 11.10 shows. This country's shortfall in comparison with Europe's leaders is therefore probably due to the high headship rates attained by young single people and divorced and separated women in parts of northern Europe. These rates are expected to increase in Britain too during the coming years, but their demands may have been underestimated.

While the equipment of our houses – their baths, hot water supplies,

---

England and Wales; Finland; France; East Germany; West Germany; Hungary (limited to persons within a single housing unit); Ireland; Poland; Spain; Scotland; Northern Ireland; Yugoslavia.

The following countries use the *housing unit* concept: Sweden; Switzerland.

Czechoslovakia uses a *family nuclei* concept, which almost certainly omits single-person households. This figure, therefore, should be treated with extreme caution.

Italy: the *Demographic Yearbook* omits to give information on the household definition used in Italy; hence this figure should also be treated with caution.

central heating, parking spaces and so on – steadily improves, their condition is deteriorating. More and more of them need fairly expensive repairs, and more of these poorly maintained houses are owner-occupied (see Table 11.8). The spread of owner-occupation has greatly increased the proportion of elderly people who own houses, many of which were built long ago for renting. Meanwhile the inflation of building costs, particularly in the labour-intensive crafts required for maintenance work, makes it increasingly difficult for poorer owners to pay for repairs. The implications for old people who have to cope single-handed with these conditions can be profound. We discuss this problem in Chapter 14.

However, for the great majority of ordinary people, housing conditions in the simpler physical sense have never been so good or so equal. For them the most pressing housing problems are now of a different kind. The general quality of the environment may be poor: many estates are squalid in appearance, thermal and sound insulation are too often flimsy, there may be no gardens and little space for the domestic economy. Families with children and elderly people may be confined to high flats (although the numbers involved should not be exaggerated: only 4 per cent of people aged 65 or more and 3 per cent of children under 16 live in flats above the first floor).[46] Access to urban services may be poor, and growing poorer as fuel costs rise and bus services deteriorate.

Somewhere on the periphery of most big cities there are neighbourhoods where no one wants to live. That is a problem we shall discuss in Chapter 15. Meanwhile many people grow increasingly concerned about the differences in legal and financial status which divide tenants from owner-occupiers, conferring on the latter all sorts of advantages which the generally poorer tenants are deprived of. These advantages, largely created by the state and the financial institutions it helps to sustain, as we show in Chapter 13, have built up powerful political pressures, not for the correction of injustices but for further extensions of owner-occupation and the protection of owner-occupiers' privileges. In contrast, the groups still excluded from the better housing in which most people now live are diverse minorities, and that makes it difficult for them to organize effective pressure on their own behalf. We explore all these issues further in the chapters which follow.

# 12
# Agenda for the Future

## Introduction

We conclude this review by asking where British housing policy stands. What issues have been resolved since the formative days immediately after the war, and what new issues now call for resolution? We explore these questions by looking at each sector of the market, starting with privately rented housing and the housing associations, and then turning to council housing and owner-occupation.

## The Private Landlord

It is now generally accepted that the private landlord will not again build new housing for a mass market. Landlords were the main providers, for rich and poor alike, before the First World War. But their share of the market fell to 58 per cent of the dwellings in England and Wales in 1938, and to 14 per cent in 1978.[1] Figure 11.1 in the last chapter shows changes in the size of the housing stock and its distribution among different tenures since the war. As the Milner Holland Report[2] first showed and Adela Nevitt later confirmed,[3] the disappearance of the private landlord, often attributed to rent controls, is to a larger extent due to other causes. We examine these more closely in Chapter 13. Every market economy in Europe has experienced a similar decline in privately rented housing for broadly similar reasons.[4]

The Housing Act of 1980, which introduced a new form of shorthold tenure and freed approved institutional landlords from the more rigorous controls, shifted the battle lines between landlord and tenant in favour of property owners, but seems unlikely to disturb the fundamental settlement, or to generate any major increase in building by private landlords. Meanwhile it is also clear that local housing authorities are unlikely to meet all demands for rented housing. However far their role is extended – and in many places it could go much further yet

– some people will be excluded, or will choose to exclude themselves, from council housing. Thus private landlords have a continuing part to play as providers of housing for newly formed and newly arrived house-holds, and for students, tourists, and all who need a temporary foothold in the market. As owner-occupation extends more widely and further 'down market' to people on lower incomes, it will probably be to home owners who let parts of their dwellings that we must increasingly look for privately rented housing. That will call for generally acceptable rules about tenure and rents which both parties to the arrangement can rely on for the future.

This brings us to the first set of unresolved issues now demanding attention. How large a part, and what kind of part, do we expect private landlords to play in future? How can tenants be given a secure home and be protected from exploitation? How can landlords be simultane-ously assured of fair rents which keep pace with inflation, and the right to regain possession of living space which forms part of their own homes? (That will not be easy: the Milner Holland report showed that harass-ment of tenants was most common when their landlords lived in the same house.) How can the poorer private tenants be subsidized in ways which ensure that more of them actually get the rent allowances to which they are entitled? (The take-up of these allowances remains obs-tinately low, particularly among private furnished tenants.)[5] We return to some of these issues in the following chapters.

## Housing Associations

Housing associations have been created and extended on a growing scale, partly to fill the gap left by the disappearing private landlord. They have performed other functions too: doing some imaginative and humane rehabilitation of decayed housing, particularly in inner-city areas; building for groups with special needs and life styles not easily accommodated in the self-contained boxes which other tenures provide;[6] developing new methods of management, more democratically account-able to tenants; and bringing some very talented people into the profes-sion of housing management, training them and giving them op-portunities for trying out new ideas. They have also housed people whom the local authorities may find it politically difficult to provide for: newcomers to the country, for example, young single people, ex-prisoners, addicts and deviant groups of various kinds.

The associations' operations have grown steadily in scale, most dram-

**12.1** *Public House Building, Slum Clearance and House Improvements, England and Wales, 1945–80*
(Annual averages in thousands)

| | Houses built by local authorities and New Towns | Slums demolished or closed | Dwellings improved with the aid of grants of all kinds |
|---|---|---|---|
| 1945–50 | 116 | 6 | |
| 1951–5 | 188 | 16 | 25[1] |
| 1956–9 | 129 | 47 | |
| 1960–64 | 167 | 62 | 122 |
| 1965–9 | 170 | 68 | 113 |
| 1970–74 | 105 | 62 | 253 |
| 1975–9 | 105 | 41 | 128 |
| 1980 | 78 | — | 176 |

*Source:* Department of the Environment, *Housing and Construction Statistics.*

*Note:*
1. Annual average 1949–59.

atically since the 1974 Housing Act. By 1977 and 1978 they were producing over 20,000 houses a year – 8 per cent of the new houses completed in the United Kingdom – and improving a similar number with the help of government grants[7] (see Tables 9.1 and 12.1). The investment this called for has tied the associations more closely to the Department of the Environment and to the Housing Corporation, through which government funds have been channelled to them. Of the associations surveyed by the Housing Corporation in May 1978, about three quarters had formal arrangements with their local authorities for nominating tenants. Of the new tenants housed by associations in a two-week period in May 1978, 28 per cent had been nominated by local authorities.[8] Some authorities and the associations working with them have made excellent use of this collaboration to do things which neither could easily manage on their own. Meanwhile the more enterprising associations have given their tenants growing responsibilities for the management of their housing. Other associations, however, have been more restricted in the needs they meet and the areas they serve than any local authority, less generous to people in urgent need, and less accountable to their tenants and to local taxpayers.[9] And because they lack the scope which local authorities have for pooling rents and subsidies on houses built over many years, building by the associations costs the central government far more in subsidies than council building does.

These trends pose dilemmas which must in time be resolved. As housing associations work in closer collaboration with central and local authorities, they align their rents and selection procedures with those of the councils, and give their tenants similar rights to buy their homes. 'What started off as an alternative may end up as more of the same thing,' to quote Barry Cullingworth.[10] If their building programmes come to an end and they give their tenants growing influence in their selection procedures, they may end up by creating a privileged enclave of well-housed families whose children inherit any vacancies which appear, without doing anything to help new generations who may be in difficulties in the future. To resolve these dilemmas will call for a delicate blend of independence and accountability, and a continuing programme of new building and rehabilitation.

## The Local Housing Authorities

Few now dispute that the local housing authorities have a permanent job to do. They have a massive stock of houses – one third of the nation's total – on which rents and subsidies are pooled. Inflation of rents and building costs has over the years enabled them to make a huge 'holding gain' on their property. This keeps the rents of new housing down by steadily raising the rents of older houses built at lower prices in the past. The troubles which housing associations and other public housing agencies encounter in neighbouring countries of Europe, where the rents of new housing for young families constantly outpace those of older housing for more affluent middle-aged people, show how successful our system has been in this respect.[11] Our local authorities have also done a better job of housing the poorest people than some of their counterparts abroad. That is because they originated not from independent cooperatives or the housing built by employers for their workers, but from the local public health and poor law authorities who were compelling landlords to improve or demolish slum property long before they started building houses themselves.

Since the Second World War, the main priorities of these authorities have switched successively from war-damage repairs to the mass production of houses for families on the waiting-lists; then to slum clearance and redevelopment and building for old people; and now, on a declining scale, to the improvement of public and private housing. (See Table 12.1 which, like Table 9.1, approximately distinguishes the periods covered by successive governments.) It is now generally agreed that henceforth this work should be focused mainly on selected towns and areas of special need, and the choice of those areas should depend as much on social as on physical criteria – criteria such as 'the concentration in the area of households likely to have special problems – for instance old age pensioners, large families, single-parent families, or families whose head is unemployed or in a low-income group'.[12] In the past, improvement has too often led to the exclusion of the people who used to live in the property improved. Henceforth the interests of the residents should be the main priority, and the social functions of the area must be respected. Housing policy is thus becoming a matter of community development. These principles, outlined in the Housing Act of 1969 and carried forward by the Housing Act of 1974, make a fundamental break from the sanitary tradition which for over a century focused attention upon physical defects such as the absence of lavatories and hot water taps, and the presence of damp and decay. In housing, as in education, social work and other fields, concepts of 'area', 'neighbourhood' and 'community' are back in fashion. So are attempts to consult and involve the public at a local level.

These generally agreed priorities leave a lot of unanswered questions. Britain's remaining housing problems are increasingly a product of social exclusion and poverty – the presence in an area of many people who are retired, sick, caring for children single-handed, unemployed or confined to low-paid jobs. Housing programmes will therefore depend for their success on selective subsidies directed to people rather than bricks and mortar, and also on social security programmes and programmes for the revival of failing local economies, and hence on policies for the national economy too. Chapter 14, which deals with some of the most striking examples of the problems caused by poverty and exclusion, takes our discussion of some of these issues a little further. But more radical action will be needed to bring central and local government services to bear more effectively upon deprived areas. The new Urban Development Corporations, to be set up in districts like the London docklands, may eventually provide a basis for that.

A continuing flow of investment will be needed for these purposes. It will be difficult to secure the funds for that until the problems of compensation and betterment, three times unsuccessfully tackled by Labour governments, are resolved. A larger and fairer redeployment of the gains created by urban development could then be achieved. The principles of the Community Land Act 1975 appear sound, but the local authorities were not an effective instrument for putting them into practice.

While some local authorities still have a lot of expensive building to do, most of them will be mainly concerned with the maintenance and improvement of their housing, and perfectly capable of making a modest profit on it. Equally important therefore was the Conservatives' attempt, made in the 1972 Housing Finance Act, to redistribute the burdens of housing debt, and to establish a nationally consistent pattern of rents and subsidies for tenants with low incomes in the public and private sectors of the market. Because it rode roughshod over the local authorities, provoking rebellions of the sort immortalized by Clay Cross, and was demonstrably unfair in cutting subsidies to tenants while subsidies to owner-occupiers went on growing, the measure was repealed in 1975. But the problems it sought to resolve still demand a solution. We return to these issues in Chapter 13.

Can local housing authorities develop a strategy which matches their increasingly varied needs, while remaining properly accountable to their ratepayers and through central government to the national taxpayer? The principles to be decided in answering that question will offer guidance in dealing with many other contemporary issues. Policy for the sale of council houses is one of those issues. It should be decided not on crude ideological grounds – for or against – but by weighing in particular neighbourhoods the need for an expansion of opportunities for house purchase against the need for subsidized, rented housing allocated without regard to the income of tenants. In Australia, where over half of the public housing built since the war has been sold to its tenants, this policy has enabled many people with modest incomes to join the two thirds of Australians who own their homes. It has also created an urban landscape of small houses with gardens, and discouraged the erection of flats too brutally impersonal for anyone to consider investing his own money in them. However, the costs in rent rebates to the very poor tenants left in public housing are now becoming high and politically unpopular.[13]

If local authorities are to sell housing, there is no reason why they should not go into the market and buy it too. The great city architects' departments have produced some fine buildings, but far too much public architecture is dreary or worse. In Canada the Ontario Housing Corporation – one of the more creative of the Commonwealth's public housing authorities – now rarely builds its own housing. Instead it buys houses and flats in the areas where it needs them from developers building for sale to owner-occupiers and private landlords.[14] In Australia the Housing Department of the State of Victoria is adopting a similar policy. In Britain, too, there is no reason why councils should not buy and sell in the open market to match their stock to the changing needs that have to be met. The standard council estate is not the only instrument for this purpose and may not be the best.

To pursue successfully the developments foreshadowed by these trends, the local housing authorities will need staff capable of working in sophisticated, innovative, yet accountable ways. Some will have to understand the economic and social structure of cities, and others will have to buy and sell in the urban housing market; some must help owner-occupiers to improve their homes, and others must work with deprived communities, with squatters and communes, and with difficult tenants who, thanks to the Housing (Homeless Persons) Act, can no longer be got rid of by eviction. Yet of all the major public service professions, housing managers have least systematic training for their difficult and varied task. A major investment in training is clearly going to be needed.

## Owner-occupation

We turn finally to owner-occupation. All the main spokesmen in British debates about housing now agree that people who can buy and maintain their own homes should be encouraged and helped to do so. The option mortgage scheme which was designed to help house buyers with incomes too low to pay the standard rate of tax was introduced by a Labour government. Ordinary tax reliefs and improvement grants, which have played much larger parts in encouraging home ownership, have also been accepted by all parties as major features of their housing policies.

Building societies, whose operations have increased enormously as owner-occupation has spread, were once regarded as independent and purely financial institutions, beyond the control of the state. No longer: their interest rates and lending policies are now a constant concern of government. Meanwhile, with the encouragement of Housing Ministers, they have extended their operations, lending on the security of secondary earners' incomes, lending in improvement areas, putting pressure on the builders of new houses to serve people living in such areas, and trying in general to revive the traditions of a movement originally concerned more with housing conditions than with lending.

Meanwhile, tax reliefs on mortgage interest payments are recognized as being a form of subsidy – if not to individuals, then to owner-occupied housing as against other sectors of the market. The option mortgage scheme, and the restriction of tax reliefs on ordinary mortgages to one house at a time with a maximum loan of £25,000, show that governments now treat this as a form of subsidy which can be deliberately manipulated for the purposes of housing policy.

But how far can house purchase be extended without putting intolerable burdens, now or later in old age, on people ill equipped to bear them? How far 'down market' can the building societies or other lenders responsibly go? What new financial devices may extend the range of people capable of acquiring at least some of the equity in their home? How may subsidies for the house buyer be placed on a footing which can be more fairly related to the subsidies offered to tenants? How should the social security system be related to housing benefits of all kinds? Many of the most difficult of the unresolved questions of housing policy now spring from the spread of owner-occupation. We say more about some of them in Chapters 13 and 14.

## Conclusion

Can we assure everyone in Britain that, as a basic right of citizenship, they will get an adequate and secure home if they are prepared to pay for it a price which is fair in relation to their household's income? That is the central theme of this discussion.

To pose the question that way is to give priority to needs rather than demands in the continuing debate about housing policy. But in an increasingly affluent world, needs and demands must be considered together. Demands are important partly because people should be given as much choice as possible and the freedom which choice confers. As we pointed out in Chapter 6 on eastern Europe, free housing allocated at prices so low that they play no part in the process of distribution is in fact rationed housing. It enormously reinforces the power of the bureaucracies which decide who gets what. East European experience also shows that if those who can afford to do so are prevented from buying housing of their own choice, they are apt to gain the lion's share of collective, subsidized housing which might otherwise have been available for people in greater need.

On the other hand, a society which relies wholly on provisions to meet demand as a solution for its housing problems will find that, unless it goes much further in equalizing the distribution of income and wealth than any market economy has yet attempted, many potential demands will not gain a hearing. They do not become 'effective'. People too poor to contend with their more affluent competitors get squeezed out. That is what seems likely to happen in Britain during the coming years if the successful grow richer, the low-paid and the larger families grow poorer, unemployment increases, the building of new public sector housing is drastically curtailed, and a considerable proportion of the best council housing is indiscriminately sold off to richer council tenants. If that is the path we tread, it will lead, as it has done before, to increasingly turbulent times until government is once more compelled to resume a more responsible role.

# Part III
## Agenda for Action

We have shown that the housing circumstances of Britain and the more mature urban industrial economies of Europe are converging. With large stocks of good housing, sophisticated bureaucracies, and populations which now grow and move very slowly, the old problems of general scarcity and squalor which seemed so daunting a generation ago have been solved, or are within sight of solution. If governments forget the lessons they have learnt, allow public provision to fall into decay, and turn their backs on the people who can get decent housing only with their help, those problems will in time re-emerge. But whether these countries press on to reach a complete solution of the basic quantitative and qualitative housing problems, or whether they allow the supply of houses to be overtaken again by unmet needs, is now a matter of political choice, no longer dictated by brute scarcities of resources.

In future the main problems of housing policy in these countries will be of different kinds. They will no longer be measured with statistics about unfit houses, persons per room, shared and unshared bathrooms, indoor and outdoor lavatories – the traditional measures of quantitative and qualitative housing standards. Already, three clusters of related questions define the main themes of the new debate. First, *tenure*: questions about access to housing of different tenures and the financial and other benefits associated with each of them. Second, *location*: questions about the character and quality of neighbourhoods and the access they give their residents to everything else in an urban society. Third, *minority needs*: questions about the housing of people who tend systematically to be excluded from the normal housing markets, and about those who have unusual or extreme needs which cannot adequately be met within those markets – questions which reveal remaining problems of scarcity and squalor, but which cannot be resolved simply by building more houses. These problems pose important further questions – about housing management, for example, and the training of those who do this work.

We explore some of these questions in the third and last part of this book. As in previous chapters, we try first of all to clarify problems and the dilemmas they pose. But we go further than we did in previous chapters to suggest the directions in which solutions should be sought.

We start, in Chapter 13, entitled 'Housing Tenure and Finance', by comparing the financial benefits which people in housing of different tenures gain from the state, at different stages of their lives, and the dilemmas posed by any attempt to distribute these benefits more fairly. At this stage we focus on the mass of ordinary households in the middle of the income distribution. Then, in Chapter 14, 'The Needs of the Poor', we look at the problems of various groups at the bottom end of the market, and suggest some general principles which may help to improve a system now so complicated that few of those intended to benefit from it can understand it. Chapter 15, 'Empty Flats', deals with neighbourhoods now to be found in nearly every large British city and in other countries too – neighbourhoods where it is growing increasingly difficult to find tenants for public housing. We discuss the responses which should be made to problems which often owe more to the neighbourhood and its place within the city than to its houses. Then, in Chapter 16, 'Housing the Homeless', we trace recent developments which led, through the passing of the Housing (Homeless Persons) Act of 1977, to an important extension of government responsibilities for meeting minority needs. We treat this both as an opportunity to discuss the problems of the homeless, and as a case study in the politics of housing.

# 13
# Housing Tenure and Finance

## Introduction

The combined expenditure of central and local government on housing grew from 6·3 per cent of total public expenditure in 1968 to 8·8 per cent in 1976, since when both the total and the percentage have slightly fallen. That increase was largely due to the growth of central government subsidies and grants. These subsidies increased over the same period from 1·0 per cent to 2·6 per cent of the central government's current expenditure.[1] Meanwhile, revenue forgone by the Exchequer owing to tax relief on mortgage interest payments and the option mortgage subsidy rose from £395 million in 1966–7 to an estimated £1,240 million in 1976–7 at constant 1976 prices.[2] The rising costs of these commitments, shown in Tables 13.2 and 13.3, was unforeseen and unintended. It was due partly to the inflation of building costs and house prices which took place around 1973 (shown in Figure 13.1) and partly to the continuing spread of owner-occupation, coupled with rising tax rates, falling tax thresholds and rising house prices. Together these influences overwhelmed the determined attempt, made in the Housing Finance Act of 1972, to bring expenditure on public housing under control. As a result governments, regardless of party, have become increasingly concerned about housing finance.

Official concern has been reinforced by growing public concern. The decline of the private landlord has divided the British people increasingly starkly into owner-occupiers and council tenants. Rising house prices and interest rates demand greater sacrifices of those who choose to buy, and later confer greater gains on those who achieve this ambition – at the point when the same processes tend to push up the rents of council tenants. The resulting injustices seem increasingly glaring to many people. That was why the Housing Finance Review, as it was at first called, was set up by Anthony Crosland, Secretary of State for the Environment, in 1975. He hoped to formulate arrangements which would place buyers and tenants on a more equal footing.

**13.1** *Increases in House Prices and Earnings, United Kingdom, 1956–80*

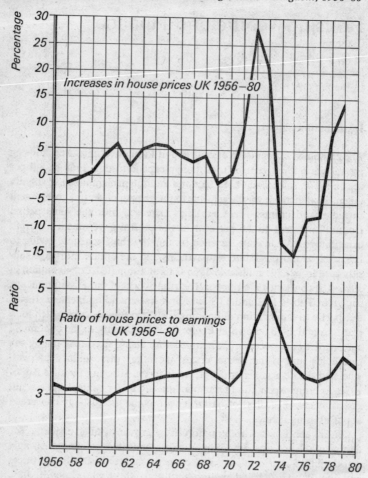

Notes: Source: *Building Societies Association Bulletin No. 27*, July 1981, p. 19.

1. The BSA says of the series for all house prices: 'The series is far from perfect, especially prior to 1966, but should be adequate to enable long-term trends to be analysed.'
2. The figures showing the 'real' increase in house prices are equal to the increase in house prices less the increase in the retail price index (the latter taken from *Economic Trends*).
3. The house price/earnings ratio is calculated by dividing the average price for all houses by average earnings of fully employed men aged 21 and over.

Public and private studies generated by these concerns have taken the analysis of the whole system of housing finance further than ever before, and much further than we can pursue it in this book. Our aim in this chapter is to draw on this work in order to clarify the main issues, and to suggest the general directions in which the system should evolve. We focus particularly on the needs and problems of ordinary householders. In the next chapter we consider the needs of poorer people.

## How the System Has Evolved

Procedures for paying for housing have grown up over the years into a system so complicated that it cannot be understood without some appreciation of its history. We start by describing as simply and briefly as possible the successive strata on which this system has been built.

But first it is essential to recall that in an urban society housing has become an expensive and complex good which plays an integral part in people's life styles and consumption patterns. Its price tends to rise faster than the prices of other things, roughly in line with incomes. Figure 13.1 shows how incomes and prices have moved over twenty years, which included in the early seventies a sharp inflation in house prices followed by a return to a more gently rising income-related trend. This trend is rising slightly faster now, probably because house prices increasingly reflect what two-earner households are willing and able to pay. Houses cost a lot, far more than anything else that most people will ever buy. Thus they can only get a home with the help of borrowed money which they need for a long time and have to repay very slowly. But this home, thanks to its long life and buoyant price, provides good security for a loan.

Until the First World War, most of the capital for house building was lent by local people through local solicitors, banks and similar institutions to landlords, who often divided the burden of repayments between ground landlords, long-lease holders, their tenants and subtenants. With proper management, each could rely on a continuing flow of rents from which to pay interest on loans which therefore never had to be repaid.[3] Some argued that no man should be entitled to draw an income without working for it. This view was held by medievalists who regarded usury as sin, by radicals and anarchists who regarded property as theft, and by Irishmen who regarded landlords as fair game for assassination. But these arguments, although still to be heard, amounted to an attack not only on the sources of finance for housing, but on the whole capitalist system. Others argued that small-scale capitalism performed reasonably well in the housing field, creating a massive stock of houses which, decayed though their survivors may now seem, were widely regarded in their day as the finest artisans' dwellings in Europe.

The next layer in the successive strata of our system of housing finance was the building society, invented towards the end of the eighteenth century.[4] These societies were in effect clubs whose members agreed to subscribe regular contributions to a fund which was used to build or buy houses for them. When the last house was completed and the last subscription paid, the association came to an end. This was the 'terminating' building society. Its members were usually skilled artisans and it never spread very widely.

Much more important was the discovery that the societies' lenders and borrowers could be entirely different people: thousands of lenders could deposit funds, secured on the value of houses built for a much smaller number of borrowers. Lenders could join and leave the society at any time. Equally important, the buyers – because they wished to acquire their houses outright – were prepared to repay their loans as well as the interest on them. The societies could therefore survive and grow indefinitely, harvesting a double flow of funds – deposits from investors and repayments from borrowers, both of which could be channelled as fast as new borrowers and builders could be found into further house building. The 'permanent' building society was invented in the middle of the nineteenth century. It provided a means for borrowing short-term and lending long-term without going bankrupt, and for drawing in savings from a much larger population for house purchase and thus spreading risks more widely. The increasingly affluent middle and lower middle classes who dominated these societies were looking for safe places to put the money they were saving. The societies survived difficult years, during which their corporate status was established under the Building Societies Act of 1874, and their scope and limits were clarified. Then they began to grow more rapidly after the First World War.

By then the taxpayers were lending a hand too. The government helped the building societies by giving them and their depositors somewhat more generous tax treatment than banks and other financial institutions received. Meanwhile landlords received less generous tax treatment than other entrepreneurs. They still do. Their houses, unlike other productive capital such as factories and the machinery inside them, are assumed by the Inland Revenue to last for ever. Money set aside year by year in depreciation funds to replace them or to repay the loans which financed their construction is not deductible from landlords' profits before they are taxed – although if the same people were to build factories instead, their depreciation funds would be tax-deductible.

In 1915, following wartime disturbances amongst munitions workers in Glasgow, controls were imposed on the rents of private housing, and tenants were given security of tenure. These controls were repeatedly extended and amended between the wars, but were abolished entirely for new building after April 1919. Complete control was re-imposed in 1939 at the start of the Second World War, and then reduced in 1957 by freeing a top slice of the market and all new tenancies, and by raising the rent maxima on the remainder. In 1965 a new system was introduced which for the first time detached rent control from security of tenure: all normal unfurnished tenancies were henceforth to be secure, but rents were regulated in more flexible ways, later extended to furnished tenancies. In effect these arrangements gave private tenants, particularly those with the longest-running unfurnished tenancies, a share in the ownership and value of the housing they lived in. Some landlords recognized this by paying their tenants to move out or selling them the property on favourable terms – in this way offering them part (often a very small part) of the increase in value which would be brought about by their departure.

Support for the financing of house building for owner-occupation was extended with the taxpayers' help by giving buyers tax reliefs on their interest payments. Tax relief of this kind had been established much earlier in the first half of the nineteenth century, long before owner-occupation became common. It was in the 1950s, as owner-occupation spread, as tax thresholds fell and as the starting rates for tax rose, that tax relief became a major element in housing finance.[5] Table 13.2 shows the scale on which it has since grown.

Since income tax began at the start of the nineteenth century, landlords were taxed on their rents by paying the central government a charge which was based on the valuation of their property for the purposes of local taxation. As a by-product of this arrangement, owner-occupiers, who were still fairly rare until after the First World War, paid the same charge. They were allowed, like landlords, to deduct from it their expenditure on repairs and maintenance. Because the valuations made in 1936 were not revised for many years, the real burden of this Schedule A tax fell to very low levels, and in 1963 it was abolished altogether. As recently as 1955 the Royal Commission on the Taxation of Profits and Income had argued that this tax was justified because it treated tenants (who paid taxed rents) and owner-occupiers (whose

**13.2** *Tax Relief on Mortgage Interest and Option Mortgage Subsidy, 1965–77*
(£ million)

| | Current prices | Constant 1976–7 survey prices |
|---|---|---|
| 1965–6 | 135 | 355 |
| 1966–7 | 155 | 395 |
| 1967–8 | 180 | 445 |
| 1968–9 | 200 | 470 |
| 1969–70 | 245 | 540 |
| 1970–71 | 300 | 620 |
| 1971–2 | 330 | 635 |
| 1972–3 | 395 | 710 |
| 1973–4 | 560 | 925 |
| 1974–5 | 770 | 1,075 |
| 1975–6 | 970 | 1,095 |
| 1976–7 (estimate) | 1,240 | 1,240 |

*Source: Housing Policy*, Technical Volume, Part II, p. 60.

property enabled them to live rent-free) on an equal footing. If that view – which treats tenancy as the norm – is accepted, then the abolition of the tax amounts to a major subsidy. (It might now be over £1,000 million a year.)[6] But in that case house buyers who do not yet own their property must be entitled to tax relief on their mortgage interest payments, for both forms of tax relief cannot be regarded as subsidies. Alternatively, the American and Canadian view – treating owner-occupation as the norm – may be adopted. In that case no tax should be levied on the imputed rents of owner-occupied houses, and its abolition is not a subsidy. But tax relief on interest payments is a subsidy.

House building by local authorities, which began on a sporadic local scale towards the end of the nineteenth century, became widespread after the First World War. In areas of housing shortage there was no other way to fill the gap left by the wartime interruption of building, and to meet the demands of millions of returning servicemen. Later, as this building programme for the general needs of the working class was reduced and finally brought to an end in the 1930s, the local authorities turned to slum clearance. It was at last recognized that it was pointless to try to get rid of the worst housing by building something better to take its place unless rents were subsidized. Compelling landlords to improve or close slum houses without helping poor people to get something better only shifted housing problems from one street to another.

Subsidies from the Exchequer and the ratepayers for council building were initially generous, later reduced, but always remained important.[7] Table 13.3 shows the flow of funds coming from this source in recent years. Yet another means of extending the resources for the funding of house building had been discovered. During the 1960s, total assistance from the state, expressed as a proportion of the gross costs of local authority housing, fluctuated between 25 and 27 per cent. Then the explosive inflation of the early 1970s, coupled with the return of a Labour government determined to increase council building, pushed subsidies up from 27 per cent of gross cost in 1971–2, to 38 per cent in 1973–4 and 52 per cent in 1975–6.[8] Subsidies stayed at that level thereafter till the Conservatives resumed power in 1979.

**13.3** *Subsidies on Local Authority Housing at 1979 Survey Prices, United Kingdom, 1974–80*
(£ million)

|  | Subsidies other than rent rebates from | | Rent rebates | Total assistance |
|---|---|---|---|---|
|  | Exchequer | Local rates |  |  |
| 1974–5 | 1,152 | 350 | 422 | 1,924 |
| 1975–6 | 1,210 | 341 | 404 | 1,955 |
| 1976–7 | 1,379 | 264 | 432 | 2,075 |
| 1977–8 | 1,279 | 244 | 462 | 1,985 |
| 1978–9 | 1,384 | 302 | 456 | 2,142 |
| 1979–80 | 1,447 | 349 | 447 | 2,243 |

*Source: The Government's Expenditure Plans, 1980–81 to 1983–84, Cmnd 7841, 1980.*

For many years the houses built, the Exchequer subsidies earned and the rents charged under each Act of Parliament had to be distinguished from those applying to houses built under earlier and later Acts. But since 1935 these payments have been pooled. That gave the local authorities greater scope for redeploying rent revenues and subsidies to bring the maximum financial support to bear where it was most needed. The rents of houses built in earlier years at lower prices and interest rates than those ruling today can be increased to generate what amounts to a profit which the authority uses to keep down the rents of houses built more recently at higher prices and higher rates of interest

Since the Second World War, and particularly during the last decade, inflation has come to exert a growing influence on housing finance. Because repayments of loans and interest tend to continue with little change in money terms, while house prices tend to rise faster than other prices (as Figure 13.1 showed), anyone who owns a house holds an asset which tends to appreciate in real value at a rate that outpaces the dwindling real burden of the loans raised to finance its construction. That windfall – sometimes called a capital gain, but more accurately described as a holding gain – goes to local housing authorities, owner-occupiers and private landlords. If the local authority passes these gains on to its tenants in reduced rents, rather than to its ratepayers in reduced subsidies, council tenants benefit collectively from it. Along with their subsidies, this gain forms a tax-free addition to their incomes.

Owner-occupiers are in an even stronger position because they can decide for themselves what to do with their holding gains. They can raise further mortgages on their houses (to buy a car or a country cottage perhaps), or they can sell their houses and use the proceeds as down payments on bigger and better houses, or they can purchase annuities when they retire if they move to smaller and cheaper houses at that stage in their lives. This flexible, tax-free benefit is clearly a subsidy of a kind. If they had rented their homes instead of buying them, and invested their savings in industrial shares, and if these shares had appreciated in value to a similar extent (which is most unlikely), they would have had to pay tax on their dividends and capital gains tax on their shares when they were sold.

All sorts of additional subsidies have been introduced to help the poorest householders meet the costs of their housing. The oldest and largest are the payments made to householders living on means-tested supplementary benefits. These benefits in nearly every case cover their rates and (for tenants) their rents or (for owner-occupiers) their mortgage interest payments and a contribution towards repairs and insurance. In Great Britain in November 1979 there were 1·4 million householders living on supplementary benefit who were council tenants, 0·5 million who were private tenants, and 0·4 million who were owner-occupiers.[9] It could be argued that the full payment made to them in respect of their housing costs should be regarded as a housing subsidy. If so, it would have amounted during that year to £900 million. Or it could be argued that since most claimants have other income (most often a retirement pension) part of which will be devoted to rent, there should only be attributed to housing a proportion of their total benefit equal to the proportion of the average claimant's total expenditure which is devoted

**13.4** *Rent Rebates, Rent Allowances and Rate Rebates, England and Wales, 1975 and 1979*

|  | Number granted (thousands) | Average weekly rebate or allowance (£) | Estimated take-up (Per cent) |
|---|---|---|---|
| *Rent rebates*[1] | | | |
| 1975 | 820 | 2·42 weekly | 70–75 |
| 1979 | 975 | 3·47 weekly | 70–75 |
| | | | |
| *Rent allowances*[1] | | | |
| to unfurnished tenants | | | |
| 1975 | 135 | 2·30 weekly | 30–35 |
| 1979 | 195 | 3·43 weekly | 50–55 |
| | | | |
| to furnished tenants | | | |
| 1975 | 9 | 2·80 weekly | Not known |
| 1979 | 8 | 3·56 weekly | Not known |
| | | | |
| *Rate rebates*[2] | | | |
| 1975 | 2,300 | 36·50 annually | 60–65 |
| 1979 | 2,680 | 55·80 annually | About 70 |

*Source:* Department of the Environment, *Housing and Construction Statistics.*

*Notes:*
1. In January.      2. In March.

to rent. That would have amounted to about £590 million in 1979. Alternatively it could be argued that the whole payment should be treated as deferred wages transferred through the tax system, and should not be regarded as a subsidy to housing at all.

Since 1972, when a uniform national scheme was introduced, growing numbers of poorer council tenants have received rent rebates which reduce their rent payments. Rent allowances – a cash payment to private tenants which serves a similar purpose – were introduced the following year. The percentage of those eligible who actually claim these benefits is much higher for council tenants than for private unfurnished tenants. It is probably lower still for furnished tenants.[10] Rate rebates, introduced in 1966 and generously extended in 1974, go to larger numbers still. The take-up rates are much higher for owner-occupiers than for private tenants.[11] Table 13.4 shows, for England and Wales, how these subsidies have grown. For Great Britain as a whole the total expenditure on these schemes amounted in 1979–80 to £222 million on rent rebates, £38 million on rent allowances, and £201 million on rate rebates.

Perhaps the clearest recognition that tax relief on mortgage interest should be regarded as a subsidy came in 1967 when the government introduced the option mortgage scheme, which gave a payment equivalent to tax relief at the standard rate of tax to house buyers with incomes too low to claim the full value of the relief in the ordinary way. The option mortgage subsidy is shown in Table 13.5. Expenditure on it has remained fairly stable in real terms since the mid 1970s. The percentage of new mortgages taken out with the help of this subsidy has fallen since the peak year of 1972.

**13.5** *The Option Mortgage Subsidy, United Kingdom and Great Britain, 1969–79*

|  | Option mortgage as a percentage of all new mortgages (GB)[1] | Total expenditure (£ million) | |
|---|---|---|---|
|  |  | At current prices (GB)[2] | At 1979 survey prices (UK)[3] |
| 1969 | 6 | * | * |
| 1972 | 21 | 28 | * |
| 1975 | 16 | 109 | 175 |
| 1978 | 13 | 148 | 170 |
| 1979 | 11 (UK) | 186 | 193 |

*Notes:*

1. *Source:* Department of the Environment, *Housing and Construction Statistics.*
2. *Source:* Central Statistical Office, *Social Trends.* [*Financial years.*]
3. *Source: The Government's Expenditure Plans, 1980–81 to 1983–84,* Cmnd 7841, March 1980.

* Not known.

Although they may not strictly be housing costs, there are other payments which householders cannot escape. Their local taxes – the rates – are the most important of these. Some would argue that rate rebates, reducing the burden of taxation for poorer households, are a kind of housing subsidy. That is why we included them in Table 13.4. Fuel and light, now constantly rising in price, are the householder's other main commitments. An unfuelled house is an uninhabitable house. At the rates applying from November 1979, the Supplementary Benefits Commission paid £95 million a year in additions to benefit for heating purposes for its claimants. From November 1980 this expenditure was increased to about £195 million, including an increase in family income supplement for working families with low wages paid for the same purpose.

One further layer in the successive strata of arrangements which play a part in Britain's system of housing finance should be noted. It will become increasingly important in future. More and more people own their own home, and this asset tends to retain its real value well. Other financial assets, such as shares in companies, have tended to fall in real value as profits have fallen. Since the ownership of shares is more heavily concentrated amongst the rich, these changes have led to an appreciable equalization in the distribution of wealth. Figure 13.6, taken from a

**13.6** *Asset Composition of Gross Personal Wealth, United Kingdom, 1960 and 1975*

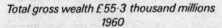

*Total gross wealth £55·3 thousand millions*
*1960*

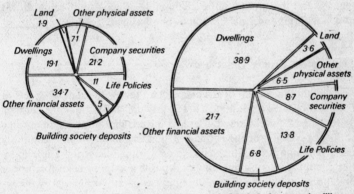

*Total gross wealth £210·3 thousand millions*
*1975*

*Source:* Royal Commission on the Distribution of Income and Wealth, Cmnd 6999, 1977.

Report of the Royal Commission on the Distribution of Income and Wealth,[12] shows how personal wealth has increased in volume and changed in character. In a later Report the Commission concluded that: 'The share of total net wealth of the top 1 per cent declined by over 3 percentage points between 1971 and 1976, on the unadjusted basis ... In contrast the bottom 80 per cent group increased its share of total net wealth by 4 percentage points between 1971 and 1976. This would seem largely due to their increased holdings of total net dwellings (a gain of over 5 percentage points over this period).[13]

Already about half the male householders over pension age are owner-occupiers (see Table 11.13 on page 182). This means that a growing proportion of the population will in time inherit a house. Those who have been able to buy one will thus pass on to their heirs a major asset which may play a part in improving the housing standards of the next generation. Their heirs may choose to live in it, use it as a second home, pass it on to their own children, or sell it and use the proceeds for these or other purposes. Not surprisingly, the children of owner-occupiers are much more likely than the children of tenants to buy houses.[14] Thus, if the arrangements we have described confer privileges on owner-occupiers which tenants are deprived of, that bias tends to be redoubled from generation to generation.

To a much more limited extent, tenants too can inherit some of their forebears' housing advantages if they are living with them when they die. Councils and private landlords usually accept the survivors as tenants. But this asset is not exchangeable or capable of being shifted into new forms and places as the owner-occupiers' is.

## The System Briefly Described

Concluding this section of the chapter, we review the general effects of these complicated arrangements. The private landlord was the bedrock underlying all that followed. The first big advance on this system came with the invention of the permanent building society – an enormously important innovation, still envied in many other countries. These societies generated a continuing flow of deposits and repayments for further investment in housing. Their strength was greatly enhanced by tax reliefs, which have become increasingly important in recent years as tax thresholds have fallen and tax rates have risen.

The next great invention was the local housing authority, drawing subsidies from the national and the local taxpayer. The authorities' strength was greatly enhanced when they were enabled to pool their rents and subsidies on housing built at different times. The public sector housing agencies of many other countries are still unable to do this: as a result, the rents of new housing intended for young families tend to be too high, while the rents of older housing occupied by older and more affluent people tend to be low.

These two great 'engines' for raising and investing capital in the hous-

ing market have each been greatly strengthened in recent years by inflation, which has reduced the real burden of loans charges on householders
and conferred enormous, tax-free holding gains on owners. The lenders
have generally been the losers. Figure 13.7 illustrates the increasingly
dramatic way in which successively higher rates of inflation reduce the
proportion of income which a house buyer has to devote to his mortgage
payments. These holding gains have enriched existing owner-occupiers –
fairly quickly for those who have been able to realize them, much later

**13.7** *Mortgage Payments as a Proportion of Income Given Various Rates
of Income Inflation*

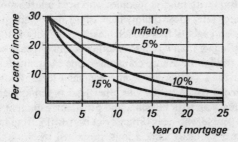

Shows average mortgage payments for a typical loan repaid over 25 years with the mortgage
rate at 11 per cent, as a percentage of average income in the mid 1970s.

*Source:* Martin Boddy, *The Building Societies*, Macmillan, 1980, p. 170.

for those who have simply accumulated an asset to bequeath to their
heirs. The price of these gains has been paid partly by the taxpayers who
were unable to gain the advantage of these tax reliefs. But much of it is
paid by people buying their way into owner-occupation for the first
time – young couples who have to pay a constantly rising price for
home ownership, inflated by the excessive demands encouraged by this
system. The whole national distribution of wealth has been shifted in
the process. Where local authorities have passed on their holding gains
to tenants by using them to keep rents down, council tenants too have
benefited collectively from what amounts to a tax-free addition to their
incomes. Where the gains have been used to reduce subsidies from the
ratepayers, it is the whole local population which has benefited.

To these, the main strata of the system, have been added a whole
cluster of additional arrangements to help the poorest people meet the
cost of their housing. Payments for rent and mortgage interest from the
Supplementary Benefits Commission and its predecessors go back to the

days of the old local poor law. Rent allowances and rebates, and rate rebates have become widespread in the last fifteen years. Finally there are the growing effects, which will become increasingly important in the future, of the inheritance of owner-occupied property, the 'inheritance' of subsidized and controlled tenancies, and the privileged access to cut-price owner-occupation which many council tenants are now being offered.

Even this rather complicated summary of the British system of housing finance greatly oversimplifies reality. We have said nothing, for example, about the constantly changing basis for subsidies to local authorities, or about the fluctuating flow of loans which they make to house buyers (directed more often than the building societies' loans to first-time buyers with modest incomes who need a large mortgage). The effects of water rates (now rapidly increasing) and of stamp duty, solicitors' charges and agents' fees (which make the cost of buying and selling houses much higher than it is in some other countries) have been ignored. So have the roles of insurance companies (operating much like building societies but on a smaller scale, and generally lending to people with higher incomes), fringe banks and other lenders (concerned more with money lending than with housing, and providing capital at higher interest rates for people who have difficulty in borrowing from more conventional sources). Housing associations, promoted to create a non-profit-making alternative to the private landlord, have grown more rapidly in the past five years than any other sector of the market: we have neglected them too. Neither have we discussed the criteria and priorities of building societies and other lenders who deploy vast sums of money through a small staff who have to be given fairly simple rules to follow. Not surprisingly, these rules often favour the more conventional, salaried households with secure jobs, buying good and readily saleable property in popular neighbourhoods.

## The Effects of This System

What are the main redistributive effects of the whole system? Who gains and who loses from it? Many official and independent studies have been made of this difficult question.[15] They demonstrate that there can be no single authoritative answer to it.

For a start there is no consensus about what constitutes a subsidy. Most would agree that subsidies to council tenants should figure in the reckoning, but some would argue that a portion of them should be attributed to the general well-being of the whole community, which benefits from a healthier and more attractive city, cleared of its slums. Many would exclude tax reliefs – and particularly the tax relief on capital gains, which may be difficult for home owners to realize because they usually have to go on living in their houses or buy another at equally inflated prices. And what about rent rebates and allowances – are they housing subsidies or a form of income maintenance? What about rent controls – a subsidy paid by private landlords to their tenants, which is often recouped by failing to maintain the house? Some would regard supplementary benefit payments for rent not as a subsidy but as a form of income maintenance; others would include only a small proportion of that payment, equivalent to the share of the claimant's total expenditure which is devoted to rent. The questions are endless.

If some agreement could be reached about how to reckon up the amounts of government assistance given to householders living in different sectors of the market, it would then be equally difficult to decide what this assistance should be related to. Should the total paid to all householders in one tenure be compared with the total paid to all in some other tenure? Should average payments per household be compared? Should the proportion of housing costs (also an exceedingly tricky concept) met by subsidy be compared in different tenures? Should average net payments for housing, after subsidy, be compared? Or should subsidies be related to the capital borrowed or the interest charges paid in respect of households in different tenures? These five different questions were examined in the Housing Policy Review, producing five different answers – generally, but not unanimously, leading to the conclusion that council tenants gained more assistance than owner-occupiers.

A more sophisticated but exceedingly complicated analysis has since been made by Dr Kerrie Bigsworth, who compares assistance of various kinds with estimates of 'residual' income, assuming that each household needs for non-housing expenditure at least the scale rates its members would receive if they were living on supplementary benefit, and that this sum must be deducted from their net incomes before deciding how much of that income is potentially available for housing. She shows how residual income, housing payments and assistance from the state vary over the life span for people living in different kinds of housing and in different kinds of place.[16]

If we want conclusive answers, these may not be very fruitful questions to ask. But we should not therefore withdraw defeated, abandoning the whole attempt to create a better system. There is a large measure of agreement about the main defects of this system, and a growing consensus about some of the things which must be done.

If investment in housing of different tenures is compared, rather than the experience of particular households, it is clear that owner-occupation and public rented housing are both massively subsidized competitors of private landlords. Not surprisingly, they have driven private landlords out of the market, with the exception of relatively small corners of it which cater for people not interested in the other tenures or unable for the time being to get into them – the kind of housing that is used by students, holiday-makers, newly arrived immigrants, and young couples saving up the deposit for a mortgage or accumulating points on a council waiting-list, for example. With or without rent control and security of tenure, the private landlord would be disappearing as a large-scale provider of new housing.

If we compare the distribution of housing debt burdens, subsidies and rent levels between different local authorities, it is clear that authorities which made wise or lucky choices about the time to borrow, authorities which built their houses with subsidies secured under the most generous legislation, and – above all – authorities which have given up building altogether are in the financially easiest position. The central government's attempts to channel funds into areas of high need and cost, such as the London boroughs, have gone only part of the way to equalize resources and burdens.

If we compare the general principles used to channel assistance to people within different tenures, it is clear that subsidies for council tenants are very widely distributed. The range of council rents is relatively restricted, and it has grown more so, thanks to attempts to use restrictions on rents to hold down the general increase in the cost of living. The general pattern is roughly progressive, however, giving most help to the poorest tenants, thanks partly to the effect of rent rebates. Dr Bigsworth shows that if, instead of looking at net incomes, you examine residual incomes which take account of family needs, the public sector presents a less encouraging picture. Viewed in this way, council tenants with children generally get much less help in relation to their needs than middle-aged people and pensioners. (Since that is a general problem not confined to council tenants, the solution may be a redistribution of funds between child benefits, tax allowances and pensions, rather than a redistribution of housing subsidies for council tenants.)

But Dr Bigsworth confirms, as every other researcher has done, that subsidies for the house buyer are frankly regressive, giving most help to the richest people who borrow most money, buy the most expensive houses and pay the highest rates of tax. Meanwhile private tenants, who tend on average to be the poorest of all (see Table 11.14 on page 184), clearly get less help than people in either of the other tenures. Even rent allowances and rate rebates, which are designed to help the poorest of them, are much less successful in reaching private tenants than the equivalent subsidies are in reaching council tenants and owner-occupiers. Tables 13.8 and 13.9 present the main conclusions of the Housing Policy Review on the distribution of assistance within tenures.

If we examine the general effects of this system on investment and prices, it is clear that it tends to draw a growing share of savings into the building societies and away from other forms of investment in which they might be at least as productive for the nation. It tends to inflate house prices; indeed, the lenders and (once into the charmed circle) the borrowers each have an interest in allowing prices to rise. As funds flow in and out of the building societies, fluctuations in their resources can produce destructive fluctuations in price levels and in the fortunes

**13.8** *Distribution by Income of Local Authority and New Town Housing Subsidies, 1974–5*

| Income (head of household and wife) | Number of households (thousands) | Total general subsidy (£ million) | Average general subsidy (£) | Average rebate (£)[1] | Total rebate (£ million) | Total all subsidies (£ million) |
|---|---|---|---|---|---|---|
| Under £1,000 | 1,230 | 148 | 120 | 46 | 56 | 204 |
| £1,000–1,499 | 660 | 87 | 132 | 48 | 32 | 119 |
| £1,500–1,999 | 510 | 78 | 152 | 28 | 14 | 92 |
| £2,000–2,499 | 660 | 90 | 137 | 7 | 5 | 95 |
| £2,500–2,999 | 660 | 97 | 147 | — | — | 97 |
| £3,000–3,499 | 430 | 67 | 154 | — | — | 67 |
| £3,500–3,999 | 260 | 38 | 148 | — | — | 38 |
| £4,000–4,999 | 240 | 39 | 164 | — | — | 39 |
| £5,000 and over | 50 | 7 | 154 | — | — | 7 |
| All ranges | 4,700 | 651 | 139 | 23 | 107 | 758 |

*Source: Housing Policy*, Technical Volume, Part I, Table IV.35 (see paras. 87–92 for greater detail about assumptions used).

*Note:*
The method used here is to (i) work out the national average rent that would just suffice to meet unsubsidized historic cost; (ii) express that as a ratio to gross value for the whole local authority and New Town housing stock; (iii) within each income range apply that ratio to average gross value to derive the average 'unsubsidized' rent; (iv) subtract the average unrebated rent in each income band from the average 'unsubsidized' rent to arrive at the average subsidy per household in each income band.

1. Averaged over all tenant households in the range, not just over those receiving rebates.

**13.9** *Distribution by Income of Tax Relief on Mortgage Interest and Option Mortgage Subsidy 1974–5*

| Income of head of household and wife | Number of households (thousands) | Total tax relief and subsidy (£ million) | Average subsidy or tax relief (£) |
|---|---|---|---|
| Under £1,000 | 100 | 6 | 59 |
| £1,000–1,499 | 170 | 12 | 73 |
| £1,500–1,999 | 380 | 34 | 91 |
| £2,000–2,499 | 590 | 61 | 104 |
| £2,500–2,999 | 720 | 73 | 101 |
| £3,000–3,499 | 850 | 110 | 129 |
| £3,500–3,999 | 640 | 82 | 129 |
| £4,000–4,999 | 910 | 135 | 148 |
| £5,000–5,999 | 370 | 66 | 179 |
| £6,000 or over | 380 | 139 | 369 |
| TOTAL | 5,100 | 718 | 141 |

*Source: Housing Policy*, Technical Volume, Part I, Table IV.34 (see paras. 83–6 for description of assumptions used).

*Note:*
Number of households rounded to nearest hundred thousand, but average tax relief calculated from unrounded figures.

of the building industry. The building societies' operations exacerbated the jagged trends illustrated in Figure 13.1. By helping to fuel inflation and the rise in interest rates it has produced, this system has imposed particularly heavy costs on young people when they take out their first mortgages. Later on it has reduced their housing costs when, in middle age and with higher incomes, they could more easily bear the burden.

The experience of the years since the Second World War has taught people that if they want to protect themselves from inflation, maximize their wealth and minimize their tax payments, they should buy a house as soon as they can, and repeatedly increase their stake in the market later by taking out new mortgages and buying bigger houses. They should not move to smaller and cheaper houses when their families grow up and leave home, despite the fact that other young people may need the excessive space they occupy. Not surprisingly, this is exactly what large numbers of people have done.

Finally, if the system is assessed by its capacity to help the poorest households, the mixture it offers of supplementary benefit payments, rent allowances and rebates, and rate rebates (involving three quite different means tests administered through two or three different offices) is unnecessarily complicated, bewildering to the public, likely to reinforce disincentives to work, and leaves many of those entitled to help claiming the wrong benefit or none at all. We look more closely at these arrangements in the next chapter.

British political debate tends to be obsessed with distributional problems. We showed in Chapters 9 and 10 that the still unresolved questions of compensation and betterment are usually posed as an argument about the distribution of the profits of urban development, not about how to make the process of development more convenient, attractive or efficient. That may be why the argument remains unresolved. Likewise questions about housing finance have often been posed simply as an argument about the distribution of government assistance between owner-occupiers and council tenants – an argument which can never be satisfactorily resolved. By focusing instead on the defects of the system about which most people agree, better progress may be made.

## Future Directions[17]

Taking each tenure in turn, we outline the general directions in which the debate is leading. The aims of any reform have already been well summarized:

We assume that the objectives of a pricing and subsidy system are both economic and social. The economic objectives are:
a the provision of sufficient housing of the right sizes and types and in the right places to accommodate everybody at or above the minimum standard which society considers desirable;
b the best use of existing housing, in the sense that the under-utilization of housing space (e.g. vacant dwellings, unused rooms in occupied dwellings) is discouraged;
c the maintenance of housing in good condition;
d the minimum disincentives to mobility between dwellings which may or may not be in the same geographical area, or the same tenure (owner-occupied, rented privately, or rented from the council). The social objectives are:
e subsidies to ensure that there is no one who cannot afford housing of at least the minimum standard;
f a fair distribution of subsidies: at the very least the avoidance of a regressive system;

**g** a reasonable amount of choice between dwellings (of different qualities, types, sizes, etc.), tenures, locations, etc.
**h** the minimum of bureaucratic interference with the freedom of the individual.[18]

Most of the voters now live in owner-occupied houses, many of the remainder hope to do so some day, and all parties agree that for those who can afford it this is a good thing. Thus no party which intends to win an election will suddenly or completely withdraw tax relief on mortgage interest, or reimpose a Schedule A tax on the notional rent which an owner-occupier secures from his home. A Labour Minister of Housing made that clear fifteen years ago. 'Of course we wooed the owner-occupier during the [1964] general election.' 'My plan,' he said on another occasion, '. . . is primarily concerned to increase the production of owner-occupied houses; we only build council houses where it is clear they are needed . . . My aim is to make owner-occupation a possibility for a whole group of average and below-average workers at present excluded because they can't afford the current mortgage rates . . .'[19]

However, as the drive to restrain public expenditure compels governments to make unpopular choices, it is clear that the present unlimited growth in tax reliefs will somehow have to be brought under control. Already, since 1974, tax relief for house buyers has been confined to one house at a time and to a maximum loan of £25,000. If that ceiling is left unchanged, further inflation of house prices will in time reduce its real value. But, with the median building society loan standing at only £11,770 in 1979,[20] – less than half the ceiling – that process will be slow. Relief should be given at the standard rate of income tax, instead of treating people who pay higher rates of tax more generously. But, if reductions in this subsidy are to be imposed fairly, they must be phased in gradually, and directed particularly at people in middle age with high incomes and shrinking households, rather than at young couples struggling to raise a family and buy their first homes. Hence the interest attracted by the Housing Centre's proposal, made in evidence to the Housing Policy Review, that house buyers should each be entitled to one 'ration' of tax relief extending over, say, twenty-five years and transferable from one mortgage to another as they move from one house to another. Someone who moved house to buy for a second time after, say, eight years would then get tax relief on his new mortgage, credited at the rate appropriate for the eighth year of repayment of a loan of the new amount.[21] This proposal, as the government pointed out, presents all sorts of administrative problems. But simpler versions of it could be devised. Meanwhile it shows the directions in which informed thinking is moving.

Other developments which are already taking shape will help to ensure a more predictable flow of funds for the building societies and, through them, the house-building industry. Meanwhile, in Britain as in other countries, various schemes are being devised to help people with lower incomes buy their own homes, through local authority lending and low-start mortgages for selected borrowers, 'homesteading' (which enables those capable of reconditioning dilapidated property to buy it cheaply), 'equity sharing' (which enables buyers, in effect, to continue renting half their homes while getting a foothold on the house-purchase escalator in respect of the other half), new forms of loan calling for lower interest payments on a capital sum which is increased in value each year to keep pace with the general price level, and cut-price sales of council houses to sitting tenants.

All these schemes call for some redistribution of the burden of house purchase which makes the early years easier at the cost of increasing payments in later years. The scope for progress in this direction depends heavily on the rate of inflation assumed, as Figure 13.7 made clear. Studies like Dr Bigsworth's suggest that young couples buying a house generally find the first years easier than the next few years. The most difficult period often comes when wives stop full-time work to have children, who then become steadily more expensive to maintain until they start work. It is not until some twenty years after they first started to buy a house, when the couple are about 45 years old and their children leaving home, that their residual incomes (which take account of the costs of a family) really start to rise.

The same problems of ill-controlled public expenditure, and the destructive effects of inflation, irrationally distributed subsidies and unnecessary restrictions of choice, appear in council housing but in different guises. Here too there is some measure of agreement about the directions in which solutions should be sought. All parties want to give council tenants legal security of tenure, greater freedom to sublet their houses and to improve and adapt them, and some opportunity to secure for themselves the enhanced value they create in that way. These are among the practical advantages of owner-occupation which could be extended to tenants.

Although sales of council housing to sitting tenants have been more rapid under Conservative governments, central and local, there have been many under Labour rule too. A total of 95,900 council houses were sold between 1974 and 1979, for most of which time Labour was in power at Westminster. Dispute centres around plans for indiscriminate sales at heavy discounts of up to 50 per cent – even in neighbourhoods where publicly owned and subsidized housing is scarce and will always be needed, and at a time when new building is being virtually brought to a halt.

Meanwhile, with the remaining problems of scarcity and substandard housing concentrated in a few places, and with many local authorities needing little or no new building, it is clear that, unless steps are taken to prevent it, continuing inflation will impose constantly rising costs on the minority of active builders amongst them, while conferring handsome surpluses on some of their less active neighbours. Local rent pooling, which subsidizes tenants of the most expensive new housing with the help of 'profits' reaped from those in cheaper, older housing, has long been a welcome weapon in the battle to keep building going and rents low in face of rising costs and interest rates. A national system of rent pooling, applying between authorities the same principles which already apply within authorities, should be the next stage. Many would agree that this should keep the total of housing subsidies provided by the national taxpayer unchanged, while giving extra help to areas of high need. In its evidence to the Housing Policy Review, the Housing Centre Trust argued that if the Exchequer's standard contribution to a pool of this sort was calculated as a percentage of the interest on outstanding debt which was equivalent to the standard rate of tax relief for owner-occupiers, the public would regard that as rough and ready justice between tenants and house buyers. The local authorities must retain some scope for fixing their own rent levels. But if there is to be a comprehensive national scheme for subsidizing the poorest households, as we argue in the next chapter, then there must also be national rent ceilings – annually uprated – for council rents. Otherwise, irresponsible authorities could transfer their burdens to the national taxpayer by putting all their rents up and telling their tenants to claim help from the national scheme. To preserve incentives for efficiency, the cost of management and maintenance should be excluded from the national pool and remain a local responsibility.

The case for a national pool of this sort will become more convincing as housing authorities come to recognize that they have a permanent but changing job to do which will throw fluctuating burdens upon them for the foreseeable future. Some old industrial towns where the slums have all been cleared away and population is now falling have assembled a massive stock of new council houses and can virtually close down their building programmes. But only for a while. There will come a time when houses without central heating and flats without private open space or a car park will be regarded as obsolete. Some believe they already are. These towns will then have to undertake big improvement and rebuilding programmes if their more affluent tenants are not all to move away. Meanwhile, other authorities which now have a lot of work on hand will by then have reached a quiescent phase and become net contributors to the national rent and subsidy pool. Membership of the pool will provide an insurance for each authority which protects it during periods when there are heavy demands on its resources.

We argued in Chapter 12 that as sales of council housing become increasingly commonplace, it should also become natural for local authorities to buy houses in the open market too, both second-hand from private owners and new from speculative builders. That would enable them to expand, contract and diversify their stock to ensure that it matches, in sizes, types and locations, the constantly changing needs which they have to meet. Council housing does not have to be specially commissioned or conform to distinctive styles: it should simply be the councils' current holding within a varied market of good housing, in which the different sectors are not visibly distinguishable by their ownership. Growing variety in the public sector is already to be seen in the bigger cities, where municipal authorities own housing acquired from private landlords and built by themselves to varying standards over sixty years. That will call for harder thought about policies for allocations, transfers and rent fixing. Many authorities make little attempt to reflect the relative value of the houses they offer in the prices they charge. Flats often have higher rents than houses with gardens; peripheral estates often have higher rents than similar property in more central areas; and housing in vandalized streets in which bus services are deteriorating may be no cheaper than well-maintained housing served by good public transport. Only the gross values of the houses fixed for rating purposes seem to bear any consistent relationship to the rents charged. These valuations were described by Grey and his colleagues as 'more related to a private art than a rigorous science, and ... not significantly correlated with the variables that we would normally expect to influence the popularity of estates'.[22] Several things are needed: first, a more rational pricing policy; second, adequate rent and rate rebates (or the better system of housing allowances which should succeed them); and third, a published and clearly understood points system – a second 'currency' in effect – which awards priorities to the factors to be taken into account when allocating council houses and arranging transfers between them (factors such as family size, time spent in the queue, physical disabilities, the location of close relatives, and so on). Armed with their 'points', and with any rebates or housing allowance to which they may be entitled, tenants could then choose a house on which prices would be set, both in points and in money. Carefully devised systems of this kind, which some local authorities are beginning to introduce, can give tenants greater choice and reduce the burden of allocation decisions now resting on housing managers – burdens which to the tenants may seem more like a tyranny.

We turn finally to privately rented housing. A few years ago the prospects for this apparently moribund sector of the market seemed generally agreed. But some of the things recently said by advocates of the Housing Act of 1980, which is reducing security of tenure and relaxing rent control, show that hopes for the resurgence of the private landlord are once again abroad, as they were when the last big measure of decontrol – the 1957 Rent Act – was passed. So the topic calls for more thorough discussion.

Since privately rented housing is more varied in its character, its occupiers and its owners than any other sector of the market, it is harder to generalize about it. Studies[23] of the people who own this housing show that they range from a few large, professionally managed companies to a much bigger number of small owners – mostly elderly, many of them women, and mostly poorer than their tenants – who let one or two houses only. Institutions such as the National Coal Board and the Church of England, still letting the residue of the much larger stock they once owned, a handful of sharks operating in areas of scarcity, owner-occupiers letting off parts of their homes, and people who let flats and caravans through the summer to holiday-makers in the resorts – these also play their parts in this sector of the market. Most of them fall into one of four types: **1.** a few large and middle-sized professionally managed companies, typically owning purpose-built flats, still of fairly good quality, put up before the First World War in the inner parts of big cities, and more recently in the inter-war suburbs of London and the bigger towns; **2.** a large number of predominantly elderly people who let one or two houses, mainly built before the First World War, many of which were acquired rather accidentally (by inheritance, for example, or because the owner wanted the house or shop next door and was obliged to buy the rented house with it); **3.** a smaller number of more commercially minded landlords letting rooms and 'flatlets' – often poorly adapted and ill equipped, and sometimes furnished or partly furnished – particularly in the inner parts of London and other big cities; and **4.** owner-occupiers in all kinds of property who may let off rooms or flats in their homes during the early and later years of their occupation, or let off a whole house temporarily while working abroad.

A recent report[24] shows that landlords' reactions to the levels of rent they can charge and the security of tenure they have to grant their tenants differ widely. On the whole, large corporate landlords and many smaller non-residential landlords think their rent income insufficient to keep their business going. They want higher rents, lower taxes and less security for tenants. Their share of the market is shrinking as they steadily transfer their resources into more lucrative and secure forms of investment. A change in the law which reduced security of tenure would only hasten the disappearance of this kind of landlord by making it easier for them to gain vacant possession of their property and sell it at an enhanced price to owner-occupiers or developers. That is what happened after the 1957 Rent Act, as previous studies of our own showed.[25] Meanwhile smaller landlords, many of whom let parts of the houses they live in, are less discontented with rent levels and more concerned about the type of tenant they get. They do worry, however, about security of tenure. Changes in security of tenure may encourage more owner-occupiers to let parts of their houses for income or companionship, but only if they are convinced a future government will not reverse these changes. That, however, is unlikely to halt the overall decline of the private landlord. Many owner-occupiers who are willing to let parts of their homes live in neighbourhoods where there is no great demand from tenants.

It would now only be profitable to build privately rented housing for people who cannot get a council house or buy a home of their own, or do not want to do so. That confines the market mainly to students, foreign visitors, holiday-makers, recently arrived immigrants, and people who are saving a deposit for house purchase, or serving their time on the waiting-lists for council housing. These are not very stable or profitable demands. They are probably the demands served by most landlords of the third and fourth types – the people letting furnished or unfurnished rooms and flatlets in the inner city, and owner-occupiers who let parts of their own homes, together with others such as the owners of seaside flats for holiday-makers, the people who let caravans to migrant oil workers in north-east Scotland, and so on. There has been some investment in these markets, but not much. The constant possibility that the laws about rents and security of tenure will be changed, as they have been repeatedly since 1915 (and as Labour Party spokesmen in recent debates made clear will happen again), means that the returns from such an investment have to be quickly harvested. That precludes anything more extensive than quick conversions and small-scale improvements. Much of this property, moreover, is attractive more for its location – the access it affords to central parts of London, for example – than for its value as a home. Central London is not a territory where new building is easy or cheap.

A study recently made by Michael Harloe with the help of an international team of expert consultants compared privately rented housing in the USA, France, West Germany, Denmark and the Netherlands. In all five countries the private landlord used to dominate the urban housing market. Each country has in recent years had a more buoyant economy than our own. In the USA competition from the public rented sector is negligible in scale. There and in West Germany the private landlord has been fairly heavily subsidized. All these countries imposed rent controls during and after the Second World War, but their controls have been more flexible and sooner relaxed than Britain's. None has conducted a programme of slum clearance on the British scale.

Despite these differences, which all favour private enterprise, private landlords are losing ground in all five countries, and for the same fundamental reasons as in Britain. Other systems for investing in housing are more efficient and cope much better with inflation. The private landlord's competitors are more heavily subsidized. Even when attempts are made to correct this by offering grants to landlords and their tenants, owner-occupiers and public sector tenants are quicker to take up these benefits and gain more from them. Every householder who can get into the growing sectors of the market does so, and that leaves private landlords with older, less attractive housing, serving poorer people from whose payments less profit can be made.[26]

These conclusions are still as true as they were when we included somewhat similar findings in *The Government of Housing* many years ago. But it seems necessary, yet again, to explain that relaxation of rent controls and security of tenure will do something for the minority of commercially minded landlords, but little for tenants – with the possible but potentially important exception of tenants who rent from owner-occupiers. We cannot rest content with that conclusion however. There will still be people who can neither get a council house nor buy their own home: indeed, there will be more and more of them if the current slump in building continues. If decontrol will not help them, what else should be done for them?

The way forward is the same as ever: to persuade local authorities to accept people whom they have previously excluded; to ensure that local authorities can, and do, go on building in the areas of greatest scarcity, and do not sell houses in the neighbourhoods where subsidized rented housing will always be needed; to develop housing associations and ensure that they meet real needs, giving priority to the people whom councils find it politically difficult to house (newcomers who have recently arrived from other towns, for example); and – for those who want life styles which the standard semi-detached box cannot provide – to extend the range of shelter available to include various kinds of communal housing and caring community. We say more about several of these possibilities in the next chapters.

## In Conclusion

Meanwhile we must remember that what emerge as some of the most intractable housing problems are not principally housing problems at all. Bad housing conditions are a product of poverty. If we retain a very unequal distribution of income and wealth, we shall not easily achieve a more equal distribution of housing. If we try to solve people's housing problems by placing some of the poorest people in high-cost environments – where the flats are centrally heated by the most expensive methods, where there are no shops, and buses are few and far between – we transform but do not resolve their difficulties. Over recent years, we have allowed prices to move in ways which penalize poorer families with children (the prices of food and fuel, on which they spend large proportions of their incomes, have risen faster than most). Taxation has evolved in ways which penalize the same people (reducing the real value of the threshold incomes at which families start to pay tax, and increasing the rates of tax they then pay). Social benefits have developed in ways which again penalize poorer working families with children more severely than the childless. Pensions, like tax allowances for childless people, have kept pace with inflation, but the real value of child benefits has fallen. Free school meals, educational maintenance allowances and other benefits for families with low incomes have borne the brunt of recent cuts in the social services. Thus it is not surprising if some of these people find themselves in trouble. That trouble will often include difficulties in getting a decent home and paying for it.

Those concerned with housing should neither wrestle unaided with problems which originate elsewhere, nor think that by passing the buck to those responsible for other fields of policy they can wash their hands of these dilemmas. They must constantly remind people that these are the marks of a society which, by comparison with many of its neighbours, does not greatly care for children and their families, and is more inclined than most to regard the poor as defective people, responsible for their own difficulties, rather than as victims of the society and economy in which they live.[27] These attitudes and the policies which flow from them can be changed. We shall not make much progress towards the solution of housing problems until they are.

# 14
# The Needs of the Poor[1]

## Introduction

In the previous chapter we discussed Britain's system of housing tenure and finance and advocated changes which would suit the needs of the average citizen better. In this chapter we turn to the needs of the poor and the excluded. The plight of families who may become homeless is discussed in the next chapters: here we focus on three other issues. Each is quite different, but all appear to be growing more urgent.

First we consider poorer people in all sectors of the housing market, and the problems posed by the increasingly complicated and partly ineffective arrangements made to help them pay for housing. Then we turn to elderly owner-occupiers, many of whom live in houses which badly need repair, as we showed in Chapter 11. Finally we consider homeless and rootless people without a settled way of living.

## Housing Subsidies for the Poor

We start with the biggest of these issues: the mixture of schemes devised to help people with low incomes to pay for their housing. As the last chapter showed, vast sums of money are now spent on this in confusingly different ways under arrangements originally devised for different purposes. As a result, people with similar needs get treated differently, depending on whether they are in work or out of work, and on whether they are tenants or owner-occupiers – irrelevant distinctions which should be brushed aside. Instead, we need a single, income-related housing benefit which treats equal needs equally.

The present system can be briefly summarized. The poorest households of all live on supplementary benefit: under that scheme the state meets the total housing costs of over 99 per cent of its householder claimants – about 2·3 million of them in 1979 – by bringing their incomes up to the scale rates laid down each year by parliament, plus their rent or mortgage interest and their rates. Alongside this help there are, for people slightly better off, the benefits available to about 1·9 million people under the rent rebate and allowance schemes, and to 3·1 million people under the rate rebate scheme. Although it is not strictly speaking means-tested, the option mortgage scheme which helps about 850,000 people is designed to benefit house buyers with low incomes. These overlapping arrangements create all sorts of problems and dilemmas for those people (mainly retired pensioners) who could claim either supplementary benefit, or the rebates and allowances. At the margin most people cannot tell which of these benefits, with their different means tests and different levels of entitlement, would make them better off. They have to make complicated comparisons based on information obtained from their social security office and the town hall. Even with expert advice it may be impossible to decide what would be their 'best buy' because of the constantly changing discretionary payments, fuel discounts and other benefits which may be available only to people claiming supplementary benefit.

As a result, a lot of poor householders fail to get benefits which they ought to have. By going through over a million files in 1975 and 1976, the Department of Health and Social Security (DHSS) transferred 90,000 supplementary benefit claimants to rent and rate rebates which were a better buy for them. But the DHSS believed that there were many more drawing rebates who would have been better off on supplementary benefit – but no one was telling these people about that. In total the Department estimated that about 400,000 people were in 1979 getting the 'wrong' benefit. Many others entitled to one or other of these benefits were so bewildered that they did not apply for any of them.

This state of affairs is intolerable. What Britain needs is a single housing benefit for all householders with low incomes. The Supplementary Benefits Commission called for that for years.[2] Official proposals of this sort are now afoot and may be on the statute book soon. Ideally, such a scheme would replace rate rebates, rent rebates and allowances, and the rent element of supplementary benefit. It would also extend to the owner-occupier and replace the option mortgage scheme too. It would meet 100 per cent of reasonable housing costs for all supplementary benefit claimants, and should do the same for others with similar incomes, including people in full-time work. The new benefit would then taper off as incomes rise above these levels.

There would be many advantages in such a comprehensive and unified benefit. Once it was clear that help with housing costs for poor people came from a single benefit, regardless of the source of the claimant's income, everything would be easier to understand. Research done for the Supplementary Benefits Commission suggests that many people think the complexities of the present system are devised deliberately to confuse them and obstruct them in getting what they are entitled to. It also suggests that most people would prefer to go to the town hall, rather than a social security office, for help in meeting their housing costs. If it was administered by the housing authorities, such a benefit would help to sort out these confusions and encourage more people to claim their rights.

A comprehensive housing benefit should also help to remove discouragements to work, because people with low incomes would be entitled to the same kind of help, whether they were in or out of work. At present they get more generously treated when they are on supplementary benefit, which normally meets their entire housing costs. In future, when claimants go back to work their housing benefit would continue on an unchanged basis, adjusted only to take account of their earnings. Comparisons between those in and out of work could also be made more easily and more fairly. Today people compare supplementary benefit, which includes an allowance for rent, with the workers' take-home pay, without noting the value of the rent allowances and rate rebates which the lower-paid worker gets. If rents are dealt with quite separately, the comparison will be fairer and will look fairer.

As we showed in the previous chapter, take-up rates for the present rebates and allowances remain obstinately low, particularly for private tenants. Henceforth, under a unified scheme, the man who claims supplementary benefit would automatically get his housing benefit, even if he had not known how to claim it while he was in work. Then, when he returns to work, he would be invited to continue claiming a housing benefit if his income was low enough to entitle him to do that.

Local authorities would have to deal with claims for the new benefit from those now on supplementary benefit. But they could handle that; they are already doing this job for more than twice as many people on rent and rate rebates. Meanwhile, they would find that the problem of recovering arrears of rent from defaulters on low incomes would be greatly eased. So too would the huge volume of communication which now has to take place between social security offices and local authority housing departments on individual cases about the amounts of rent and arrears, direct payments of rent, dates and amounts of rent increases, and so on. There is no doubt that a significant saving in work and public service manpower could be achieved over central and local government services together.

A scheme of this sort would pose problems which should be recognized realistically. If public expenditure on housing is not to grow, a benefit which gives the lowest-paid workers the same amount of money as people on supplementary benefit get, and which also includes the owner-occupier, must call for a transfer of resources from the better-off beneficiaries of the present rebate schemes to people in lower income groups – a transfer from the rather poor to the very poor. The only alternative would be to spend more on subsidizing housing.

The familiar problem of the poverty trap, arising from the gradual withdrawal of benefits as incomes rise, coupled with the gradual increase in income tax and national insurance contributions, might also be intensified. To keep within current expenditure limits, there would have to be a relatively sharp 'taper' in benefits, making large reductions as incomes increase. Again, this drawback could be reduced if more money were found for the scheme.

Some people – chronically unemployed or chronically sick – move in and out of work frequently. They may sometimes get the wrong amount of benefit when their incomes are interrupted, but if they seek supplementary benefit they usually get some money very quickly: about 70 per cent of claims for supplementary benefit are paid within five working days. Before a new comprehensive benefit could be introduced, the local housing authorities would have to learn to respond as quickly: otherwise people with high rents would suffer hardship or run up disastrous arrears.

Local authorities would not willingly take over payment of what now amounts to around £600 million a year in supplementary benefit unless they were assured that this expenditure would be met entirely by the central government. There might be additional administrative costs to meet too.

If a single, fairer, more comprehensible, income-related housing benefit replaced the present confusion of schemes devised to help the poor, that would pose questions about the very similar confusion of schemes invented to help poorer households meet that equally inescapable price of maintaining a home – the cost of fuel. Britain also needs a national fuel discount scheme, no longer tied to supplementary benefits and family income supplement. It would go to much the same people – about 30 per cent of households – who now draw supplementary benefits, family income supplement, or rent and rate rebates and allowances. To conserve increasingly scarce energy supplies and to pay for the steady growth now required in generating capacity, there are powerful arguments for increasing the price of fuel. That would only be tolerable, however, if ways can first be found to protect poorer households through a comprehensive fuel benefit which is not tied to the supplementary benefits scheme. The enormous profits conferred upon the fuel industries by their rising prices mean that there need be no difficulty about finding the resources for a benefit of this sort.

## The Poorer Owner-occupier

We turn to the problems of the poor, and particularly the elderly, owner-occupier. More and more people own their own homes. About half of the retired heads of households are now probably owner-occupiers, and that figure is still rising. More and more of these pensioners are very old. Few of them will be able to do their own major repairs to roofs, wiring, plumbing and paintwork. And for demographic reasons, fewer, as the years go by, will have children, nephews or grandchildren capable of helping them; for families have been growing smaller, generation by generation. So they will depend increasingly on the labour-intensive jobbing builder whose costs have risen dramatically in recent years.

The poorer pensioners were usually poorer than most when they were young. Many of those who bought houses would therefore have bought cheap ones, and possibly had to repay loans at higher rates of interest and with much less help from tax relief and the option mortgage scheme than younger and richer buyers get. If they bought houses in the sort of neighbourhood where the cheapest property stood, they were also less likely to get loans from conventional building societies. The only advantage they had – if indeed it is an advantage – was that the lenders to whom many of them turned were unlikely to impose any obligation to repair and repaint their homes regularly. But that means these houses are more likely to become dilapidated later.

In view of these developments, it is not surprising – as we showed in Chapter 11 – that more and more houses need major repairs, more of them are owner-occupied, and old age and poverty play central parts in creating that problem. The repairs grants for owner-occupied housing which may soon be available from local authorities will help some people. But they are likely to be restricted in value and total volume, and confined to particular neighbourhoods (housing action areas, perhaps) and particular types of property (pre-1919 houses, for example). Many of those who need help will thus be excluded. For home owners living on supplementary benefit, the DHSS contributes a sum of 98 pence a week, increased from time to time, for insurance and repairs. That is quite inadequate for major repairs. But major repairs are only needed occasionally. Thus to increase this sum substantially would in effect give many owner-occupiers a higher rate of weekly benefit than tenants get. The DHSS can meet the interest which has to be paid on money borrowed to meet the cost of repairs. But it is not easy for poor people to get loans for relatively small sums, and the Department is therefore prepared, in the case of exceptional needs, to make payments of a limited amount – £200 or £300 – to claimants who have no other way of financing essential repairs. For major repairs, however, the claimant has to look to a building society or his local authority. If you are old, however, and have no outstanding mortgage, building societies are not interested in you. They do not lend to that kind of borrower. In the future they should do.

There are other solutions to this problem too. Section 37 of the 1974 Local Government Act gives local authorities the power to grant loans to owner-occupiers who are unable to obtain a mortgage in the normal way. Such loans are usually maturity loans, which only call for a regular payment of interest. The principal is recovered from the value of the property when the house is sold. For borrowers living on supplementary benefit the DHSS can pay this interest. These lending powers, however, are permissive, not mandatory, and many local authorities are not using them. What is needed is a recognized and regular service of maturity loans to help poorer home owners to keep their houses in better repair. For lack of such a service, the housing authorities, and the country, will eventually be faced with a costly programme of slum clearance, far sooner than is necessary.

Maturity loans will not solve the problem everywhere. In areas like Clydeside and south Wales there are still houses which change hands for a few hundred pounds. The local authorities cannot – indeed, they legally may not – lend £3,000 on a house worth £300. In these cases the best solution may be for them to buy the house, repair it, and rent it to the tenant – if the tenant is willing.

A government which is determined to sell off publicly owned housing and promote owner-occupation at all costs has a duty to protect people who can only just afford to buy and cannot afford to do major repairs – particularly in their old age, when they cannot turn for help to anyone else. A scheme of this sort provides home owners with no more than the basic protection required to make the present government's main policies for boosting owner-occupation feasible and fair.

## People without a Settled Way of Living

We turn finally to those with the most extreme needs of all: the people who are described as 'homeless and rootless', the 'single homeless', 'without a settled way of living', or 'of no fixed abode'. None of these phrases exactly defines them. They may in fact be married, not single. And, far from having no settled 'abode' or way of life, they may have lived in the same way in the same place for many years. But they lack any secure and convenient home; they probably 'sleep rough' in the open or in derelict buildings and similar places for parts of the year; they do paid work intermittently if at all; and they have no family that cares for them if they fall ill or need help. They may wander from place to place, and they use the cheapest lodging houses, hostels and reception centres. Some of them have alcohol problems and bouts of mental illness. Many have spent periods of their lives in institutions: children's homes, prisons, mental hospitals, and the regular armed forces, for example. They congregate most heavily in the inner parts of the biggest cities and seaports. A fairly large proportion of them came originally from Ireland and Scotland – the peripheral and more poverty-stricken regions of the British Isles. There are a few women amongst them, but the great majority are men.

This description emerges from successive studies,[3] but it would be a mistake to define too precisely those to whom it applies. Many people move in and out of this group or rest upon its fringes at some stage of their lives – roving agricultural workers and builders' labourers, men and women whose marriages have broken up or whose spouses have died, and young people just out of college and not yet into regular work, for example. They are usually very poor for much of the time, but their condition is not necessarily unhappy. To label them too distinctively would be both misleading, because untrue, and destructive, because it makes it harder for them to move back into a more settled community when they are ready to do so.

The numbers involved are small, far smaller than they used to be. In 1932, in the depths of the depression, the local poor law authorities sheltered about 16,000 homeless and wandering people in their casual wards. The DHSS, whose predecessors took over in 1948 215 of these casual wards, was able to close the great majority of them. It now administers only 22 reception centres and resettlement units, sheltering about 1,800 people on an average night.[4] Salvation Army hostels, Rowton houses, night shelters, common lodging houses and other accommodation used by the homeless and rootless have also declined dramatically in numbers since pre-war days. That change has probably come about because opportunities for work have until recently been much better, social security payments and welfare services are more generous, subsidized housing and old people's homes are more plentiful, and private tenants have greater security of tenure. Many of the old hostels and lodging houses have either been demolished in redevelopment schemes, or have improved their standards and now charge higher rents to a more settled population of single working men.

But there are still homeless and rootless people about; and rising unemployment may now be adding to their numbers. The disappearance of cheap, privately rented housing, severe reductions in council building programmes, and the sale of council housing may soon make it harder for them to find anywhere to live. Already there are reports that there are more and more homeless youngsters of a sort not seen since the 1930s. Meanwhile the public, participating increasingly aggressively in planning inquiries, is directing newly discovered capacities for belligerent advocacy against homeless people and other unpopular neighbours. Voluntary bodies which try to convert houses to shelter half a dozen ex-mental-patients or ex-prisoners, central government when it tries to build resettlement units for homeless people, and local authorities when they build hostels for unattached youngsters and others, all find it harder to make progress than they used to.[5] Thus needs appear to be growing; the resources for meeting them have shrunk; and the political obstacles confronting those who try to do something about them are in many places becoming harder to surmount.

The experience of those working in this field and the research we have quoted show that various well-coordinated responses are required. The only thing which the homeless and rootless all lack is secure and decent housing. They may have other needs too. But until they are properly housed nothing can be done about the job opportunities, the medical care or the welfare services which they may also require. Since most of them stay in and around the same towns for long periods – for very few are real wanderers now – it is the local housing authorities which ought to find shelter for them. They are as entitled to their help as other local citizens. Experience in London, Leeds and Glasgow shows that men in reception centres and night shelters intended for the most deprived people of all can successfully make a home in council housing if they get an opportunity to do so. Others will want the support of a small group of fellow residents, possibly helped by a warden or visiting social worker. Even the most unsettled may in time move – individually, or collectively in small communities – towards more conventional life styles. If they are unable to support themselves with paid work, the social security benefits to which they are entitled can be administered in close collaboration with social workers or hostel wardens to ensure that special needs are met and rent is regularly paid. For some, occupation, shelter, and a meeting place offering social support will have to be provided during the day in a day centre of some sort.

It is not only the homeless and rootless who may want the comradeship and support of a group of fellow residents. Voluntary associations of various kinds, ranging from long-established cooperatives and communes to more transient groups of squatters, have shown that a lot of completely self-supporting and independent people value the opportunity of living, at least for a period of their lives, in a group which gives its members some privacy, yet shares the tasks of housekeeping and child care. Such groups can also accommodate and support more dependent and vulnerable members, provided the dependent proportion is not too large and their needs not too similar. Whatever his needs, each resident can contribute something to the rest of the group, and it helps no one if a house gets stereotyped in the neighbourhood as the hostel for some deprived category of people. (The continuing tendency of statutory and voluntary agencies, and the authorities which fund their work, to herd people into groups with similar needs can be destructive. It is rather as if these agencies had to display to the world 'their' collection of alcoholics, ex-prisoners or battered wives.)

The Supplementary Benefits Commission, which was responsible until its demise in 1980 for DHSS reception centres and for providing some grant aid for voluntary hostels meeting the same needs, had long made it clear that central government was unsuited for this business. By trying to help it tends to stigmatize vulnerable people, encouraging the public to treat them as social outcasts for whom specially quarantined services have to be provided. Their needs, said the Commission, should in future be met by 'local housing authorities and voluntary bodies working with local authority support. If social support or care is needed, that should come from local social services authorities, and if the need is for health care, this should be provided by local health authorities – as it is for everyone else.'[6] That view is now gaining ground, but a lot more will have to be done before the homeless and rootless get the help to which they are entitled.

Housing is the starting-point for everything else in this field. To provide it, in the face of what will sometimes be fierce local opposition, the planning authorities which control development – together with the planning inspectorate and the central departments to which aggrieved citizens can appeal against planners' decisions – must recognize the community's responsibilities for the homeless and rootless, and for other potentially unpopular neighbours. The Good Samaritan did not first have to get his local authority's permission to shelter and succour the man who fell among thieves. But today planning committees can block sound proposals for development on pretty spurious grounds which may be no more than a thinly disguised political decision to keep unpopular people out. In future the Minister of Housing should find ways of ensuring that local authorities have to provide adequate shelter somewhere for people without a settled way of living. (He can already bring strong pressure to bear on local authorities to ensure that sites are found for gypsies – although the outcome is not yet altogether encouraging.) If an overriding obligation to do this cannot be imposed, then procedures for planning inquiries into projects of this kind will have to be reappraised. At present, the inspectors who conduct these inquiries often have little choice but to defer to overwhelming demonstrations of public feeling, however misconceived that feeling may be. That is because they are asked to pass judgement on the wrong question: Should the unpopular project be placed *here*? (We could never build a third London airport that way, let alone a nuclear power station or military base.) Government must instead decide whether there are needs to be met which call for special provision of some sort. (Conventional housing supported by community services may be all that is required.) If there is a need for something more than that, a public local inquiry can then deal with the proper questions to be debated: Where and how (not whether) these needs should be met.

## Conclusion

We have in this chapter explored three of the many housing problems which particularly concern poor people. Despite their diversity there are some general conclusions to be drawn from the discussion.

Gone are the days when the most urgent problems afflicted large proportions of the working class. These problems now arise from the special needs and circumstances of particular groups, ranging from 'skid row' to the genteel poverty found among elderly home owners.

The solutions to these problems too can no longer be found in the traditional programmes of the Left or the Right – simply by building more council houses or more houses for sale to owner-occupiers. More sophisticated, mixed strategies are needed, which offer an escape from the confines of old administrative categories, and combine the resources of statutory services, voluntary services and private enterprise.

In all cases the solutions which we have briefly outlined would call for the imposition upon local authorities of some common responsibilities and standards of service, and hence for some restraint on their freedom to do as they wish. A comprehensive national scheme of housing subsidies for poor people would call for generally accepted conventions about minimum housing standards and maximum rent levels, particularly for public tenants; otherwise every authority would be tempted to raise rents for poor people and claim extra subsidies from central government. It would be unrealistic to press local authorities to do more for people without a settled way of living unless they can first be assured that neighbouring authorities will follow suit: otherwise every council will fear that more generous initiatives will only attract demands from far and wide. These dilemmas are not unique to housing. But it is in housing policy that solutions are now urgently needed. Once their basic obligations have been settled, however, local authorities should be given as much freedom as possible to decide how these duties should be fulfilled.

# 15
# Empty Flats[1]

## Introduction

A few years ago to describe empty council housing as a 'problem' would have seemed madness to councillors and officials who had battled for two generations with what seemed insurmountable scarcities. To add that empty flats would first appear on a large scale in big, old cities where squalor and overcrowding have been worst and the waiting-lists have been longest would have seemed still more incredible. Yet this is what is happening. And not only in Britain: all across north-western Europe, public housing authorities have surpluses which, though proportionately small, have been growing. Their first reaction has usually been to ask central governments for bigger subsidies to bring rents down; but that rarely works for long. They then have to reconsider the whole question.

To explore this problem poses fruitful questions about many of the assumptions of housing policy. We start by briefly outlining the extent and character of the phenomenon. We do not go into detail: the pattern is changing and today's figures will soon be obsolete. Next we note the effects of current trends, already traced in Chapter 8, on the economies of the big cities where surplus housing is most often found. Then we discuss the impact made by public policies in these cities, looking first at housing policies and then at other programmes. After summarizing what we have learnt thus far, we consider its implications for housing and for other fields. Finally we draw some broader conclusions about housing authorities and the kind of job they should be doing in future.

## The Present Position

At the time of the 1971 census only 3·2 per cent of the dwellings in England and Wales were empty – excluding new houses not yet occupied, but including second homes and holiday cottages. Since then this figure has risen slightly.[2] More recent official figures showed that nearly 100,000 council dwellings were empty in England in 1979, amounting to 2·2 per cent of the stock. That, by the standards of the American open market, is still quite a modest vacancy rate. Of these, 22,000 houses – less than half of one per cent – had been empty for more than a year. Council housing does not, in total, exceed the demand for it. On the contrary, the waiting-lists of people queueing for a council house are still forbiddingly long, and in some places getting longer. The occupied houses in this sector of the market are more intensively used than most. They hold more people per room than owner-occupied or privately rented housing, as we showed in Table 11.7 on page 171. Many of the houses which are now empty were acquired for conversion and improvement from private owners. Unforeseen cutbacks in council building then postponed the work, leaving them with unoccupied property on their hands. In June 1979 the Greater London Council had in its own stock a vacancy rate of 3·2 per cent, amounting to 7,402 empty dwellings. Of these, 1,420 were available for letting, under offer, temporarily reserved, or accepted and not yet occupied; 506 were occupied by squatters; 172 were awaiting a management decision; and the great majority – 5,304 – were awaiting repair, improvement, sale, etc. Meanwhile there were about 175,000 people – 24 times the number of vacant dwellings – on London's waiting-list for council houses.[3] Even in the bigger cities, where apparent surpluses are most often found, they are usually concentrated in small parts of particular estates. There are three large blocks of flats in the inner parts of Liverpool, for example, which have become virtually unlettable. The council is trying to sell them. Other blocks on the edge of the city and beyond are going the same way. Some are being demolished. Those built with a 'deck access' design are most unpopular because it is so difficult to prevent vandalism, burglary and intrusion by strangers in them. Other design faults too often add to these problems: refuse chutes get blocked; poor insulation for sound destroys privacy; poor insulation for temperature makes flats cold, damp and expensive to heat. Manchester, London and other big cities have similar but less dramatic problems. In Glasgow there are a few streets of tenements, mostly built in the 1950s, with vacancy rates of 30 to 40 per cent. Some of these blocks are being demolished as unlettable. Glasgow's worst problems are concentrated not in tower blocks – though the city has more of them than any other in Britain – but in flats of four and five storeys, and not in central areas but on peripheral estates. Yet here, as in the other cities mentioned, there are other blocks within a stone's throw of the emptying flats which are fully let and beautifully cared for, with lace curtains and potted plants behind their shining clean windows.

Even worse than the vacancies are the outward signs of decay, demoralization and public hatred for the buildings so expensively constructed a few years ago to meet urgent needs. The windows of empty flats are soon shattered; doors, fireplaces and electrical fittings are torn out; lifts are polluted and defaced; litter remains uncollected; graffiti abound; and the few shops in the neighbourhood, if they remain tenanted, are often clad with steel sheet or hardboard like the bomb-scarred streets of Belfast.

Although these conditions are very rare, and heavily concentrated in a few small neighbourhoods, unlet housing has grown rapidly in recent years. If nothing is done, it is likely to spread more widely, bringing social disorder which disturbs and frightens local residents, and imposing heavy costs for repairs and rent arrears on the housing authority and its ratepayers.

Thus, while there is no cause for panic, the problem posed by empty council housing will have to be tackled seriously and soon. That is what some of the authorities concerned are already doing: Glasgow, for example, had by the end of 1978 set up six inter-departmental teams in the most afflicted areas, staffed by community development workers from the social work services and people from housing, planning and other departments of the regional and district authorities. Their aims are to gain a better understanding of the problems and to restore the morale of residents, to draw their needs to the attention of the services concerned, and to bring greater stability to these communities. Before making any proposals for action, we must explore the reasons for these surpluses. We look first at some of the underlying trends in the development of the cities concerned.

## The Urban Economy

Britain's changing patterns of urban settlement are much like those to be seen in other advanced industrial economies. The main trends now leading to the growth and decline of cities have been traced in Chapter 8. It is the big, old ports and the old centres of heavy industry, mining, and textiles which have generally declined most rapidly. So have the county boroughs which stood, before local government reorganization, at the heart of the biggest conurbations: there, people have for most of this century been moving out faster than they were moving in. The electric railways began this massive dispersal to the suburbs before the First World War; later the motor car and the loss of jobs from these central cities took the process further. The trend began earlier in Manchester and Liverpool than elsewhere.[4]

Like most migrants, the people who leave these cities tend to consist disproportionately of younger parents and their children, and the more highly qualified workers. Those who come to them are drawn disproportionately from still younger age groups, many of whom will leave again when they start their own families. Among those who stay there are higher proportions of the disabled and the elderly, the unskilled, one-parent families and ethnic minorities – various groups of people, many of them on the fringe of the labour market or excluded altogether from the working population, who lack the incentive or the opportunity to move to the expanding industries and the leafier suburbs outside the conurbations.

There are signs that these developments exacerbate social divisions in the declining cities. Workers in the big conurbations are not, as a whole, poor. The earnings of manual workers in the metropolitan areas of the United Kingdom were, on average, slightly above those for the rest of the country. Yet, as we explained in Chapter 8, these cities show more signs of poverty than other towns do, they have higher rates of unemployment, and the differences between the rates of unemployment experienced by their most skilled and their least skilled workers are greater. All classes suffer from the decline of the inner conurbations, but it is manual workers in general and the unskilled in particular who suffer most. Table 8.4 on page 138 supported that conclusion for many of the most deprived cities in Britain.

These trends can be briefly summarized. The big old industrial cities are unequal places. The incomes of those in their working age groups are likely to be rather more unequally distributed than elsewhere. Unemployment is certainly higher and more unequally distributed, inflicting particularly severe hardship on unskilled manual workers. In comparison with the rest of the country, the inner parts of these cities also have more large families, more young workers under the age of 20 (for whom unemployment tends to be high and wages low), more one-parent families, and more black ethnic minorities[5] – all of them potentially vulnerable groups. These cities therefore have to spend more on social services if they are to meet the needs of their people as effectively as other places do. But the locally borne costs of those services rest on a tax base of local incomes and property values which are falling behind those of other cities.

We have described the economic 'climate' of the cities where empty housing is most often found. But to talk in these terms should not encourage the assumption that their decline is, like the weather, un-avoidable. Difficult though it may be to change these trends, they are the outcome of market behaviour and political decisions and are capable of being reversed.

## Housing and Other Policies

We have traced the course of housing policies since the war in previous chapters. Here we need only to recall some features of that story which have particularly affected the bigger cities. Most of them spent the first years after the war repairing bomb damage and then building houses for returning servicemen. Their programmes were tightly restricted until the early 1950s, when output was increased, partly by reducing the size and quality of the new housing they built. More generous standards were introduced in the late 1960s, when the recommendations of the Parker Morris Report were put into practice. But by then most of these cities were well into massive slum-clearance programmes which, from 1960 onwards, demolished much of their inner areas. Thousands of people were moved (or 'decanted', to use the forbidding jargon of the housing managers) from inner areas to estates farther out. Many of these estates were built hastily, to poor standards, with new forms of large-scale concrete construction which were powerfully promoted by the government but had never been used in this country before. Some were to become the slums of the future.

Housing managers now face other problems too. They are masters of a continually growing proportion of the urban map, covered by housing which is increasingly varied in location, type and age – ranging from

**15.1** *Rent and Rates for a Three-Bedroom Council House at Various Distances from the Centre of Liverpool, 1979*
(Pounds per week)

|  | Distance from centre in miles | | | | | | |
|---|---|---|---|---|---|---|---|
|  | Under 1 | 1–2 | 2–3 | 3–4 | 4–5 | 5–6 | 6 or more |
| Rent | 9·30 | 8·60 | 8·25 | 7·37 | 8·07 | 8·60 | 8·42 |
| Rates | 3·35 | 3·07 | 2·93 | 2·58 | 2·87 | 3·07 | 3·00 |
| Total | 12·65 | 11·67 | 11·18 | 9·95 | 10·94 | 11·67 | 11·42 |

**15.2** *Land Values in Some Major Cities*

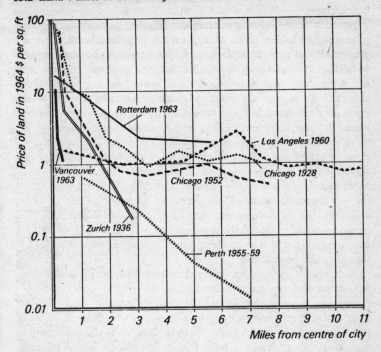

Source: Colin Clark, 'Urban Land Use Here and Abroad', *Journal of the Town Planning Institute*, No. 52, 1966. Reproduced in Alan Evans, *The Economics of Residential Location*, Macmillan, 1973, p. 61.

first-class, centrally heated units with views of the park or the river, for which private buyers would pay high prices, to bleak barracks standing in inaccessible or dreary estates, stigmatized by the reputations brought to them by residents originally drawn from the city's most notorious slums. Thanks to the financial and administrative traditions of local government, the managers are unable to let these differences in demand be reflected in the rents they charge. Thus their staff have to find some publicly defensible way of allocating lettings.

The criteria of the private landlord who often picked new tenants from the married children and friends of good tenants already on his books cannot be applied in the public sector. The formal rules, often unpublished, which have been adopted by many authorities require a good deal of interpretation in practice, and the priorities which emerge owe a lot to informal 'native law and custom' at junior levels of the bureaucracy.

People whose homes are being demolished, particularly those in good houses knocked down to widen roads or build schools, generally get first pick. If they refuse to move, major investment programmes will be held up. Housekeeping standards count for a good deal: the neat and tidy get priority over those suspected of being tight and needy. New-comers to the city and the victims of family break-down – people whose needs may be urgent, but who have spent little time on the waiting-lists – tend to come at the end of the queue. Once into council housing, the more demanding tenants seek moves and exchanges in a complicated game of snakes and ladders which carries orderly and persistent people up to the most popular estates and closer to their friends and relations. Meanwhile, poor rent-payers and less respected people are confined to the less attractive estates. There people in the prime of life are often dragged down by the numbers of children and other dependants. The environment deteriorates: the grass cannot bear the weight of running feet; windows are broken and telephone boxes vandalized more quickly than they can be repaired.

Maintenance policies sometimes reinforce these social distinctions. Manpower and expenditure allocated to the work of supervision, re-decoration and maintenance take insufficient account of the heavier wear and tear inflicted on everything in estates with large numbers of children, estates with many one-parent families, and estates designed in such massively impersonal ways that their residents can develop no sense of pride in their territory and no capacity for policing and improv-ing their own environment. Anyone who has watched a street evolve, from the stage at which nearly every family is struggling to make a home and feed and clothe young children with one income to the stage at which there are several earners in each household, knows what a big difference the resources of the community can make to the quality of the environment.

The recurring story of failures to provide new estates with adequate shopping, recreational, medical and social services, public telephones and meeting places, and reliable public transport is too familiar to be worth repeating. Government reports and circulars have often given warning about these dangers and recommended better ways of doing things. So why are such warnings disregarded? Anyone who saw the overcrowding and squalor suffered until recently by people on the wait-ing-lists in some of Britain's biggest cities must have some sympathy with elected representatives who demanded before everything else that more houses be built. To add a community centre, a bar or some shops to an estate might mean that families would have to wait longer in intolerable conditions. As a result, however, some of the people rehoused on new estates built far from urban resources of this kind have suffered severely – often at a time when they had greatest difficulty in making ends meet and could not afford cars, telephones, or long bus rides to the centre of town. Some families suffered a loss in real disposable income when rehoused, as we pointed out on page 121. That helped to give the estates on which they lived a lasting reputation for poverty.

Big city housing authorities have often been reluctant for political and administrative reasons to put a large proportion of their tenants through the means tests required by rent and rate rebate systems. Thus they tried to keep rents down, without major variations, to a level which the majority of tenants could afford. Such variations as there were reflected differences in the age and size of the dwellings, and whether they were houses or flats. These were related to valuations for rating purposes, which followed similar patterns. But the rates are little better than a crude poll tax, modified by rebates for poorer householders. They are not a means of laying financial burdens on those best able to bear them.

The general pattern of charges which resulted can be seen in Table 15.1, which shows typical rents and rates for three-bedroom council houses at various distances from the centre of Liverpool. They do not vary in any systematic way from the centre to the edge of the city. Liverpool can at least give such figures. Other cities replied to our inquiries (in a sense more revealingly) by saying, as Glasgow did, that 'distance from the city centre is not regarded as a factor in the fixing of rents, and therefore I am unable to supply these figures'.[6] In London the Greater London Council follows similar policies. Yet the rents which people are prepared to pay in order to live at more and less accessible points on the urban map vary enormously, falling sharply from the centre. Figure 15.2, which reproduces some findings about land values assembled by Alan Evans, demonstrates this. He examined many other cities besides those shown in this figure and concluded that 'only the data for Los Angeles suggest that in that city there may be no decline in land values with distance from the central business district'.[7]

If council rents are as high on the inaccessible fringes of the town as they are in the centre, there are bound to be far more people trying to get into the central areas than they can hold. Meanwhile many others will be confined unwillingly to less attractive but equally expensive neighbourhoods on the fringes. That mismatch between the patterns of price and preference is often compounded by charging higher rents for flats than for houses, despite the fact that nearly everyone prefers houses to flats. Once again the responsibility for deciding who gets what is thrown more heavily upon the shoulders of housing managers and their junior staff.

We have looked very briefly at some of the practices of 'urban management' in various branches of government. Together they tend to create what we described in Chapter 7 as discontinuities within different sectors of the urban economy, and disjunctions between these sectors. These, we suggest, are likely to restrict mobility and opportunities. Thus some people get trapped by the disjunctions in council estates from which it is difficult to gain access to the better jobs, shops, schools and other resources of their city. A few of them fail to pay the rent or disappear altogether, and may re-emerge elsewhere some day with new housing problems. Meanwhile, at the upper end of the hierarchy, some tenants encounter discontinuities which mean that they are unable to secure the better housing to which they aspire within the stock of council property because it is so uniform in structure and tenure. They may stay put; or they (and their children when they come to set up home) may move out altogether and buy homes of their own if they can afford to do that.

These disjunctions and discontinuities reinforce existing social divisions. In many occupations – in semi-skilled manual work and in the clerical and junior grades of central and local government, for example – there are people who feel compelled early in their careers either to seek promotion and a higher income, to accept the mobility required to achieve that, to buy the house which makes it easier to move on again, to postpone child bearing and rely on their wives' earnings in order to pay off the mortgage; or to stay put accumulating points on the waiting-list, seek a council house, start a family earlier, and abandon ambitions for promotion. The housing market reinforces these pressures and the social divisions they create.

Empty houses, or more often flats, emerge at the bottom of the public sector of the housing stock, which has become increasingly elaborately stratified by the allocation of tenancies and the subsequent movements of tenants who are sifted up and down the snakes and ladders of an administered market. By fixing rents and taxes for this housing at rather uniform levels which do not match the far steeper gradient of tenants' preferences, the housing authorities have gained no help from the price mechanism in distributing tenancies. They had to do the whole job themselves. Meanwhile their procedures both for letting and for maintaining houses have often made the popular estates even more popular and the unpopular even less popular. Vacancies emerge in housing for which an open-market rent might fall close to zero. Had a private land-lord built it, he would have had to reduce his rents to very low levels, or go bankrupt and sell out to someone else who would do that. Meanwhile the total demand for council housing is reduced, partly by excluding from it some of the most rapidly growing types of household, such as the young and single, or by offering them housing only in peripheral neigh-bourhoods where they cannot easily survive; and partly by physical and administrative characteristics of the public sector which drive existing tenants and their children out of it to buy homes of their own elsewhere.

These are generalizations painted with the broadest of brushes, neg-lecting many of the real dilemmas of particular cities, each of which faces a different situation. On Merseyside, for example, the decline in population, coupled with the massive building programmes completed in recent years, means that there may be a real surplus of housing – at least of some types in some areas. In London there is no general surplus, only a temporary excess supply of housing for the kinds of people whom the authorities have been prepared to house.

## Looking to the Future

Prospects for the future are not wholly depressing. We have described the small but growing surplus of council housing and the vandalism often associated with it as 'problems'. In a sense they are – and very expensive ones too. In some neighbourhoods it costs a great deal to make flats habitable again after they have been left unoccupied for a few days. But it must be a good sign that standards have risen to a point at which prospective council tenants feel able to reject some of the less attractive housing to which they have hitherto been consigned, and in this way draw public attention to unpopular estates and the conditions in which their residents live. Long waiting-lists still exist. Thus empty houses mean that many people prefer what they have to some of the council housing on offer. For some people, that is the first real choice about housing which they have ever been able to make.

Housing authorities build to meet needs, not only economically effec-tive demands. If they have surplus houses, that is partly because they have met a large proportion of the needs which they have so far been prepared to recognize. Britain still has potential but unmet demands for housing from people who do not yet form separate households. Scan-dinavian and German experience presented in Table 11.16 (page 194) shows that. Those demands, as we showed in Table 11.10 (pages 175–6), will come mainly from younger and single people for whom many housing authorities have so far made inadequate provision. Their numbers, moreover, are now rising. The increase in births which began in 1956 and continued every year till 1964 is now producing an increase in the numbers in their mid twenties in Britain as a whole (the pattern in particular towns varies). Thus if the housing authorities can successfully meet the demands of single people and young married couples, they have a growing market to serve. Between 1976 and 1986 Greater London expects a decline in population of between 3·5 and 6·2 per cent. But over the same period households are expected to increase by between 0·8 and 3·2 per cent.[8] To achieve that kind of growth in separate households, many big cities will have to redefine housing needs and extend the range of people to whom they are prepared to offer tenancies.

## Proposals for Action

So what should be done? The proposals which follow are presented, for brevity's sake, in dogmatic fashion. But each poses many practical problems. They should be read, not as instant solutions, but as signposts suggesting strategies which may be worth exploring – strategies which are in fact being tried out by housing authorities upon whose experience we have drawn in writing this chapter. Starting with action which falls largely within the housing field, these are the steps which should be considered.

The range of needs met by the local housing authorities should be extended. Indeed, it may be wiser to regard them henceforth as meeting *demands* within a framework which gives an overriding priority to certain kinds of need. Such a policy would relax the restrictions which in many authorities still prevent single people, youngsters and newcomers to the town from getting a council house.

To do that, some authorities will also have to extend the types of housing they offer by building, converting and acquiring property which would provide not only conventional unfurnished dwellings with between three and six rooms, but bedsitters, smaller flats, furnished lettings, and larger houses let as shared tenancies and hostels. In that way they can provide a greater variety of living arrangements. Authorities reluctant to use their powers to provide furnished housing may prefer to sell furniture and kitchen equipment to their tenants on hire-purchase, collecting payments along with the rent. They already have powers to do this, but rarely use them. Alternatively they can fund housing associations which operate in these ways.

If the supply of council housing and the demands which it meets are to be successfully extended, that will have to be done with some understanding of the other resources of the city to which tenants need to gain access. Universities and polytechnics are already providing furnished flats and bedsitters for their students, and those demands are by no means confined to students. As privately rented housing and landladies who let lodgings continue to dwindle, there will be growing demands for these kinds of housing which the local authorities should in future be prepared to meet. But to do that successfully, a good deal of this housing will have to be placed within reach of jobs in centrally located industries, higher education, the city's bright lights and other resources which their new tenants will want to reach. That will exclude from this treatment some of the peripheral estates on which vacancies are usually most common. Nevertheless, it may help to stem the outflow of tenants from the total stock of council housing by enlarging the range of people who are able to look for shelter to this sector of the market.

Better maintenance, prompter repairs and closer supervision will be needed in many of the more brutally vandalized estates before anyone would happily stay there. Conversions which divide and enclose the windier open spaces and longer balconies will also be needed to give residents greater privacy and a more defensible territory.

To stabilize troubled communities from which everyone wants to escape and to improve conditions there, the housing authorities should first consult local residents and confer some responsibilities and the necessary resources upon them for this purpose. That may be done through committees set up by the housing authority, or it may be worth going further and setting up cooperatives or 'community housing associations' to which some of the responsibilities and benefits of ownership can be conferred. Experience shows that residents will want money to spend on improving their housing and its surroundings. Time-consuming and patient negotiations may be needed before they will trust the authority and work with it. Before long they will also want to gain some control over the allocation of tenancies in their neighbourhood. Provided the people rehoused have a legitimate claim which the council recognizes as valid, and provided other legitimate contenders can be rehoused somewhere else before long, there are advantages in allowing people to assemble their friends and relatives around them. That is how the private landlord often operated in the past, and it can help to create a stable and happier community.

The sale of council houses will not directly affect the surplus of unlettable flats because few buyers will invest their money in this kind of property. By depriving tenants in the less popular estates of the chance of moving into the more popular ones where buyers are most likely to be found, sales may help to keep council housing fully occupied at the cost of reinforcing the segregation of the poorest people. That is a problem to be taken seriously and avoided so far as possible. But it is not a problem first created by sales, nor is it resolved by refusing to sell. The present management of public housing appears to segregate and stratify people according to social status even more sharply than the private sector of the market does.

Turning next to action which falls mainly in the fields of other departments of government, these are some of the steps to consider.

For a long while some of the most unpopular estates have lacked shops, public houses, meeting places, telephones, parks, allotments and play spaces – or at least some of these things. Since there are usually large numbers of children, one-parent families and elderly or disabled people in these neighbourhoods – all of whom have to rely heavily on local resources because they cannot afford to travel far – it is particularly important to put these things right. It is cruel, too, that communities with so little money to spend should so often be compelled to spend their pittances elsewhere, creating jobs and earnings for more fortunate people. If they are compelled to travel elsewhere for these things, then the city should at least ensure that they have good public transport services. Should other departments be unable to furnish the various services they need, the housing department may have to recognize that such areas cannot be decently inhabited and pull a lot of their houses down.

As shops, public houses, launderettes and other services are provided, as housing is repainted, parks laid out, and public services are improved, it will be important to get as many as possible of the jobs created in this way into estates which have been starved of opportunities for earning money. To bring that about, close collaboration will be needed with the employment services, whose job centres are now increasingly concentrated in city centres where they are placed to serve employers, not unemployed workers. If a shopping centre is opened in a deprived estate, it should be normal practice for the job centre to advertise for staff in that area and send its employment counsellors down to the local community centre to recruit people there.

Rents and valuations for rating purposes should be reappraised throughout public housing. If the gradient of housing costs matched the gradient of tenants' preferences more closely, with adequate rebates to protect poorer people in the more popular estates, there would be a less constant outflow of the more demanding and 'respectable' tenants from estates standing low on the ladders of esteem. While it costs far less than the market price to live in a popular estate and more than the market price to live in the streets where unlettable vacancies persist, the latter can never become stable communities. People live there not because they have chosen to, but because there is no other place they can find a home. If they get the opportunity to do so, they will move out.

How much can be done to achieve all these things will depend partly on the general health of the surrounding urban economy. Thus everything we have proposed must be related to wider policies for the old, industrial conurbations and their more depressed areas, and waits partly on the success of these policies.

## Conclusion

These proposals suggest some broader conclusions about the directions in which housing policies should evolve. Action along these lines would call for policies which are more comprehensive in three different senses: more comprehensive on the demand side (that is to say in the range of needs and demands to be met by the council), more comprehensive on the supply side (in the range of housing – owner-occupied and rented, large and small, furnished and unfurnished – required to meet these needs) and more comprehensive in the range of policies and programmes to be coordinated to this end (including those of planning, transport, employment, education, valuation, and other services).

A housing authority working in this way would have to take its tenants more closely into its confidence and confer more power and responsibility upon them. To do that will call for some changes in budgeting procedures to enable tenants' representatives to exert an influence on expenditure. It will also call for some reorganization of administrative structures which are at present designed to be controlled by, and accountable to, those at the top of the hierarchy. The householder who tries to get some action taken at the bottom of the hierarchy tends, if he goes beyond the more trivial objectives, to be defeated by a system which deprives the relatively junior people he meets of any power to initiate or coordinate action extending outside their own narrow specialisms. In future the 'organization chart' must be at least partly turned upside down, making housing managers and their staff more accountable to tenants.

Such a housing authority would also have to work with local voluntary groups such as tenants' and neighbourhood associations, housing associations and cooperatives. No longer would large, unitary bureaucracies deal with a mass of unorganized individuals. Within the administration, more power would then have to be devolved to area offices and teams working with these groups.

That prescription will make heavy demands on a service which has given its staff less formal training than any other major profession working in local government. What training they have had comes mainly on the job or in correspondence courses, and it has nothing to offer on many of the points discussed in this chapter. To make a success of the role which we envisage for them, housing authorities will have to invest more, and more imaginatively, in the training of their staff.

# 16
# Housing the Homeless

## The Moving Frontier of Social Conscience

The first local authorities to build houses in Britain were not particularly concerned about their homeless or poorest citizens. They started building in London and other big cities during the last decades of the nineteenth century, prompted by finding that they had land suitable for housing in their possession, by their determination to demolish housing which was a menace to public health, and by a general desire to set higher standards for contractors building for working-class families. In a pamphlet published in 1912, R. C. K. Ensor expressed the reformers' philosophy clearly. 'It is sometimes said reproachfully that municipal housing (except in Liverpool) has "failed" to house the very poorest. Save in very exceptional cases, it is not desirable that it should try. Its business is to provide *model* accommodation, to be an example inciting progress upwards.'[1]

But housing needs are never clearly defined for long. New ones emerge as old needs are met. Moreover, the problems to be solved by a housing service are often created by the solutions achieved by other services – by the closing of workhouses, once full of homeless elderly men, by the discharge of patients from mental hospitals and prisoners from prisons as new methods are developed for dealing with them in the community, and by the provision of assured incomes for pensioners, disabled people, unmarried mothers and deserted wives who are thus no longer compelled by poverty to live with their relatives or to seek refuge in institutions.

The range of people for whose housing the state has an obligation has been steadily extended. This frontier of the nation's collective social conscience is still moving – and not always forward. In this chapter we explore the state's present commitments and the way in which they have been enlarged by campaigns which led to the Housing (Homeless Persons) Act of 1977. That story is an interesting case-study of the evolution of housing policy and of the politics of poverty. At the end of the chapter we draw some conclusions about these wider issues.

Since medieval times the community's response to the poor and the homeless has depended on whether they were recognized as local citizens with a right to settle in the district. If they were, they could be sheltered, not under housing powers but under the Poor Laws – as happened on a massive scale. If they were not, they could be punished or ejected under the Vagrancy Acts. Elderly men, particularly the single and to a lesser extent the widowed, were those most likely to end up in workhouses administered by the poor law authorities. The census of 1911 recorded a population of 258,000 people in the poor law institutions of England and Wales. These included 5 per cent of all single women and 25 per cent of all single men aged 65 and over.[2] Thereafter the numbers living in workhouses began to fall as pensions improved, and as the numbers in hospitals, old people's homes and other residential institutions rose. The workhouses were closed after the National Assistance Act of 1948, which was designed to abolish the poor law. By then, full employment, the new free health services and more generous social security payments were enabling more and more people to maintain independent households; and more and more of their houses were built and subsidized by public authorities.

As we showed in Chapter 9, the housing authorities' first priority at the end of the Second World War was to repair bomb-damaged housing, and then to build new homes for the returning servicemen and their rapidly growing families. Young couples with children were their main customers and three-bedroom council houses their main product. A *separate* home for every *family* that *needs* one: this was their aim. As production got under way, the numbers of families housed in temporary accommodation fell. Later the authorities resumed their programmes of slum clearance set in hand during the 1930s and interrupted by the war. New roads, new schools and other projects led to further demolition and rehousing. Clauses in the legislation which had confined them since the 1920s to housing 'the working classes' had been repealed just after the war. Thus they took on wider obligations to rehouse all sorts of people. Meanwhile council tenants rehoused in earlier years were growing older and their households were dwindling in size. Many of these ageing people were still living in three-bedroom houses. By the mid 1960s most authorities were devoting a growing share of their programmes to the building of small flats and bungalows for old people, who at that time had less than their proportionate share of council housing: they now have more. In these ways the range of people whose housing needs the community felt obliged to meet was steadily extended. We concluded an earlier book optimistically by saying that 'homeless families, overcrowding and the more squalid housing conditions' were gradually coming to be regarded as 'intolerable'.[3] That was the position in the mid 1960s. A *good* home at a price they can *afford* for *everyone* who *wants* one was becoming the aim.

## The Problem of Homelessness

Nevertheless, many people's housing needs still remained unmet. Those most likely to be neglected were returning servicemen, immigrants and other mobile people who had not spent long enough in any one place to get onto the waiting-lists or to the head of the queue, unmarried mothers and fugitive wives who were expected to stay with their relatives or fend for themselves, and single and childless people who had little chance of being rehoused unless their homes were pulled down in clearance projects. Most of these found somewhere to live but some could not.

It was in London that public concern about homelessness revived in the early 1960s. The numbers of families housed by the welfare authorities in temporary accommodation, after falling from the peak figures attained just after the war, had unexpectedly begun to rise in the late fifties, slowly at first, then sharply from 1959. People still argue about the reasons for that – the relaxation of rent controls introduced by the 1957 Rent Act and the rapid growth in sales of rented housing for owner-occupation which followed; the reduction in council building for general needs; the greater confidence with which people threatened with homelessness demanded help from the local authorities: all these played a part. The London County Council set up a Committee of Inquiry into Homelessness[4] and commissioned a study of the problem by John Greve,[5] then researching at the London School of Economics and Political Science. 'Homelessness' was a Victorian word which had dropped out of general use. To most people it meant, initially, 'houselessness'. That was the condition of 'sleepers out', counted with the help of volunteers by the LCC's Welfare Department in 1963. The emergency accommodation which the council provided for homeless families was repeatedly extended in the early sixties, partly in response to genuinely increasing needs, and partly as a result of an equally genuine growth of public sensitivity to the plight of those living in conditions which were felt to be scandalous.

Before long, the term 'homeless' was extended by propagandists to include people living in every kind of bad housing. These were the years when Abel-Smith, Townsend[6] and their colleagues were redefining poverty, once regarded as a state of absolute deprivation, in more egalitarian relative terms. Henceforth, more and more people argued that anyone whose resources and living conditions excluded them from the increasingly affluent society of their fellow citizens must be regarded as being in poverty.

This new approach had important implications for housing policy. It meant that housing authorities could no longer rest content with building houses, allocating them as fairly as possible, and sending out their environmental health inspectors to impose minimum standards on the rest of the market. They would be expected to find and rehouse all whose housing conditions seemed intolerably bad. At this time most local housing departments would not have accepted any such obligation. Many authorities did not even have a housing department: the borough engineer or surveyor might see to the building of houses, the housing committee and a clerk might allocate them; and the treasurer might collect the rents. The homeless were usually the responsibility of the welfare department – a living relic of poor law practice. And outside London and the county boroughs, the welfare departments were in the counties – completely different authorities from those which were responsible for housing. Even where they were in the same authorities, the barriers between them were formidable. When John Greve's researchers sought their first interview with the London County Council's Housing Department, the opening words of the man deputed to deal with them were 'Very well, but tell me – what has homelessness to do with Housing?'

Concern soon spread to other cities, fanned by *Cathy Come Home*, a vivid television programme, and by the coverage given to the issue by the news media. But there was at this stage a great deal of confusion about the nature, extent and causes of the problems to be dealt with. Subsequent studies suggest that in provincial towns and rural districts without particularly severe housing scarcities those described as homeless had often suffered other misfortunes which deprived them of the shelter and support which most people get from their families and the communities in which they live. They were poor rent-payers, or recently released from some sort of residential care, or victims of family breakdown.[7] Many had lived in council housing, but at some stage had been evicted from it. Their plight was less a problem of housing scarcity than of housing management.

In the capital and other big cities with more severe housing problems, homelessness threatened a much wider range of people – 'ordinary, decent Londoners' as they were often called in public debate. Nevertheless, these people too tended to be in some sense marginal members of society – mobile people, men recently demobilized from the armed forces and others apt to be excluded from networks of information and support on which the long-established local citizen relies. Many of those with whom the Milner Holland Committee talked in the course of studying London's worst housing conditions came from Ireland and more distant parts of the world. The Committee also showed that the cheaper 'best buys' in the market for privately rented housing were seldom publicly advertised: these tenancies changed hands privately amongst friends and relatives. The tenancies advertised in shop windows where newcomers might see them were more expensive; those handled by estate agents were costlier still.[8]

Housing opportunities for marginal people were growing scarcer at this time. Privately rented housing was shrinking fast through transfer to owner-occupation at the upper end of the quality range and through slum clearance at the lower end. Although the numbers of people were falling and the numbers of dwellings were increasing in areas of housing pressure like London and the other inner conurbations, there was at the same time a rapid growth of small households, consisting mainly of the elderly and of young childless people. Although their incomes were often low, these people could compete successfully for living space against families with children because they could devote a larger proportion of their incomes to paying for it. Meanwhile the steadily growing numbers of married women in paid work meant that families with several children depending on one earner were increasingly disadvantaged.

Thus, although the average standards of housing were improving, more and more families with children were sharing accommodation or compelled to seek shelter in furnished flats and rooms, where they were excluded from the security of tenure conferred on unfurnished tenancies by the 1965 Rent Act.[9] There, if they could not afford to buy a house, they found themselves trapped – excluded from rehousing when unfit property was pulled down, and thus compelled to move on, often to some other borough where, as newcomers, they were again excluded from the waiting-lists. When, in desperation, they turned for help to the public services, some authorities dealt punitively with them: they separated families by sheltering mothers and children but excluding fathers; they offered them squalid housing with no privacy, and they turned the whole family out each day to tramp the streets in search of accommodation with no assurance that they would be re-admitted in the evening. Such things had often happened before. What was new was the growing public conviction that these deterrent policies were no longer tolerable.

Demonstrations by fathers separated from their wives and children at a hostel in Kent, and sit-ins by furnished tenants fighting evictions in North Kensington followed. The uproar provoked in this way brought marginal groups into conflict with public authorities. In North Kensington the local Labour Member of Parliament was one of those who opposed more generous policies. He feared, not without reason, that the generosity called for by all sorts of humane and progressive people would in practice be paid for by long-established working-class families, patiently hoping their names would come to the top of the waiting-lists. The marginality of the homeless – their exclusion from more settled communities, and the schools, political parties and other institutions which served these communities – was thus reinforced by housing policies which kept them out of council housing, on the move, and paying higher rents than other people for housing of poorer quality. These became the natural victims of rapacious landlords. As the poorer privately rented property on which they depended for shelter dwindled year by year, their plight was compared, in the Milner Holland Report, to that of rabbits in the corn, confined by the circling harvester to the dwindling shelter left in the middle of the field – ultimately to be chewed up (the Committee might have added) by the bureaucratic machine or the dogs scavenging on its flanks.

The plight of homeless families was not due only to developments in the housing market. With the growing prosperity of the late 1950s and early 1960s there came a steadily growing birth rate, rising to a peak in 1964. Families who could buy themselves a home or get one of the rapidly growing supply of council houses did well during these years. But the less affluent faced rising rents in private housing freed from control by the 1957 Rent Act, rising prices for food and other necessities as subsidies were withdrawn, and declining support from family allowances and tax allowances for the family – both of which were falling in real value at this time.

The firmest figures available about homelessness were those which recorded the numbers of families living in emergency accommodation of various kinds provided by local authorities. Their numbers were undoubtedly rising. Various studies, of which that by Greve, Page and Greve [10] was the best, made it clear that, in London at least, this was a real increase, due to changes in the economy and the housing market which we have briefly sketched. But these statistics only dealt with the kinds of people to whom the local authorities were prepared to offer emergency accommodation – mainly families with dependent children. They tended therefore to neglect single and childless people.

Meanwhile, as local authorities abandoned more deterrent policies, desperate people realized that the more humane or less hard-presssd councils would ultimately offer the homeless permanent shelter of some kind if pressed repeatedly to do so. People therefore became more willing to declare themselves homeless rather than share with friends, double up with their in-laws or allow their families to break up. That was what the less generous authorities predicted: 'You can have just as many homeless people as you are prepared to provide for' was the cynics' constant warning. Some part of the increase in homelessness – no one could say how much – was due to a growth in the supply of accommodation for the homeless, not the demand for it. That did not mean that people on the boundary lines of homelessness were well-housed opportunists manipulating the authorities to their own advantage.

Among the many people described by Glastonbury and by Greve's team who were *not* classed as 'homeless' was a man whose wife came home from hospital with a new-born baby: he sent her to live in her sister's caravan with four other people because water was pouring through a hole in the roof of their two vermin-infested rooms. His landlord gave him notice to quit when he appealed for help to the public health authority. So he handed over the key to his rooms and went to sleep in a shed at his place of work. He and his family were not accepted as homeless because they had 'voluntarily left their accommodation'.

Another couple with three children avoided this mistake by hanging on until they were legally evicted. Having nowhere to go, they divided the family and moved in temporarily with two sets of grandparents. They were refused help because they had 'made alternative arrangements'.

A confused and wandering middle-aged woman who sought shelter in south Wales said to the official who interviewed her that she had once had friends somewhere in Manchester. Although there was no reason to believe that she would find help there, a welfare officer who discovered she possessed a savings book drew out her money and spent it on a railway ticket to that city, whither she was dispatched penniless because she had 'no local connection' in south Wales.

Readers of the novel *Catch 22* will recognize the form. To get yourself accepted as homeless at this time you had to have children, determination and luck. The point persistently made by critics of this system was that it was irrelevant to debate whether its victims were 'irresponsible' or 'deprived', 'difficult tenants' or 'tenants in difficulties'. Either way, these people needed shelter, and nothing could be done about any other problems they might have unless they first had secure homes to live in. Ultimately the questions posed by pressure groups like Shelter and repeatedly taken up by the news media at this time would have to be answered. How far do the housing responsibilities of the state extend? Only to providing for reliable rent-payers with housing needs? Or to every household with potentially vulnerable members? Or to everyone who wants a separate dwelling and is prepared to pay what he can afford for it?

As alternative forms of housing dwindle, the state is expected to provide for larger and larger numbers of people. What standards of behaviour – in paying rent, caring for the property and living at peace with their neighbours – can the state properly ask of its tenants? And what can it do to enforce these standards in cities where the public sector so dominates the market that other forms of adequate and responsibly managed housing may no longer be available for people whom it evicts? Some tenants are bound to present nagging problems to housing managers. But what kind of a problem are they? A problem of poverty, delinquency, mental health, family breakdown or housing management? And which departments of central and local government should be responsible for helping them?

Whatever policies are adopted, can authorities directly accountable to local electors and ratepayers be relied on to stick to them if that means providing for people who may be unpopular in the district – people who may not be regarded as 'belonging' to the district at all? Is democratic local government a viable instrument for tackling this kind of problem? And what powers should the central government assume to ensure that local authorities do their duty, and to arbitrate between them if they dispute with each other about whose duty it is?

These were the main issues at stake.


## The Housing (Homeless Persons) Act, 1977 [11]

When the functions of the dismembered Poor Law were redistributed in 1948, the National Assistance Act of that year gave local social service authorities (now the counties of England and Wales, the metropolitan boroughs, and the regions of Scotland) a duty 'to provide . . . temporary accommodation for persons who are in urgent need thereof, being need arising in circumstances which could not reasonably have been foreseen'.[12] It also gave them power, rather than a duty, to shelter other people. The Act was designed to ensure that these authorities would provide temporary shelter in emergencies for people whose homes were burnt down or flooded out, without obliging them to rehouse people who became homeless for foreseeable reasons. Failing to pay the rent was regarded as a foreseeable cause of homelessness. The Department of Health and Social Security inherited the responsibility for overseeing the local administration of these powers.

By the early seventies the studies we have quoted by John Greve and Brian Glastonbury, official studies by the Department of the Environment (DoE) and the London County Council, the gradual accumulation of official statistics about homelessness, and the general experience of pressure groups and professionals in many quarters had together convinced reformers inside and outside the public services that more must be done to prevent homelessness. The 1948 Act provided the wrong powers (imposing a weak obligation to provide temporary shelter for small numbers, when the problem of homelessness called for strong obligations to provide permanent housing for large numbers) and these powers were in the wrong hands (resting ineffectually with the DHSS and the county social services departments instead of the DoE and the district housing authorities). Progressive local authorities were already transferring this work from social services to housing departments. A new Act was needed. But, despite general agreement among a lot of the experts, there was no political pressure in parliament for change. In central or local government, elected representatives accountable to the mass of ordinary voters were unenthusiastic about the marginal citizens who became homeless.

Then, in 1972, a late amendment to a routine Local Government Act appeared to be reducing the limited duty which local authorities had to the homeless to a discretionary power. Things seemed to be moving backwards, not forwards. Barely noticed at first, this amendment provoked five voluntary bodies and pressure groups concerned with homelessness[13] to mount a campaign to reimpose a clear duty and switch it from social services to housing authorities. Other groups joined them later: the Women's Aid movement, concerned with domestic violence, played an important part among them. The Joint Charities Group, as the whole alliance came to be called, tried to get provisions of this sort into the Local Government Act of 1974, but failed. The Conservative government then in power promised them, however, that the Secretaries of State for Social Services and the Environment would issue circulars[14] which would have the effect they sought; and Anthony Crosland, Labour's shadow spokesman for the Environment, promised that his Party would re-examine the issue if returned to power. A few weeks later came the February election of 1974 and Crosland took over as Secretary of State for the Environment in the new government. Officials and pressure groups soon formed the view, however, that the new Ministers were at best lukewarm about reform. Urged to act by the pressure groups, Crosland announced in June 1974 that there would be a wide-ranging official review of the problem. That only postponed decision. In April 1975, with no sign of the findings of this review, the pressure groups instigated a debate about homelessness, which took place in June in the House of Lords. There, sympathetic peers, mostly bishops, pressed for action. Eventually, in June 1975, the DoE published a consultation document[15] (dated April) which concluded that 'the government are not persuaded that the present is necessarily the appropriate time to introduce a major change in legislation'.

The disappointed pressure groups then set about presenting evidence derived from their own casework to the DoE to show that the circulars of 1974 were not protecting the homeless. They also worked through constituency Labour Parties and managed to get a motion calling for action to prevent homelessness passed at the Party's National Conference in 1975. They worked on MPs in all Parties and assembled a group of sympathizers, twenty-two of whom agreed to introduce private members' Bills if given the opportunity to do so. They built up support in the media too. In these ways the ground was prepared for action. But officials in the DoE, some of whom wanted a reform, still sensed no demand for legislation from MPs. This was a 'back-benchers' parliament' in which the government had no effective majority. To get their legislation through, Ministers had to wheel and deal with individual members in a fashion reminiscent of the eighteenth century. Soon the government was only surviving with the precarious support of the Liberal Party.

But DoE Ministers eventually resolved to act, and their officials began discussing the whole problem with the local authority associations – the County Councils Association, the Association of Metropolitan Authorities, the London Boroughs Association, and the Association of District Councils. From time to time they met the pressure groups whose main contribution to the debate was an unwavering demand for strong legislation, derived from deep-rooted scepticism about the local authorities' willingness to take effective action unless compelled to do so. Never were the two sets of consultations brought together. The local authority associations were bruised by the constant, ill-tempered battering they received from Shelter, and did not recognize the pressure groups' right to be consulted. In fact many authorities – particularly in London and other big cities, where most of the homeless were concentrated – dealt generously with the problem. The opposition in Labour authorities was muted by the Party's Conference resolution. It was the Conservative district authorities which were most reluctant to act. They worried and moralized constantly about the threat of being invaded by homeless 'layabouts'. These differences of opinion were not surprising. The holiday resorts, where the homeless were most feared, had in their electorates many elderly and impoverished owner-occupiers who were particularly hostile to intruders from the big cities and to any increase in the rates. The big cities were more anonymous places. Their councils had built, or recently acquired, a good deal of old housing of poor quality, let at low rents. Some of the less popular houses could be used by homeless families. Smaller district authorities had much less property of this kind. Their council houses were scarcer, and allocated in more visible ways. Councillors themselves were apt to play a larger part in the letting of these houses, and were more likely to be exposed to pressure from disappointed applicants.

The team of DoE officials working on the problem were led by a remarkable Under-Secretary – a pragmatic, friendly but purposeful reformer. They eventually persuaded most of the authorities to accept the need for a new Act. In November 1975 Crosland announced his intention of introducing a Bill the following year, and officials set about drafting one. They formed increasingly close working relations with the pressure groups, and particularly with their informally accepted leader, Nick Raynsford, then working for the Shelter Housing Aid Centre (SHAC) and later to become its Director. Raynsford and his colleagues knew exactly what was happening to people in the most stressful areas of London's housing market. He himself was a perceptive consensus builder of unquestioned integrity.

In the autumn of 1975 the pressure groups tried for a private member's Bill to be introduced by David Lane, a Conservative MP who had espoused their cause. They thought he would adopt their proposals. But his, when they appeared, were weak, and coupled in a two-part measure with provisions which would modify the Rent Acts to relax security of tenure for private tenants. His Party's principal spokesmen on housing were convinced that homelessness was an essentially temporary problem which could be resolved if the supply of rented housing could be increased. DoE officials, like the Milner Holland Committee which had made an extensive report on rented housing in London ten years earlier, believed that this was an illusion. The Conservatives relied more upon the Francis Committee. Reporting in 1971 on rented housing throughout Britain, this Committee had given a 'solemn warning' that security of tenure for furnished tenants would dry up a vital supply of housing for young people.[16] The pressure groups were dismayed and worked hard in the lobbies of the House of Commons to get what had begun as their own measure rejected. It was talked out on its second reading.

DoE officials hoped to get their Bill into the Queen's speech in November 1976, but their Ministers failed to get the Cabinet to accept it as part of the government's legislative programme. The pressure groups, hearing that the government was going to introduce tougher measures against squatters instead, leaked this news to the press and mounted a renewed campaign for action by private members. By now about forty MPs had agreed to introduce a private member's Bill if they got the chance to do so when ballots were held for them. The government promised to support a suitable private Bill.

Stephen Ross, who was one of these friendly MPs, came fourth in the ballot. That gave him a chance of getting a Bill through parliament. He was still fairly new in the House, but he was the Liberal Party spokesman on Housing. That was far more important from the pressure groups' point of view. Anxious to make sure that he did not change his mind, they got to him within thirty minutes of the announcement of the ballot results. (He was showing a party of school children round the House at the time.) Their measure was too amateurishly drafted to be of much use, but at least it looked like a Bill and Ross agreed to take it on. A surveyor and gentleman farmer with a refreshing indignation about oppressive authority, he could not be dismissed as an impractical do-gooder, or be overawed by anyone.

Ross and the pressure groups consulted DoE officials, whose Bill, they were delighted to find, was more radical than their own, and much better drafted. With the approval of their Ministers, officials were happy to hand their Bill over to him, and gave him a quick but intensive course of instruction in the whole problem, supplemented by detailed Departmental briefs. The pressure groups had secured sponsors for the Bill from all the main Parties, including the Welsh and Scottish Nationalists upon whose support the government was becoming increasingly dependent for its majority. Ross was persuaded to drop some impractical amendments he wanted to add to the Bill, but remained determined to extend it to Scotland, where Ministers and local authorities alike were determined to have none of it.

When he introduced the Bill in the House, Ross was at first given a rough time by Hugh Rossi, the principal Conservative spokesman, who had himself been a Parliamentary Under-Secretary at the DoE when its circular on homelessness – 18/74 – was issued by the previous government. This was dangerous to the measure because Rossi was the ablest and most experienced speaker in the debates on the Bill. But the two established good working relations once Ross accepted amendments sought by Rossi and the district councils. 'I persuaded Stephen Ross with the acquiescence of Department officials to import into the Bill the twin concepts of "intentional homelessness" and "district with which the applicant has the closest connection",' said Rossi.[17] These were vital departures from the absolute duty to house the homeless which the original Bill would have established. But they probably helped to make the Act which was eventually passed more widely acceptable, and hence more durable. Ernest Armstrong, Parliamentary Secretary at DoE, Robin Cook, Bruce Douglas-Mann and the late Millie Miller were helpful on the Labour side. To their more reluctant colleagues they could point out that the Bill was espoused by the Liberals without whose support the government would be compelled to call a disastrous general election. The most effective critic on the Labour benches was George Cunningham, who repeatedly pointed out that the most crucial point of all – the definition of the groups to be housed – was not prescribed in the Bill but was to be decided later in a Code of Guidance which would not be approved by parliament. Moreover, since the Code would have no legal force, it would not effectively compel the housing authorities to act. Later, at the report stage of debate on the Bill, he argued unsuccessfully that the whole measure be looked at again by a standing committee. That would have killed it, because the necessary time for further discussion could not have been found within the session.

It was vital to Ross's arguments for the Bill that he could demonstrate that there were local housing authorities, even in hard-pressed areas, which were already following the policies that all of them would be called upon to adopt if the Bill went through. Fortunately one of their housing directors – in Wellingborough – had published a paper to prove the point.[18]

Opposition came at first from small-town Conservatives. One, from Thanet, described the Bill as 'a charter for scrimshankers and scroungers'.[19] Later some of the Tribunite MPs on the Left of the Labour Party turned against the Bill because they thought too many concessions had been made to its opponents. The crucial issues concerned the criteria for selecting homeless people whose needs were to be given overriding priority; the treatment of those who appeared to have made themselves intentionally homeless and those who had no local connections in the area; the ways in which all these categories were to be defined; rights of appeal; and rights to information about reasons for refusal of housing. The pact between the Liberal and Labour Parties eventually helped the measure through. David Steel, the Liberal leader, made its passage one of the terms of the pact, and the Prime Minister himself insisted that it be extended to cover Scotland as well as England and Wales. But the willingness of leading Conservatives to support the Bill was vital too, because it removed the threat of serious opposition in the Lords. That would have killed the Bill because the government's legislative timetable was too precarious to allow a lot more debate on the measure.

The concessions made to secure an acceptable Bill meant that home-less single people were excluded from those to be given priority for housing, and there were no rights of appeal. Some members of the pressure groups' alliance – in Shelter and Women's Aid, for example – doubted whether the measure was worth having, and the unity of the movement was threatened. They had to content themselves with the hope that this reform would lead some day to something more far-reaching. The alliance held up, thanks largely to the mutual confidence forged between Raynsford and the Under-Secretary who took the lead within the DoE. Both, with their colleagues, were constantly advising MPs and meeting with interested parties inside and outside parliament.

The Act, which received royal assent in July 1977, was brought into force in England and Wales at the end of the year and in Scotland three months later. It gives housing authorities a duty to prevent homelessness or to secure rehousing (not necessarily in council property) for people in various priority groups, provided these people do not have a closer connection with some other area and have not made themselves inten-tionally homeless. For those who are homeless or in danger of becoming so but are not within the priority groups, the housing authority must offer 'advice and appropriate assistance'. Those in priority groups but without the necessary local connections must be put in touch with the authorities which should help them, and be offered temporary shelter meanwhile if they need it. Those becoming intentionally homeless must also be offered advice and assistance, and temporary accommodation if they need it.

Such Acts will achieve little by themselves. Everything depends on the ways in which the new obligations are handled. That, in a political and economic climate which has become increasingly ungenerous towards the poor and the excluded, will call for careful monitoring of individual authorities and their dealings with individual cases, firm leadership from the central departments, legal action by voluntary groups to secure enforce-ment in cases selected to establish the right precedents, and constant publicity. The central departments have done their best to play their parts in achieving these things, in consultation with local authorities and the pressure groups. The carefully prepared Code of Guidance, issued jointly by the DoE, the DHSS and the Welsh Office, lays down policies for coping with all the main problems which have provoked so much contention in recent years. It amounts to a public assertion of moral principles, as important in its field as comparable statements about race relations and equality of opportunity between the sexes. 'A person is homeless . . . if he has no accommodation which he can occupy together with any other person who normally resides with him as a member of his family . . .' People 'who are separated for no other reason than that they have no accommodation in which they can live together' are 'homeless'. So are those who have accommodation but 'cannot secure entry to it' (owing to illegal evictions for instance), those who 'would be likely to be met with violence or threats of violence likely to be carried out by someone else' if they tried to return to their homes (battered wives for instance), and those who have a caravan or house-boat but 'no place where [they are] entitled . . . to put it . . . and live in it'. 'Authorities should not treat as intentionally homeless those who have been driven to leave their accommodation because conditions had degenerated to a point when they could not . . . reasonably be expected to remain – perhaps because of overcrowding or lack of basic amenities or severe emotional stress.' Even if 'families have become homeless in- tentionally . . . children should not be received into care simply on grounds of the parents' homelessness . . .' Steps must be taken to ensure that 'such people are not left without shelter'. The authorities must do their best to 'protect the personal property' of those whom they have a duty to shelter, temporarily or permanently. 'Permanent accommoda- tion should be secured as soon as possible for those with "priority need" – broadly those with dependent children, victims of fire, flood and other emergencies, and people who are specially vulnerable on ac- count of youth, old age, physical or mental illness or disability.' 'Home- less people should not be obliged to spend a certain period in interim accommodation as a matter of policy.'[20] The guidance given to Scottish local authorities was at first much flimsier and less forthright, but they too now have a similar Code.[21]

These phrases stake out the advancing boundaries of the res- ponsibilities imposed upon the state by the community's growing com- passion for the homeless. Encouraged by pressure for action on indivi- dual cases and by a systematic monitoring of events in publications like Shelter's magazine, *Roof*, the DoE and the local authorities have made a lot of progress. None of the disasters predicted by opponents of the Act have occurred, although the numbers accepted and sheltered as homeless rose at once – in England from 32,800 in 1977 to 53,000 in 1978,[22] and further still since then. But shortage of housing has meant that growing numbers of London families have been placed temporarily in bed-and-breakfast accommodation. Some authorities have dragged their feet, particularly in interpreting the provisions of the Act which deal with those classed as 'intentionally homeless'. In general the help provided has been more of the same – more for the pregnant women, the lone parents and the elderly who were already provided for, not for new priority groups. The single homeless have gained little from the measure.

More serious setbacks may follow in future from the drastic cuts in the expenditure and building programmes of local housing authorities imposed by the new Conservative government after the 1979 election. These are bound in time to make life harder for potentially homeless people. Opposition to the Act itself seems to be changing in form. Councillor Frank Bushell, chairman of an Oxfordshire district council, and previously chairman of the Housing and Environmental Health Committee of the Association of District Councils, who describes himself as 'a Conservative on the Left of the Party', was one of the principal spokesmen opposing the measure when it went through parliament. He then feared the effects it would have on those who had spent years on the waiting-lists, but says that the Act has not proved as damaging as he and others in his Association feared, and there are few demands now for repeal in that quarter. Pressure for repeal now comes more often from inner London boroughs and parts of outer London. This is where housing scarcities remain most severe.

## Unfinished Business

This will not be the final Act on homeless families. There will in time be pressure for something more. The Act says nothing about people coming from abroad, and this has already proved to be a serious omission. Too many social service authorities have handed over their responsibilities for the homeless to housing authorities and washed their hands of the whole problem. Something may have to be done to keep them more constructively involved. Housing authorities too often assume that once they have provided the homeless with a house of some sort their task is over. Poor management and ill-considered allocation policies have created stigmatized 'sink' estates to which 'difficult tenants' are banished. There they suffer, and create, further problems of the sort which we discussed in the previous chapter. As so often when dealing with people who lack political 'clout', parliament has provided no appeals procedure, other than the cumbrous procedures of the ordinary courts, to enable the homeless to determine what rights they have. If appeals procedures can be set up to settle disputes between local authorities about their responsibilities for the homeless, as they have been, then something similar can be done for homeless people themselves.

Even if this legislation is made as effective as possible, important groups still remain outside its scope. Homeless and rootless people without any settled way of living are often excluded because they find temporary refuge in hostels and shelters run by local authorities or voluntary bodies and in the reception centres run by the DHSS, and are not therefore regarded as homeless. Even those who are recognized to be homeless will not be in the priority groups whom the authorities are obliged to house unless they are sick, disabled or particularly vulnerable in some way. We said more in Chapter 14 about these people and the action which should be taken to help them.

Gypsies and travelling people constitute an extreme example of a marginal group who are apt to be excluded from conventional housing and even from any legitimate parking place – both by their own way of life and by the operations of public services designed to help the rest of the population. With more comprehensive regulation of land uses, better protection of the environment and more efficient policing of the highways, it has grown harder for gypsies to find legitimate camp sites.

Policies towards the homeless and rootless and towards gypsies are passing through phases made familiar by the story told in this chapter. There has been some useful research in both fields.[23] There are officials and a few elected members of central and local government who have long been advocating action on behalf of both groups, and a good deal has already been done for them by progressive local authorities. Pressure groups working in this field, such as the Campaign for the Homeless and Rootless, the Gypsy Council and the National Council for Civil Liberties, have so far been more divided and have wielded less influence than those which helped to secure the Housing (Homeless Persons) Act; but they are not insignificant. There has already been legislation on behalf of gypsies in the Caravan Sites Act of 1968. With somewhat hesitant pressure from the central government, this Act has obliged local authorities to provide sites for gypsy families. But, like the Housing (Homeless Persons) Act, it can be used to protect the authorities as well as the people it purports to help. Once they have provided the minimum number of sites required of them, local authorities gain stronger powers to expel travellers who exceed these numbers. Everything depends in practice on the humanity and vigour with which this measure is implemented. Meanwhile, attempts to provide for gypsies, like attempts to provide for the homeless and rootless, have often been blocked by the hostility of the rest of the community. Marginal groups perceived as deviant are always apt to suffer from the tyranny of the majority.

## Conclusions

What conclusions can be drawn from this chapter? Anyone who wants to know what should be done about homelessness will find plenty of good advice readily available in the Code of Guidance and in official and independent reports which we have quoted. The more intractable problems which remain are not administrative or technical but political.

The people whose needs we have discussed in this chapter range from battered wives to unattached teenagers, from ex-servicemen and their families trying to find a way back into normal civilian life to travelling people who have no intention of settling anywhere and only want temporary resting places for their caravans, and from Bangladeshi families – hard-working and highly disciplined but wholly unfamiliar with British social services and the English language – to ageing, enuretic alcoholics for whom each day spent outside a prison or mental hospital may be a considerable achievement. They have nothing in common except their need for secure and adequate shelter – or, for travellers, a caravan site – at a price which they can afford to pay. They may have other needs too – legal advice and social security payments for battered wives, English language classes for Bangladeshis, and social support and medical care for men who have been sleeping rough, for example. But nothing can be done about these needs until the people concerned are housed. Indeed, other needs may arise largely from the difficulties they have experienced in finding decent housing. No policy can succeed unless it starts from this basic assumption, as the government's Code of Guidance makes clear.

What kinds of shelter the homeless may need, and with what support from other services, will be as varied as the infinite variety of people involved. Battered wives and their children may need to recover their own homes and be protected from molestation. Bangladeshis may only need an opportunity to buy a house of their own. Homeless and rootless men may need the social support they can gain in a small, well-managed house, with opportunities to move gradually back towards more settled life styles. An authority which can only offer standard council houses, coupled with a scarce supply of somewhat institutional 'Part III accommodation',[24] will be unable to meet these needs.

Thus an effective programme to prevent homelessness and to help the homeless find their way back into secure housing calls for imaginative housing management and an experienced housing advisory service, supported by all the services the housing authority can bring to bear – for mortgage lending, improvement grants, public health inspection and rent regulation, as well as the provision of council housing. Authorities which only dump the homeless in decaying short-life housing or in the least popular council estates will find they have transposed the problem of homelessness into more expensive problems of high turnover, vandalism, unpaid rents and fuel bills, and general demoralization in increasingly unlettable housing. Meanwhile the housing departments cannot resolve all these problems unaided: they need the help of other services, statutory and voluntary – the social services departments, the social security and health services and housing associations in particular. That collaboration calls for more than efficient administration. No matter how wisely drafted the circulars and how carefully planned the coordinating case conferences, to accept responsibility for the homeless is an essentially moral and political step which has to be taken on a national scale. It is unrealistic in a matter of this kind to expect one authority to go far ahead of its neighbours.

The story told in this chapter shows the main phases through which important extensions of public responsibility frequently proceed. First, studies of the problem must be made and widely reported, not only to assemble reliable information but – equally important – to formulate the questions and establish what they are about. To revive the word 'homelessness' and get it into popular usage again was itself a major step, helping to convey a standpoint about the issues at stake. These studies must attract the interest of the communications media and their specialist correspondents who can convey to a wider public that these are significant issues which well-informed people should know something about. The media played important parts throughout this story.

Mobilizing and bringing together innovative people inside and outside government is the next essential step – people with humane concerns, a capacity for getting things done, and up-to-date, practical knowledge of the problems derived from daily work on cases. The progressive outsiders and the progressive insiders often appear to be in conflict, but each in reality depends upon the other to achieve any progress. By themselves the mere administrator, the mere propagandist or the mere case worker, no matter how talented, cannot bring about change.

Through their campaigns and conferences, their publications and their informal contacts with people in many walks of life, the pressure groups play important parts in creating – and sometimes destroying – these innovative networks.

The politicians and the movements to which they are accountable also have irreplaceable roles in the story. Innovations in policy virtually never start with them, but they cannot proceed far without them. The most important person in a Ministry is the Minister, and his capacity for convincing other Ministers and gaining their support in Cabinet is the most important thing about him. Local government plays a vital part in the story too. Changes calling for national legislation are usually based on proven local experiments, begun years earlier and often carried out with scant support from central government, or even in face of central opposition. Ultimately action has to be taken by central government to ensure that the laggard authorities follow in the footsteps of the pioneers. In the same way Anglesey, Leicestershire and the London County Council played crucial parts in the reorganization of secondary education by showing, in the 1950s, how it could be done.

Changing the law to create new powers and duties will achieve nothing by itself – the history of race relations and women's rights makes that clear. New laws provide no more than an opportunity for creating a more sustained impetus: they are a notice of intent and a legitimation for action. If they are not followed by a laboriously persistent and effective programme to monitor what happens, interpret policies, disseminate experience, press reluctant authorities to act, and later to amend and improve the law, then nothing much will happen. During this implementation phase of reform, researchers, independent voluntary bodies, administrators, politicians and journalists again have important parts to play.

We have told this story from a national viewpoint. Equally patient and determined work will be needed at local levels. When the people to be served are potentially unpopular neighbours, local authorities are always tempted to call upon central government to assume the burden. That may transform the problem, but rarely solves it. As public concern about the homeless grew increasingly strident in the early 1960s, the London County Council succeeded in handing over its enormous and appalling old reception centre for homeless men in Camberwell to the Supplementary Benefits Commission. Although the Commission made some improvement in the standards of care provided there, they were in many ways less well equipped to help people without a settled way of living to secure normal housing and support themselves, or to surmount public hostility towards them. The Commission, until it was disbanded in 1980, had for a long time been trying to close the Camberwell centre and extricate itself from housing responsibilities for which it was ill suited.[25] The job of the central government is to establish a national consensus about what needs to be done about such problems, to formulate in consultation with local authorities the standards of service to be provided and the range of people entitled to it, to monitor and advise about the action taken, to keep all concerned up to the mark, and to ensure that people who cannot earn their own living get social security benefits which enable them to pay a fair rent for whatever housing they occupy. Within that framework, it is local government which must work out how to handle housing problems and do the job required.

# 17
## Conclusion[1]

Housing and rents have often provided the set-piece battles of British politics. As we conclude this book, in the autumn of 1980, council building has been halted and a new Act, which gives private landlords greater freedom to raise rents and get rid of their tenants, has just come into force. Thus the old controversies should all be blazing. Yet there are few signs of public concern. Why? Do the British no longer care about housing?

If housing conditions are allowed to deteriorate far, the government will again be compelled to play a more active part, as it was in the 1960s. But the battle lines of housing politics, staked out two generations ago, are dissolving, and new policies will be needed to tackle the new problems now coming into view. In this final chapter we draw some general conclusions about the priorities for housing policy.

It was just after the First World War that British governments committed themselves – hesitantly at first, and then with growing conviction – to one of the great national objectives of the century: getting working-class people into houses of a standard hitherto attained only by the middle class. These new houses provided separate bedrooms and living rooms, a bathroom, hot and cold running water, an indoor lavatory and a garden. It is easy to forget what big steps forward these were. Octavia Hill, the great housing reformer of pre-war days, had built tenements, and said, 'If you have water on every floor, that is quite sufficient for working people. It is no hardship to have to carry a pail of water along a flat surface . . . the same thing applies to the drains . . .'[2] You can still see the imprint of the new standards in every English town where denser stone-clad streets and pavements built before the war give way to the semi-detached houses and their front gardens which have dominated the scene since the 1920s. (Scotland's continuing tradition of tenement building produces a different landscape; but indoors the change in standards is just as dramatic.)

The movement for better housing was passionately espoused. People devoted their lives to it. Their task was enormous, but their cause was simple. It was the cause of the whole working class. The instruments of this campaign were fairly simple too: they were the local housing authorities, supported by subsidies from the central government and the rates. In time these authorities became powerful, vertically organized bureaucracies, pressing on with their work without much concern for other needs or for the departments concerned with town planning, transport, social services and other branches of government.

The movement was interrupted by the Second World War. After the war, the whole array of British social policies was overhauled with the help of major public inquiries: Beveridge on social security, Curtis on child care, Rushcliffe on legal aid, and a host of other committees on town planning, the health services and other matters. But policy-makers in housing simply re-enacted, on a bigger scale with more public funds, the campaigns of the inter-war years. Their aims and instruments were unchanged. The last comprehensive public reappraisal of housing policy in Britain was – and still is – that conducted by the Royal Commission on the Housing of the Working Classes, which reported in 1885.

Meanwhile the reformers' ideology was shaped and hardened by a contrasting approach which made equal sense to Conservatives. To the programmes of those who sought to meet needs and achieve social justice through the public sector, Conservatives responded with policies designed to meet demands and extend freedom of choice through the private sector of the market. In no country were the politics of housing so contentious. (Although the French have had Conservative governments with scarcely a break since the war, they never doubted the need for an active and heavily subsidized public sector. And although the Swedes have had Labour governments for even longer, they were prepared to use the contribution of private landlords and gave them a good deal of help from the state.)

Nevertheless, although policies swung more drunkenly back and forth in Britain, successive governments made reasonably good progress between them down the road to better housing. Although Britain is now one of the poorest countries in western Europe, she has completed a bigger slum-clearance programme and a bigger subsidized house-improvement programme than any other country in the world, and her housing standards are among the best.

But things are now changing. On each side old battle cries are becoming increasingly irrelevant to new problems. Mass shortages are over. Only a minority of the housing authorities still have a lot of building to do. Yet subsidies for council housing have grown massively over the years. They are unnecessarily generous for many authorities, but insufficient for the few with big building programmes ahead. Uniform policies will no longer do, for the problems to be solved are increasingly varied and they could be tackled in many different ways.

More than half of British houses are now owner-occupied. Tax reliefs for house buyers have grown even more rapidly than subsidies on council housing, and far more regressively – conferring their biggest benefits on richer people who need them least. They have helped to bring about a major redistribution of assets, conferring wealth on people in the middle and upper ranges of affluence and dividing them more sharply from tenants. Inheritance of house property tends to reinforce these distinctions in succeeding generations. The spread of home ownership also means that future house-building programmes will have to be based increasingly on economic forecasts of demand, and demand itself will be shaped partly by government policies for interest rates and taxation. Social forecasts based on demographic trends will no longer be the main basis for planning housing policy.

Like all the mature industrial economies, Britain is finding that her housing problems are becoming qualitative rather than quantitative. New strategies have steadily evolved. Priority switched first from new building to replacement; then from replacement to improvement; and then from improvement aimed at the houses (with scant regard for their surroundings, or the people living in them) to an extending concern for the whole environment, and for the people involved. Dissatisfied now with programmes confined to housing and the physical environment, we are turning to the wider aims of regenerating local economies, raising incomes, and tackling at source the poverty which always underlies poor housing conditions. But we are still very uncertain how to solve these increasingly difficult problems. The maintenance of owner-occupied houses – more and more of which belong to old people with low incomes – also poses increasingly urgent problems. As council tenants are given more responsibility for maintaining their housing and as this housing grows older, similar problems will demand increasing attention in the public sector too. Now that the community has assumed, through government, so much responsibility for grant-aiding improvements to older housing, is it also entitled to impose higher standards of maintenance upon householders? These major questions of civic duty and civil liberty (touched on, too briefly, in the Denington Report[3]) have yet to be resolved. Higher standards can be imposed only if the poor are helped to meet their share of the resulting costs.

Meanwhile, despite all the progress we have made, there are still people at the bottom of the housing market for whom no one takes any effective responsibility: homeless single people without a settled way of living, for example, who are not protected by the Housing (Homeless Persons) Act. The needs of such groups may be extreme, but their numbers are small. The problems to be solved in helping them are essentially political. That is one reason why so much of the steam has gone out of the housing movement. It is no longer the mass of working people who suffer the worst hardships; it is a wide variety of unorganized and less popular minorities.

So what should Britain's housing policies now be? Their aim is clear. It is no longer enough to provide a separate home for every family that needs one (as governments used to say). We are trying to provide a good home for everyone who wants one, at a price they can afford. But how? Every government will have to rely mainly on the existing stock of housing and the flows of subsidies already associated with it, for we only add to this stock at a rate of about 1 per cent a year.

The first concern of anyone engaged in housing must be with jobs and opportunities for earning money; and next with child benefits, pensions and other provisions of the social security and fiscal systems which redistribute money. Rising numbers out of work, coupled with cuts in the real value of child benefits and insurance benefits, must now be producing growing poverty which will make it harder for many people to meet their rent or mortgage payments. Most housing problems are really problems of unemployment, poverty and inequality.

But 'housers' cannot sit back and wait for those who manage the economy and the social security system to solve their problems for them. There is a great deal they could do to make more effective use of the resources already devoted to housing. Exchequer subsidies for council housing, frozen at no more than their present real value, should be concentrated on the authorities which need them most. As other authorities stop building, much of the 'profit' which inflation enables them to make on their housing revenue accounts should go into the national pool of subsidies for the public sector. That would be their insurance against the day when they will have to start building, buying or improving houses once again. Even if they need no more publicly owned housing in future, all of them will eventually have to modernize or replace their own ageing property.

Meanwhile, tax reliefs for house buyers should be placed on a footing that is more comparable with subsidies for council housing, and perceived therefore as fairer. More important still, they should give most help to those who need it most. It was the failure of the last Labour government to grasp this nettle which led their rivals to offer council tenants more help in buying their own homes. Once it was clear that public support for house buyers was not to be put on an equal footing with the support given to tenants, the more affluent tenants were bound to want to join the more privileged of these two clubs.

Extra subsidies for the poorest householders should be considered separately. Again, without increasing present expenditure, the government could make much better use of the funds it already deploys through rent and rate rebates, rent allowances, the supplementary benefit scheme, and the option mortgage scheme – each operating in confusingly different ways which produce low rates of take-up and unnecessarily heavy administrative costs.

As important as these financial and administrative priorities is the political priority of getting the community to recognize that homelessness is a scandal as intolerable as untreated illness or children for whom there is no place in a school. Everyone entitled to live and work in this country should be entitled to housing provided on terms which do not isolate them from the rest of the community or make scapegoats of them.

Provided these objectives are clear, local housing authorities should be given as much freedom as possible to work towards them in ways of their own choosing. Some will want to lend money to house buyers, to help people convert and improve their own homes, or to work through housing associations. Others will want to rely more heavily on the public sector. All will have to help the poorer private tenants to pay their rents. As for their own housing, they should buy and sell in the market to ensure that they have at their command a stock which is capable of meeting the changing demands that will be made on it. For most authorities there is no reason to go on building their own distinctive estates. Henceforth, if they need more houses of particular kinds or in particular neighbourhoods, they should go out and buy them. Likewise, if they need fewer units of particular kinds, they should sell.

The housing authority of the future will have a complex mixture of roles for which the old slogans will be a poor guide. In all these roles they will have to work more closely with people in the neighbourhoods where they operate, and respond where they can to their demands.

Housing committees and their staff have until now been public builders and landlords working in a cause which has successfully transformed large areas of the nation's life. But the boundaries which once distinguished public housing management from urban planning, from the regeneration of local economies and from community development are breaking down. 'Housers' will have to move into all these fields, and acquire some of the outlook and skills of those who work in them. High on the agenda, therefore, of this most under-trained of the big public services must come a major programme of professional education.

# Appendix

**Clusters of Towns discussed in Chapter 8.**

*See map on page 127.*

**Group I**
*Cluster 1   London*
  Cambridge
 *London

**Group II**
*Cluster 2*
*Regional Service Centres*
  Reading
 *Wallasey
 *Exeter
 *Plymouth
 *Bristol
  Cheltenham
 *Portsmouth
 *Southampton
  Tynemouth
 *Oxford
 *Bath
 *Brighton
 *York
 *Cardiff
  Aberdeen
 *Edinburgh

*Cluster 3    Resorts*
  Torbay
 *Southend

 *The populations living within the constituency boundaries which define the
towns used in this analysis and the local authority boundaries differ by less than
five per cent.

*Bournemouth
 Christchurch and Lymington
 Thanet
*Blackpool
*Southport
*Hastings
 Hove
 Worthing

*Cluster 4    Residential Suburbs*
   Cheadle
   Hazelgrove
   Crosby
   Chertsey and
      Walton-on-Thames
   Epsom and Ewell
   Esher
   Reigate
   Spelthorne
   Solihull
   Sutton Coldfield

*Cluster 5*
*New Industrial Suburbs*
   Runcorn
   Altrincham and Sale
   Poole
   Fareham
   Watford
   Gillingham
   Middleton and Prestwich
   Newcastle under Lyme
   Halesowen and Stourbridge
   Worcester
   Pudsey
   Monmouth

**Group III**
*Cluster 6    New Towns*
   Wokingham
   Harlow

Basildon
Havant and Waterloo
Hemel Hempstead
Hertford and Stevenage
Welwyn and Hatfield
Aldridge and Brownhills
Horsham and Crawley
East Kilbride

**Group IV**
*Cluster 7*
*Welsh Mining Towns*
Aberdare
*Merthyr Tydfil
Rhondda

*Cluster 8   Engineering Towns*
*Stockport
*Carlisle
Chesterfield
*Derby
Blaydon
*Darlington
Barrow in Furness
Eccles
*Lincoln
*Norwich
Northampton
Wallsend
*Ipswich
Brighouse
Doncaster
*Sheffield
Wakefield
*Swansea
*Newport

*Cluster 9   Textile Towns*
Accrington
Ashton under Lyne
Blackburn

*Bolton
*Burnley
  Bury and Radcliffe
  Nelson and Colne
  Oldham
  Preston
*Rochdale
  Rossendale
*Leicester
  Bradford
  Halifax
  Huddersfield
  Keighley

*Cluster 10*
*Growing Manufacturing Towns*
  *Luton
  Eton and Slough
  Bebington and Ellesmere Port
  Thurrock
*Gloucester
  Gosport
  Peterborough
  Rochester and Chatham
  Ormskirk
  Stretford
*Grimsby
*Coventry
  Swindon
  Teesside


**Group V**
*Cluster 11   Heavy*
*Engineering and Coal Towns*
  Chester le Street
  Easington
*Hartlepool
  Jarrow
  Farnworth
  Ince

Leigh
*St Helens
*Wigan
Blyth
*Dudley
*Stoke on Trent
*Walsall
*West Bromwich
*Wolverhampton
Nuneaton
Warley
Barnsley
Natley and Morley
Dewsbury
Pontefract and Castleford
*Rotherham

*Cluster 12*
*Inner Conurbations*
Birkenhead
Gateshead
*South Shields
*Sunderland
Bootle
*Liverpool
Manchester
*Salford
*Warrington
Newcastle upon Tyne
*Nottingham
*Birmingham
*Hull
*Leeds

*Cluster 13   Central Scotland*
*Dundee
Coatbridge and Airdrie
Motherwell
*Glasgow
Greenock and Port Glasgow
Paisley

# Further Reading

We have referred to publications in notes throughout this book. They provide the best guide for readers who want to explore particular questions in greater depth. Readers who want to assemble a small shelf of books about housing will find these particularly useful.

Department of the Environment, *Housing Policy: A Consultative Document*, Cmnd 6851, HMSO, 1977; and *Technical Volumes*.

Ministry of Housing and Local Government, *Council Housing: Purposes, Procedures and Priorities*, HMSO, 1969.

Scottish Development Department, *Assessing Housing Needs: A Manual of Guidance*, HMSO, 1977.

United Nations Economic Commission for Europe, *Major Trends in Housing Policy in ECE Countries*, United Nations, 1980.

Martin Boddy, *The Building Societies*, Macmillan, 1980.

Larry S. Bourne, *The Geography of Housing*, Edward Arnold, 1981.

John Burnett, *A Social History of Housing, 1815–1970*, David and Charles, 1978.

Gordon Cameron (ed.), *The Future of the British Conurbations*, Longman, 1980.

J. B. Cullingworth, *Essays on Housing Policy: The British Scene*, Allen and Unwin, 1979.

J. B. Cullingworth, *Problems of an Urban Society*, Allen and Unwin, 1973.

Roger H. Duclaud-Williams, *The Politics of Housing in Britain and France*, Heinemann, 1978.

Patrick Dunleavy, *The Politics of Mass Housing in Britain, 1945–1975: A Study of Corporate Power and Professional Influence in the Welfare State*, Clarendon Press, 1981.

Michael Harloe, Ruth Issacharoff and Richard Minns, *The Organization of Housing: Public and Private Enterprise in London*, Heinemann, 1974.

N. Hepworth, A. Gray and J. Odling-Smee, *Housing Costs, Rents and Subsidies* (2nd edn), Chartered Institute of Public Finance and Accountancy (1 Buckingham Place, London, SW1E 6HS), 1981.

John R. Lambert, Chris Paris and Bob Blackaby, *Housing Policy and the State: Allocation, Access and Control*, Macmillan, 1978.

Stewart Lansley, *Housing and Public Policy*, Croom Helm, 1979.

Duncan Maclennan, *Housing Economics: An Applied Approach*, Longman, 1982.

Stephen Merrett, *State Housing in Britain*, Routledge and Kegan Paul, 1979.

Alan Murie, Pat Niner and Christopher Watson, *Housing Policy and the Housing System*, Allen and Unwin, 1976.

Adela Adam Nevitt, *Housing, Taxation, and Subsidies: A Study of Housing in the United Kingdom*, Nelson, 1966.

John Rex and Robert Moore, *Race, Community, and Conflict: A Study of Sparkbrook*, Oxford University Press, 1976.

Ray Robinson, *Housing Economics and Public Policy*, Macmillan, 1979.

Hugh Stretton, *Housing and Government*, 1974 Boyer Lectures, Australian Broadcasting Commission (GPO Box 487, Sydney, NSW, 2001).

Hugh Stretton, *Urban Planning in Rich and Poor Countries*, Oxford University Press, 1978.

The most useful official statistics about housing which appear regularly are in *Housing and Construction Statistics*, published quarterly and in an annual publication with the same title by the Department of the Environment. The section about housing which appears each year in *Social Trends*, published by the Central Statistical Office, is also very useful. All these can be obtained from the Stationery Office and government bookshops.

Information about other European countries can be found in the United Nations' *Annual Bulletin of Housing and Building Statistics*, available from the UN in Geneva, New York, and through government bookshops.

The most useful journals are:

*Roof*, published six times a year by Shelter, 157 Waterloo Road, London, SE1 8UU.

*The Housing Review*, published monthly by the Housing Centre Trust, 33 Alfred Place, London, WC1E 7JU.

# Notes

## Part I: Problems and Policies

### Chapter 1: Housing Problems and Policies

1. D. V. Donnison, *The Government of Housing*, Penguin, 1967.
2. Peter Townsend, *Poverty in the United Kingdom*, Penguin, 1979, Ch. 4.

### Chapter 2: Demands and Needs

1. UN Economic Commission for Europe, *The Financing of Housing in Europe*, United Nations, 1958, pp. 40–41.
2. Building Research Station, *International Comparisons of the Cost of House Building*, October 1962, Note No. C918.
3. UN Economic Commission for Europe, *Economic Survey of Europe in 1974. Part II*, United Nations, 1975.
4. UN, *Economic Survey of Europe in 1977. Part II*, 1979.
5. Central Statistical Office, *Social Trends, 10*, HMSO, 1980, Table 5.1.
6. UN, *Economic Survey of Europe in 1974. Part II*, p. 2.
7. 1971 census.
8. Peter Townsend, *Poverty in the United Kingdom*, Penguin, 1979, p. 286.
9. UN, *Economic Survey of Europe in 1974. Part II*, p. 45.
10. Clive Thornton, Chief General Manager, Abbey National Building Society, at SHAC Conference on Home Ownership in the 1980s.
11. UN, *Economic Survey of Europe in 1977. Part II*, pp. 135–6.
12. See, for example, S. Castles and G. Kosack, *Immigrant Workers and Class Structure in Western Europe*, Institute of Race Relations, Oxford University Press, 1973; and Minority Rights Group, *Western Europe's Migrant Workers*, MRG Report No. 28, 1976.
13. See, for example, Ivo Baucic, 'Some Economic Consequences of Yugoslav External Migrations', in L. A. Kosinski, *Demographic Developments in Eastern Europe*, Praeger, 1977.
14. UN, *Economic Survey of Europe in 1977. Part II*, p. 239.
15. UN, *Economic Survey of Europe in 1974. Part II*, p. 22.

### Chapter 3: The Supply of Housing

1. Conference of European Statisticians, *European Programme of Current Housing Statistics*, Statistical Standards and Studies No. 7, United Nations, 1966.
2. Valerie A. Karn, *Housing Standards and Costs: A Comparison of British*

*Standards and Costs with Those in the USA, Canada, and Europe*, Centre for Urban and Regional Studies, University of Birmingham, 1973, p. 9.

3. See, for example, Hugh Stretton, *Urban Planning in Rich and Poor Countries*, Oxford University Press, 1978, p. 57; and J. I. Gershuny and R. E. Pahl, 'Work outside Employment: Some Preliminary Speculations', *New Universities Quarterly*, Vol. 34, No. 1, Winter 1979/80.
4. Kevin Lynch (ed.), *Growing Up in Cities*, UNESCO and MIT Press, 1977.
5. Peter Wedge and Hilary Prosser, *Born to Fail?*, Arrow, 1973.
6. Hugh Stretton makes the point vividly in *Housing and Government*, 1974 Boyer Lectures, Australian Broadcasting Commission.

## Chapter 4: First Interventions in the Housing Market

1. Ian McAllister *et al.*, *United Kingdom Rankings*, Studies in Public Policy No. 44, Centre for the Study of Public Policy, University of Strathclyde, 1979.
2. OECD Economic Surveys, *Turkey, August 1976*, OECD, 1976.
3. UN Economic Commission for Europe, *Annual Bulletin of Housing and Building Statistics*, United Nations, 1967 and 1976, Table 4.
4. Bruce Headey, *Housing Policy in the Developed Economy: The United Kingdom, Sweden, and the United States*, Croom Helm, 1978.

## Chapter 5: Towards a Comprehensive Commitment

1. UN Economic Commission for Europe, *Study in Housing Policy in ECE Countries*, United Nations, 1980, p. 54.
2. ibid., p. 47.

## Chapter 6: Housing in Eastern Europe

1. Frederick Engels, *The Housing Question*, Lawrence and Wishart, 1963, pp. 32, 13, 21, and 98.
2. Timothy Sosnovy, *The Housing Problem in the Soviet Union*, Research Programme on the USSR, New York, 1954.
3. Quoted in Alfred J. Dimaio, Jr, *Soviet Urban Housing: Problems and Policies*, Praeger, 1974.
4. UN Economic Commission for Europe, *Annual Bulletin of Housing and Building Statistics*, United Nations, 1978.
5. See Alfred J. Dimaio, Jr, op. cit., p. 79, for a diagram of how the adult Muscovite spends his or her time at home.
6. UN Economic Commission for Europe, *Major Trends in Housing Policy in ECE Countries*, United Nations, 1980, p. 67.
7. A. Giertz, 'Housing Policy in Poland: Its Social and Economic Problems', in United Nations, *Management, Maintenance and Modernization of Housing* (ST/EEC/HOU/28).

8. Ivan Szelenyi, 'Urban Sociology and Community Studies in Eastern Europe: Reflections and Comparisons with American Approaches', *Comparative Urban Research*, Vol. IV, Nos. 2,3/1977.

9. György Konrad and Ivan Szelenyi, 'Social Conflicts of Under-Urbanization', in Michael Harloe (ed.), *Captive Cities*, Wiley, 1977.

10. UN, *Major Trends in Housing Policy in EEC Countries*, 1980, p. 29.

11. For further reading on housing in Eastern Europe, see Michael Ball and Michael Harloe, *Housing Policy in a Socialist Country: the Case of Poland*, Centre for Environmental Studies, London, 1974; A. J. Dimaio, Jr, op. cit.; R. A. French and F. Ian Hamilton (eds.), *The Socialist City*, Wiley, 1979; Tibor Gaspar, 'Housing in Hungary', in J. S. Fuerst (ed.), *Public Housing in Europe and America*, Croom Helm, 1974; Vic George and Nick Manning, *Socialism, Social Welfare and the Soviet Union*, Routledge and Kegan Paul, 1980, Ch. 5; Hugh Stretton, *Urban Planning in Rich and Poor Countries*, Oxford University Press, 1978, Ch. 12; and Ivan Szelenyi, 'Housing System and Social Structure', *Sociological Review Monograph 17*, University of Keele, 1972.

## Part II: Housing in Britain

### *Chapter 7: Housing in an Urban Context*

1. For reviews of the literature on urban analysis, see Alan Evans, *The Economics of Residential Location*, Macmillan, 1973; R. J. Johnston, *Urban Residential Patterns*, Bell, 1971; B. T. Robson, *Urban Analysis*, Cambridge University Press, 1969; and D. W. G. Timms, *The Urban Mosaic*, Cambridge University Press, 1971.

2. Emrys Jones, *A Social Geography of Belfast*, University Microfilms Ltd, 1965; and Frederick W. Boal *et al. The Spatial Distribution of Some Social Problems in the Belfast Urban Area*, N. Ireland Community Relations Commission, 1974.

3. B. T. Robson, *Urban Analysis*, Cambridge University Press, 1969.

4. Department of the Environment, *Inner Area Studies: Birmingham*, HMSO, 1978.

5. R. M. Pritchard, *Intra-Urban Migration in Leicester, 1860–1965*, D. Phil. Thesis, Cambridge University, 1972.

6. For example, Charles Booth, *Life and Labour of the People in London*, Macmillan, 1902, and selections from it in Albert Fried and Richard M. Elman (eds.), *Charles Booth's London*, Penguin, 1971; Ruth Glass (ed.), *London: Aspects of Change*, MacGibbon and Kee, 1964; Michael Young and Peter Willmott, *The Symmetrical Family: A Study of Work and Leisure in the London Region*, Routledge and Kegan Paul, 1973; John Shepherd, John Westerway and Trevor Lee, *A Social Atlas of London*, Oxford University

Press, 1974; and Department of the Environment, *Inner London: Policies for Dispersal and Balance*, Final Report of the Lambeth Inner Area Study, HMSO, 1979.

7. James Simmie, *Power, Property and Corporatism: The Political Sociology of Planning*, Macmillan, 1981; and Peter Saunders, *Urban Politics: A Sociological Interpretation*, Hutchinson, 1979, Part 2.

8. Michael Harloe, Ruth Issacharoff and Richard Minns, *The Organization of Housing*, Heinemann, 1974.

9. Hugh Stretton, *Ideas for Australian Cities*, Georgian House, 1970.

10. Gordon Cameron (ed.), *The Future of the British Conurbations*, Longman, 1980, Ch. 3; and Alan Evans and David Eversley (eds.), *The Inner City*, Heinemann, 1980.

11. Alan Evans, *The Economics of Residential Location*, Macmillan, 1973.

12. ibid.

13. Frederick W. Boal, 'Social Space in the Belfast Urban Area', *Irish Geographical Studies*, 1970; and 'Territoriality and Class: A Study of Two Residential Areas in Belfast', *Irish Geography*, Vol. VI, No. 3, 1971.

14. I. Henderson and A. Whalley (eds.), *Personal Mobility and Transport Policy*, Political and Economic Planning, 1973; Kevin Lynch (ed.), *Growing Up in Cities*, MIT Press and UNESCO, 1977; Colin Ward, *The Child in the City*, Architectural Press, 1978; and Harriet Wilson and G. W. Herbert, *Parents and Children in the Inner City*, Routledge and Kegan Paul, 1978.

15. Peter Wedge and Hilary Prosser, *Born to Fail?*, Arrow, 1973.

16. Nicholas Deakin and Clare Ungerson, *Leaving London*, Heinemann, 1977.

17. Tim Mason, *Inner City Housing and Urban Renewal Policy*, Centre for Environmental Studies, Series No. 23, 1977.

18. Michael Harloe, Ruth Issacharoff and Richard Minns, op. cit.; and Nicholas Deakin and Clare Ungerson, op. cit.

19. Alan Evans, op. cit.

20. op.cit.

21. Michael J. Bannon, *The Development and Organization of Office Activities in Central Dublin*, Ph. D. thesis, Trinity College, Dublin, 1972.

22. Hirschel Kasper, *Measuring the Labour Market Costs of Housing Dislocation*, Discussion Paper No. 4, Urban and Regional Studies Discussion Papers, University of Glasgow, 1971.

23. I. S. Holtermann, *Census Indicators of Urban Deprivation: Great Britain*, Department of the Environment, Working Note No. 6, 1975.

## Chapter 8: Different Kinds of Towns

1. Peter Hall and Marion Clawson, *Planning and Urban Growth: An Anglo-American Comparison*, John Hopkins University Press, 1973. C. A. Moser and Wolf Scott, *British Towns*, Oliver and Boyd, 1961.

2. Oliver P. Williams, *Metropolitan Political Analysis*, Free Press and Collier-Macmillan, 1971, Ch. 2.

3. David Donnison with Paul Soto, *The Good City: A Study of Urban Development and Policy in Britain*, Heinemann, 1980, Chs. 6 and 7.
4. This cluster is described as Engineering II in Donnison and Soto, op. cit., where it is discussed in more detail in Chapter 10.
5. Department of the Environment, *English House Condition Survey, 1976*, HMSO, Part I, p. 4.
6. The evidence for these assertions appears in Donnison and Soto, op. cit., Chs. 8–11.
7. For an account of Swindon's history, see Michael Harloe, *Swindon: A Town in Transition*, Heinemann, 1975.
8. ibid.

## Chapter 9: Housing Policy: The Issues Formulated

1. See, for example, Marian Bowley, *Housing and the State 1919–44*, Allen and Unwin, 1945; *Report of the [Milner Holland] Committee on Housing in Greater London*, Cmnd 2605, HMSO, Appendix I; and R. H. Duclaud-Williams, *The Politics of Housing in Britain and France*, Heinemann, 1978.
2. *The Government's Expenditure Plans 1980–81 to 1983–84*, Cmnd 7841, HMSO, p. 179.
3. Department of the Environment, *Housing and Construction Statistics*, HMSO.
4. *Report of the Expert Committee on Compensation and Betterment*, Cmd 6386, HMSO, 1942.
5. J. B. Cullingworth, *Environmental Planning. Volume I: Reconstruction and Land Use Planning 1939–1947*, HMSO, 1975, pp. 244–8.
6. Cmnd 8996, HMSO, 1953.
7. F. S. W. Craig, *British General Election Manifestoes, 1918–1966*, Political Reference Publications, 1970.
8. *1951 Census: Housing Report*, HMSO, pp. cxxviii and cxxix.
9. Joint Committee on Labour Problems After the War, *A Million New Houses after the War*, 1917.
10. *Papers of the Royal Commission on Population. Report of the Economics Committee*, Vol. III, HMSO, 1950.
11. *Housing in Greater London*, Cmnd 2605, HMSO, 1965.

## Chapter 10: New Times, New Policies

1. D. V. Donnison, *The Government of Housing*, Penguin, 1967, p. 248.
2. Central Housing Advisory Committee, *Homes for Today and Tomorrow*, HMSO, 1961.
3. *The Future of Development Plans*, HMSO, 1965.
4. *People and Planning*, HMSO, 1968.
5. Central Housing Advisory Committee, *Our Older Homes: A Call for Action*, HMSO, 1966; and Scottish Housing Advisory Committee, *Scotland's Older Houses*, HMSO, 1967.

6. Cmnd 2838, 1965.

7. D. V. Donnison, op. cit., pp. 375 and 384.

8. John Burrows, 'Vacant Urban Land: A Continuing Crisis', *Planner*, Vol. 64, No. 1, January 1978.

9. Richard Crossman, *The Diaries of a Cabinet Minister. Volume I*, Hamish Hamilton, 1975; cf. pp. 124 and 125.

10. R. M. Kirwan and D. B. Martin, *The Economics of Urban Residential Renewal and Improvement*, Centre for Environmental Studies, 1972.

11. Chris Paris and Bob Blackaby, *Not Much Improvement*, Heinemann, 1979; see particularly Ch. 2.

12. *Report of the [Redcliffe-Maud] Royal Commission on Local Government in England, 1966–1969*, Cmnd 4040, HMSO, 1969.

13. Department of the Environment, *Housing Policy. A Consultative Document*, HMSO, 1977.

14. D. V. Donnison, op. cit., p. 385.

15. *Hansard*, Vol. 976, No. 95, 15 January 1980, Col. 1472.

## Chapter 11: Progress and Prospects

1. A dwelling is a building or part of one which forms a separate and self-contained unit designed to be occupied by a single family.

2. Households are either one person living alone, or a group of people (who may or may not be related) living at the same address and keeping house in common. Since the 1971 census, the definition of a dwelling has become slightly clearer. It is a 'household space', or a collection of 'household spaces', which one or more households inhabit. For a full definition, see *Census 1971: General Explanatory Notes*, HMSO, pp. 6–7.

3. Department of the Environment, *Housing Policy*, Technical Volume, Part I, HMSO, 1977, p. 56.

4. Department of the Environment, *English House Condition Survey, 1976. Part I*, HMSO, p. 8.

5. ibid, p. 11.

6. The definition and measurement of sharing always presents problems, but Table 11.11, which shows that households consisting of two or more families have declined, provides some more reliable evidence.

7. Department of the Environment, *National Dwelling and Housing Survey*, HMSO, 1979, p. 18.

8. Office of Population Censuses and Surveys, *General Household Survey, 1978*, HMSO, 1980.

9. D. V. Donnison, *The Government of Housing*, Penguin, 1967, p. 203.

10. Central Housing Advisory Committee, *Council Housing: Purposes, Procedures, and Priorities* (Cullingworth Report), HMSO, 1969; and A. Murie, P. Niner and C. Watson, *Housing Policy and the Housing System*, Allen and Unwin, 1976.

11. Department of the Environment, *Housing and Construction Statistics*.

12. pp. 200–204.

13. Building Societies Association, *Studies in Building Society Activity, 1974–1979*, BSA, 1980, p. 89.

14. Department of the Environment, *Housing and Construction Statistics*, No. 31, HMSO, p. 75.

15. The figures are for England and Wales, 1977 (Central Statistical Office, *Social Trends, 10*, HMSO, p. 204).

16. The figures are for Great Britain, 1976 (Department of the Environment, *Housing Policy*, Technical Volume, Part I, p. 134).

17. D. V. Donnison, op. cit., p. 202.

18. Department of the Environment, *Housing Policy*, Technical Volume, Part I, pp. 95 and 98.

19. ibid., p. 70.

20. Department of the Environment, *Housing and Construction Statistics*, derived from Family Expenditure Survey. Strictly speaking, these figures are means of the individual percentage ratios for different income groups. The average payments would in all cases be slightly lower as percentages of average incomes.

21. Charles Booth, *Life and Labour of the People in London*, Macmillan, 1902. B. Seebohm Rowntree, *Poverty: A Study of Town Life*, Macmillan, 1901.

22. Figure supplied by Department of the Environment.

23. Department of the Environment, *Housing Policy*, Technical Volume, Part III, p. 40.

24. Central Statistical Office, *Social Trends*, 1979, Table 5.2.

25. Department of the Environment, *English House Condition Survey, 1976*, Housing Survey Reports 10 and 11, HMSO, 1978 and 1979.

26. As defined in Part II of the 1957 and 1969 Housing Acts.

27. A fixed bath or shower in a bathroom, a WC with entrance inside the dwelling, a wash hand basin, hot and cold water at three points (bath, basin and kitchen sink), and a kitchen sink.

28. Eight of the more important jobs in a longer list of potentially needed repairs; see *English House Condition Survey, 1976*, p. 29.

29. ibid., Part 2, p. 39.

30. ibid., para. 7.19, p. 24.

31. See Tables 8.2 and 8.3.

32. Central Statistical Office, *Social Trends, 10*, p. 48.

33. ibid., p. 206.

34. *Building Construction: Report of a Committee Appointed to Consider Questions of Building Construction in Connection with the Provision of Dwellings for the Working Classes*, Cd 9191, 1918.

35. Central Housing Advisory Committee, *Homes for Today and Tomorrow*, HMSO, 1961.

36. Malcolm Wicks, *Old and Cold: Hypothermia and Social Policy*, Heinemann, 1978, Ch. 6.

37. Central Statistical Office, *Social Trends, 10*, p. 106.

38. ibid., p. 198.
39. In England. Department of the Environment, *Housing and Construction Statistics*, Tables XX to XXVI.
40. Pat Niner, *Local Authority Housing Policy and Practice*, Centre for Urban and Regional Studies, University of Birmingham, 1975. Department of the Environment, *Housing and Construction Statistics*, No. 30, Table XXXIX.
41. Cynthia Cockburn, *The Local State*, Pluto Press, 1977.
42. Jan O'Malley, *The Politics of Community Action*, Spokesman Books, 1977.
43. Shelter Neighbourhood Action Project, *Another Chance for Cities*, SNAP, 1972.
44. C. G. Pickvance (ed.), *Urban Sociology: Critical Essays*, Tavistock, 1976.
45. Department of the Environment, *Housing Policy*, Technical Volume, Part I, p. 144.
46. Central Statistical Office, *Social Trends, 10*, pp. 95 and 99.

## *Chapter 12: Agenda for the Future*

1. Department of the Environment, *Housing Policy*, Technical Volume, Part I, HMSO, 1977, p. 38, and *Housing and Construction Statistics*, HMSO.
2. *Report of the Committee on Housing in Greater London*, Cmnd 2605, 1965.
3. Adela Nevitt, *Housing, Taxation and Subsidies*, Nelson, 1966.
4. Michael Harloe, 'Decline and Fall of Private Renting', *Centre for Environmental Studies Review*, No. 9, May 1980; and 'Current Trends in Housing Policy – Some European Comparisons', *Royal Society of Health Journal*, No. 6, 1980, p. 207.
5. Peter Townsend, *Poverty in the United Kingdom*, Penguin, 1979, p. 892.
6. Building Research Establishment, *Housing Association Tenants*, The Housing Corporation, 1979.
7. Department of the Environment, *Housing and Construction Statistics*, Table 16.
8. Building Research Establishment, op. cit., p. 17.
9. Michael Harloe, Ruth Issacharoff and Richard Minns, *The Organization of Housing: Public and Private Enterprise in London*, Heinemann, 1974, Ch. 3.
10. *Essays on Housing Policy: The British Scene*, Allen and Unwin, 1977, p. 130.
11. Department of the Environment, *Housing Policy*, Technical Volume, Part III, Review of Foreign Housing Policies, Ch. 11.
12. Department of the Environment, Circular 14/75.
13. Jim Kemeny, 'Selling Out in Australia', *Roof*, September 1979.
14. Albert Rose, *Canadian Housing Policies*, Butterworth, 1980.

## **Part III: Agenda for Action**

## *Chapter 13: Housing Tenure and Finance*

1. Central Statistical Office, *National Income and Expenditure*, HMSO, 1979, Tables 7.1 and 9.4.

2. Department of the Environment, *Housing Policy*, Technical Volume, Part II, HMSO, 1977, p. 60.
3. Adela Nevitt, *Housing, Taxation and Subsidies*, Nelson, 1966.
4. Martin Boddy, *The Building Societies*, Macmillan, 1980, p. 5.
5. Department of the Environment, *Housing Policy*, Technical Volume, Part II, p. 57.
6. Martin Boddy, op. cit., p. 134.
7. For the inter-war history of council housing, see Marian Bowley, *Housing and the State*, Allen and Unwin, 1945, and Stephen Merrett, *State Housing in Britain*, Routledge and Kegan Paul, 1979.
8. Department of the Environment, *Housing and Construction Statistics*, HMSO.
9. Supplementary Benefits Commission, *Annual Report 1979*, Cmnd 8033, HMSO, 1980, para. 4.2.
10. Peter Townsend, *Poverty in the United Kingdom*, Penguin, 1979, p. 892.
11. ibid.
12. Royal Commission on the Distribution of Income and Wealth, *Third Report on the Standing Reference*, Cmnd 6999, HMSO, 1977.
13. Royal Commission on the Distribution of Income and Wealth, *Fourth Report on the Standing Reference*, Cmnd 7595, HMSO, 1979, para. 6.30.
14. Department of the Environment, *Housing Policy*, Technical Volume, Part I, p. 100.
15. See, for example, Adela Nevitt, *Housing, Taxation and Subsidies*, Nelson, 1966; *Housing Policy*, Technical Volume, Part II, HMSO, 1977; Peter Townsend, *Poverty in the United Kingdom*, Penguin, 1979, pp. 505–514; and Kerrie Bigsworth, *Public Sector Housing and the Distribution of Income: The Impact of Housing Policies on the Income Distribution of Public Sector Households in Great Britain, 1952–77*, Ph.D. thesis, University of Cambridge, 1981.
16. Kerrie Bigsworth, op. cit.
17. This summary owes a good deal to Bernard Kilroy and the Housing Centre Trust. See, for example, Bernard Kilroy, *Housing Finance – Organic Reform?*, Labour Economic Finance and Taxation Association (72 Albert St, London NW1 7NR), 1978; and Housing Centre Trust, *Housing Finance Review: Evidence to the Secretary of State for the Environment*, HCT, November 1975.
18. A. Grey, N. P. Hepworth and J. Odling-Smee, *Housing Rents, Costs and Subsidies*, Chartered Institute of Public Finance and Accountancy, 1978, p.3.
19. Richard Crossman, *The Diaries of a Cabinet Minister. Volume I*, Hamish Hamilton, 1975, pp. 383 and 325.
20. Department of the Environment, *Housing and Construction Statistics*, Table VIII.
21. Bernard Kilroy, op. cit.
22. A. Grey, N. P. Hepworth and J. Odling-Smee, op. cit.
23. John Greve, *Private Landlords in England*, Bell, 1965; *Report of the [Milner Holland] Committee on Housing in Greater London*, Cmnd 2605, 1965, pp.

147–161; *Report of the [Francis] Committee on the Rent Acts*, Cmnd 4609, 1971; and Bobbie Paley, *Attitudes to Letting in 1976*, OPCS, HMSO, 1978.

24. Bobbie Paley, op. cit.
25. D. V. Donnison *et al.*, Essays on Housing, Codicote Press, 1964.
26. Michael Harloe, *Private Rented Housing in Europe and the USA*, Centre for Environmental Studies, May 1979, Draft Report.
27. Commission of the European Communities, *Final Report from the Commission to the Council on the First Programme of Pilot Schemes and Studies to Combat Poverty*, 1981, p. 55.

## Chapter 14: The Needs of the Poor

1. Earlier drafts of much of this chapter were discussed at the Annual Conference of Shelter in 1978 and at three meetings convened by the Housing Centre Trust the following year. We are grateful to both of them for their help.
2. See Supplementary Benefits Commission, *Annual Reports*, 1975–9, Cmnd 6615, 6910, 7392, 7725, 8033, HMSO, 1976–80.
3. For example: National Assistance Board, *Homeless Single Persons*, HMSO, 1966; David Tidmarsh, Suzanne Wood and John Wing, *Research at Camberwell Reception Centre* (unpublished), Institute of Psychiatry, 1972; J. Stewart, *Of No Fixed Abode*, Manchester University Press, 1975; and Madeline Drake and Tony Biebuyck, *Policy and Provision for the Single Homeless*, Personal Social Services Council, 1977.
4. Supplementary Benefits Commission, *Annual Report 1976*, Cmnd 6910, HMSO, 1977.
5. Supplementary Benefits Commission, *Annual Report 1978*, Cmnd 7725, HMSO, 1979, para. 17.8.
6. Supplementary Benefits Commission, *Annual Report 1979*, Cmnd 8033, HMSO, 1980, para. 10.25.

## Chapter 15: Empty Flats

1. Earlier versions of this chapter were discussed at a seminar convened by the Housing Centre Trust and published in *New Society*.
2. Department of the Environment, *Housing Policy*, Technical Volume, Part I, HMSO, 1977, p. 74.
3. Letter from the Controller of Housing.
4. J. Douglas McCallum, 'Statistical Trends of the British Conurbations', in Gordon Cameron (ed.), *The Future of the British Conurbations*, Longman, 1980.
5. David Donnison with Paul Soto, *The Good City*, Heinemann, 1980, p. 135.
6. Letter from the Deputy Director of Housing.
7. Alan Evans, *The Economics of Residential Location*, Macmillan, 1973, p. 60.
8. Greater London Council, *London's Housing Needs*, GLC Housing Strategy Office, July 1979.

*Chapter 16: Housing the Homeless*

1. R. C. K. Ensor, *Healthy Homes for All,* National Committee for the Prevention of Destitution, 1912, p. 18.
2. D. V. Donnison and Clare Ungerson, 'Trends in Residential Care, 1911–61', *Social and Economic Administration*, Vol. 2, April 1968, pp. 75–91.
3. D. V. Donnison, *The Government of Housing*, Penguin, 1967, p. 385.
4. London County Council, *Report of Research Team to the Committee of Inquiry into Homelessness*, General Purposes Committee Report (No. 3), July 1962.
5. John Greve, *London's Homeless*, Codicote Press, 1964.
6. For a more recent review of the evidence and a statement of the relative approach to poverty, see Peter Townsend, *Poverty in the United Kingdom*, Penguin, 1979.
7. Bryan Glastonbury, *Homeless Near a Thousand Homes*, Allen and Unwin, 1971, Ch. 3.
8. *Report of the [Milner Holland] Committee on Housing in Greater London*, Cmnd 2065, HMSO, 1965, pp. 290–91.
9. D. V. Donnison *et al.*, *Essays on Housing*, Codicote Press, 1964, p. 24.
10. *Homelessness in London*, Scottish Academic Press, 1971.
11. This section is derived from interviews and correspondence with most of the main people involved in the events described. It draws heavily on *A Case Study* by Nick Raynsford, to whom we are particularly indebted (papers drawn from a series of seminars on campaigning and lobbying, published in 1978 by the Directory of Social Change).
12. S.21.1.6.
13. The Shelter Housing Aid Centre, Shelter, the Campaign for the Homeless and Rootless, the Child Poverty Action Group and the Catholic Housing Aid Society.
14. 18/74 (Department of the Environment), and 13/74 and 4/74 (Department of Health and Social Security).
15. Department of the Environment, *Homelessness: A Consultation Paper*, HMSO, 1975.
16. *Report of the Committee on the Rent Acts*, Cmnd 4609, 1971, p. 205.
17. Letter to the authors.
18. Colin Schofield, 'Homelessness – Facts not Fears', *Municipal Journal*, 25 March 1977.
19. W. R. Rees-Davies, House of Commons Official Report, Vol. 926, No. 52, 18 February 1977, Col. 905.
20. Department of the Environment, *Code of Guidance to England and Wales. Housing (Homeless Persons) Act 1977*, para. 4.4.
21. Scottish Development Department, *The Housing (Homeless Persons) Act 1977. Circular 41/1977*, 21 September 1977.
22. Nick Raynsford, 'Cold Water on Homeless Myths', *New Society*, 18 October 1979.
23. For research on the homeless and rootless, see the sources noted in Chapter

14. For research on gypsies, see Barbara Adams, Judith Okely, David Morgan and David Smith, *Gypsies and Government Policy in England*, Heinemann, 1975.

24. Accommodation provided under Part III of the National Assistance Act, 1948.

25. Supplementary Benefits Commission, *Annual Reports*, 1975–9.

## Chapter 17: Conclusion

1. An earlier draft of this chapter appeared in *New Society*.

2. *Royal Commission on the Housing of the Working Classes*, 1884–85, Minutes of Evidence, C.4402, para. 8852.

3. Ministry of Housing and Local Government, *Our Older Homes*, HMSO, 1966. See reservation by J. B. Cullingworth, p. 37.

# Index

## More About Penguins
## and Pelicans

For further information about books available from Penguins please write to Dept EP, Penguin Books Ltd, Harmondsworth, Middlesex UB7 0DA.

*In the U.S.A.:* For a complete list of books available from Penguins in the United States write to Dept CS, Penguin Books, 625 Madison Avenue, New York, New York 10022.

*In Canada:* For a complete list of books available from Penguins in Canada write to Penguin Books Canada Ltd, 2801 John Street, Markham, Ontario L3R 1B4.

*In Australia:* For a complete list of books available from Penguins in Australia write to the Marketing Department, Penguin Books Australia Ltd, P.O. Box 257, Ringwood, Victoria 3134.

*In New Zealand:* For a complete list of books available from Penguins in New Zealand write to the Marketing Department, Penguin Books (N.Z.) Ltd, P.O. Box 4019, Auckland 10.

*Published in Pelicans*

# FAMILY AND KINSHIP IN EAST LONDON

## Michael Young and Peter Willmott

The two authors of this most human of surveys are sociologists.
They spent three years on 'field work' in Bethnal Green and on a new housing estate in Essex. The result is a fascinating study, made during a period of extensive rehousing, of family and community ties and the pull of the 'wider family' on working-class people. Since its first publication their report has come to be recognized as a classic of modern sociology.

'Probably not only the fullest, but virtually the only account of working-class family relationships in any country. The general reader will find it full of meat and free of jargon' – *New Statesman*

'This shrewd – and in places extremely amusing – book combines warmth of feeling with careful sociological method' – *Financial Times*

'Observant, tactful, sympathetic, humorous ... I really feel that nobody who wants to know how our society is changing can afford not to read Young and Willmott' – Kingsley Amis in the *Spectator*

'No short account can do justice to this book, charmingly written, engaging, absorbing' – *British Medical Journal*

Published in Penguin Education

# URBAN AND REGIONAL PLANNING
Second Edition
*Peter Hall*

'Chucking a planner in the works' appears no bad thing to a community scarred by industrial or urban dereliction, or threatened by a new motorway or airport. Urban and regional planning is a response to urgent problems of the contemporary world: the growth and spread of urban populations; the need to provide new jobs; the renewal of antiquated housing and circulation systems; the conservation of a threatened heritage and containment of the explosive force of leisure.

Peter Hall's book provides an excellent historical perspective in the evolution of modern planning. He begins by describing and explaining the unplanned urban sprawl which followed the Industrial Revolution and the transport serving it. He then looks at the age of 'The Seers' – such men as Ebenezer Howard, who created Letchworth Garden City, and Patrick Abercrombie, who fathered the Greater London Plan of 1944. After discussing the influential Barlow Report of 1940, which set the style for post-war planning machinery, he gives the reader an extremely useful survey of legislation and planning progress from the immediate post-war years up to the present. Though the book is mainly based on experience in Britain, two chapters cover the very different course of events in continental Europe and the United States.

Finally, Peter Hall outlines the increasingly flexible techniques of modern spatial planning to complete a book which can be read with pleasure by anyone and with profit by students, those involved with decision-making in local government, as well as the general reader.

*Published in Penguin Education*

# GREAT PLANNING DISASTERS
*Peter Hall*

This book deals with a series of great planning decisions – ones costing tens of hundreds or even thousands of millions of pounds or dollars. It analyses the planning processes that were involved and isolates those which were disasters either because they were abandoned after much effort, or because they went ahead and were widely criticized as major mistakes.

Among the first group – *negative disasters* – the book looks at London's third airport and the abandoned London motorways. Among the many examples of *positive disasters* it considers Concorde, the Bay Area Rapid Transit System in San Francisco, and the Sydney Opera House. Lastly it probes two cases of near-disasters that became relative successes: California's plan for new university campuses, and Britain's plans for a new national library in London.

From these case studies, in the second part of the book Peter Hall seeks to distil some general lessons. He looks at the role of key actors in the planning processes: at community activists, at professional bureaucrats, at the politicians. His analysis, which synthesizes a large body of recent research in politics and related fields of social sciences, is often unflattering but always illuminating. Finally, drawing again on research – in fields as diverse as long-term future forecasting, welfare economics and ethical philosophy – he offers some tentative suggestions for improved decision-making in the future.

'Should be prescribed reading in every council chamber in the land' – *Edinburgh Evening News*

Published in Pelicans

# THE CLASSIC SLUM
Salford Life in the First Quarter of the Century

*Robert Roberts*

Shaw said that poverty is the greatest crime; *The Classic Slum* provides a grim affirmation of the truth of his remark. In a study which combines personal reminiscences with careful historical research, the myth of the 'good old days' is summarily dispensed with; Robert Roberts describes the period of his childhood, when a man could lose his job for belonging to a union and when a family's best clothes were likely to spend most weekdays at the pawnshop. The main effect of poverty in Edwardian Salford was degradation, and, despite great reserves of human courage, few could escape such a prison. The environment of slum housing and the atmosphere of hunger and insecurity created a culture blighted by ignorance, tedium, repression and a rigorous social stratification.

'An admirable blend of personal record and social history' – *Sunday Telegraph*

'It should be compulsory reading for all those who still uphold the British Empire as an ideal' – *Scotsman*

'Mr Roberts has written what may well be a classic book' – *Daily Telegraph*